"This fascinating study by Mark Fairchild persuasively argues that the apostle Paul had grown up enslaved and was later freed and that this traumatic experience pervades his vocabulary and theology. The book represents a tremendous amount of research that broadly surveys slavery in the first-century Roman Empire and more deeply analyzes the instances of slavery-related terms in the letters of Paul. When Paul identifies himself as a 'slave of Christ,' it serves as a touchstone for understanding his identity, message, and mission."

—MARK G. VITALIS HOFFMAN, Glatfelter Professor of Biblical Studies, United Lutheran Seminary

"One of this generation's most intrepid interpreters of the New Testament and its world, Fairchild is a bold guide along an excursion into the ancient territory of a tantalizing suggestion that the pre-Christian Paul was himself shaped by the experience of Roman enslavement and manumission. He provides a well-curated tour of some recent scholarship about slavery conventions in the Roman period, a refresher on Judean resistance movements, and new angles on biographical details about the apostle along with close exploration of Paul's distinctive references to enslavement and freedom. Inviting his readers along for a fresh romp around the dangerous terrain with which we are too often supposed to be familiar, Fairchild delivers a visual treasure trove of relevant images captured during his many visits throughout the Mediterranean. *Paul's Enslavement* promises to be an insightful accompaniment text for courses on Paul's letters and theology."

—DAVID R. MCCABE, professor of New Testament and Greek, Bethel University

"History is filled with ideas that deserved to go nowhere and died off. But it is also filled with discoveries, inventions, and knowledge that was so far ahead of its time, it went unaccepted by the guild of its era. Only centuries later was that knowledge taken as common knowledge. This book is one of those ideas. It's both ahead of its time and remarkably behind, in that it takes the early church's memory of Saul of Tarsus seriously. One of the great mysteries for future Pauline scholars will be how so many centuries could go by in which we forgot what the early church told us—that Paul was from a family of slaves."

—JORDAN K. MONSON, professor of missions and Old Testament, Huntington University; author of *Katharine Barnwell: How One Woman Revolutionized Modern Missions*

"Dr. Fairchild is a close friend and scholar and has been fellow traveler throughout Anatolia (Turkey) for many years. *Paul's Enslavement* is groundbreaking and very thought-provoking. I highly recommend it to those who desire to dive into a new perspective on the early life of the apostle Paul."

—DR. ANDREW JACKSON, pastor, teacher, author

"This study is a presentation of evidence, much as in a trial, that Paul was a former slave. Making the case like a lawyer, Mark Fairchild's wide-ranging argument assembles testimony from early church tradition, writings from church fathers, ancient historians, Roman law and practices, and hints in Scripture from Acts and Paul's own letters. This volume is brilliantly and thoroughly informative and thought-provoking. Wrestling with reasonable doubts or rethinking the slave imagery of Paul makes this volume fascinating for the reader. Whether one agrees with Fairchild's conclusions, the insight into Paul's world makes this book valuable. The celebration of freedom from slavery through faith in Jesus, described by Paul, is for everyone for all time—whether Jew or Greek, slave or free."

—LINFORD STUTZMAN, professor emeritus
of religion and culture, Eastern Mennonite University

"Building on his extensive understanding of first-century culture in general, first-century slavery in particular, and the contents of the Pauline Epistles, Dr. Fairchild delivers a strong set of arguments that the apostle Paul was at one time, early in life, a slave but then was freed and given Roman citizenship status. The thesis advanced in *Paul's Enslavement* is interesting, thought-provoking, and an important consideration. Fairchild demonstrates how this conclusion provides a unique perspective on the language employed by Paul in his epistles. I am thankful for Dr. Fairchild's clear and concise work. I am pleased to add this volume to my library, and I recommend that you do the same."

—PAUL D. WEAVER, associate professor of
Bible exposition, Dallas Theological Seminary

PAUL'S ENSLAVEMENT

The Early Life of Saul the Zealot

MARK R. FAIRCHILD

Paul's Enslavement: The Early Life of Saul the Zealot

Published by Hendrickson Publishers
3 Centennial Drive
Peabody, Massachusetts 01960
www.hendricksonpublishers.com

ISBN 979-8-4005-0793-9
ISBN 979-8-4005-0794-6 (Kindle ebook)
ISBN 979-8-4005-0795-3 (epub)
ISBN 979-8-4005-0796-0 (Apple epub)

Printed in the United States of America

First Printing — November 2025

All photos by Mark R. Fairchild.

Library of Congress Control Number: 2025941726

Dedicated to the memory of my brother, Gary Alan Fairchild, who unexpectedly passed away August 19, 2024.

ơ

Contents

Illustrations

Acknowledgments

I ENJOY HIKING THE ANCIENT Anatolian roads of Türkiye. While most of those still visible are less than a mile in length, the Derebucak-Gölcük Roman road is much longer. The Romans constructed this road in an attempt to control the recalcitrant Homonadeis people living in the Taurus Mountains. The road traverses the heights wandering through forests, *yayla* highlands, and mountain passes as it negotiates the terrain. Constructed of well-prepared paving stones bordered by stone curbs, the road is a tribute to Roman engineering. They even constructed steps for wagons and carts to deal with the elevations.

Walking these roads in the summer heat can be arduous, but the pristine nature, scenery, and aura of the mountains are exhilarating. My work on this volume reminds me of these long roads. The writing of this book has been a journey. The thought of Paul as a freed slave began more than twenty-five years ago as I studied his letter to the Galatians. Paul's personal tone, as he wove the issue of slavery into his arguments, stimulated me to wonder if the apostle's first-person personal pronouns throughout the letter were simply a rhetorical device or a reflection of his own experiences. Paul's words in 1:10 were particularly intriguing: "If I was *still* acting as a man-pleaser, I would not be a slave of Christ." "Man-pleaser" was a term referring to a slave who strove to please his master. The implication of the word *still* is that Paul was once a slave serving a human master, but now he claimed to be a slave of Christ. The letter concluded with Paul exclaiming that he bore the brand-marks of Christ on his body (6:17). "Brand-marks" (stigmata) were the brands or tattoos that slaveowners used to identify their possessions.

In 1999, I published "Paul's Pre-Christian Zealot Associations: A Reexamination of Gal. 1:14 and Acts 22:3" in *New Testament Studies*. In the article, I argued that Paul claimed he had been "an extraordinary Zealot," a connection with ties to the Zealot movement described by Josephus. This stance accounted for Paul's persecution of the Christians (Gal 1:13-14). As time passed in my studies, I collected notes that pointed back to Paul's past suggesting he had a secret that had been lost over the centuries. Finally, after years of following the breadcrumbs on this road, I wrote this book.

While hiking on those mountain roads, I often described my research to Benoit Hanquet, a trusty traveling companion on some of my journeys in Türkiye. I wish to thank him for lending me his ears. I also want to thank Levent Oral and his staff at Tutku Educational Travel for arranging many of these journeys into the mountains. They have assisted me in Türkiye countless times. I also want to extend my thanks to the U.S. Fulbright Commission for a Senior Scholar Research Grant and Huntington University for a sabbatical that greatly contributed to this work.

In addition, I need to mention the excellent library staff at Huntington University's RichLyn Library who helped me track down many of my resources. My colleague at Huntington University, Jordan Monson, took a great deal of interest in this topic. Together, we wrote "Paul Unchained: What If the Apostle Grew Up a Slave?," an article for *Christianity Today* (May 2024), based on this book.

It has been a pleasure to work with Patricia Anders, my editor at Hendrickson Publishers, whose insights have made this a better book. Thank you also to Madi Cannon for her expert copyediting help, to Ann Sierks Smith for her expert proofreading, and to Meg Rusick for her typesetting work. My nephew, Dustin Fairchild, did an excellent job compiling the index.

Finally, and most importantly, I want to express my everlasting love and gratitude for my wife, Darlene, who has helped with corrections and suggestions and has endured with much patience my absences from home.

Abbreviations

AB	Anchor Bible
ANRW	*Aufstieg und Niedergang der römischen Welt: Geschichte und Kultur Roms im Spiegel der neueren Forschung.* Part 2, *Principat.* Edited by Hildegard Temporini and Wolfgang Haase. De Gruyter, 1972–
BECNT	Baker Exegetical Commentary on the New Testament
BHT	Beiträge zur historischen Theologie
BJS	Brown Judaic Studies
BZNW	Beihefte zur Zeitschrift für die neutestamentliche Wissenschaft
CBQ	*Catholic Biblical Quarterly*
CJ	*Classical Journal*
ClQ	*Classical Quarterly*
CSSRB	*Council of Societies for the Study of Religion Bulletin*
ECC	Eerdmans Critical Commentary
Historia	*Historia: Zeitschrift für alte Geschichte*
HNTC	Harper's New Testament Commentaries
HTR	*Harvard Theological Review*
HTS	Harvard Theological Studies
ICC	International Critical Commentary
JBL	*Journal of Biblical Literature*
JNES	*Journal of Near Eastern Studies*
JR	*Journal of Religion*
JRS	*Journal of Roman Studies*
LCL	Loeb Classical Library

LSJ Liddell, Henry George, Robert Scott, Henry Stuart Jones. *A Greek-English Lexicon*. 9th ed. with revised supplement. Clarendon, 1996

NICNT New International Commentary on the New Testament

NIDNTT *New International Dictionary of New Testament Theology*. Edited by Colin Brown. 4 vols. Zondervan, 1975–1978

NIGTC New International Greek Testament Commentary

NovT *Novum Testamentum*

NTD Das Neue Testament Deutsch

NTL New Testament Library

NTM New Testament Message

NTS *New Testament Studies*

PL Patrologia Latina [= *Patrologiae Cursus Completus*: Series Latina]. Edited by Jacques-Paul Migne. 217 vols. Paris, 1844–1864

PNTC Pelican New Testament Commentaries

RB *Revue biblique*

REJ *Revue des études juives*

RevQ *Revue de Qumran*

SBS Stuttgarter Bibelstudien

TDNT *Theological Dictionary of the New Testament*. Edited by Gerhard Kittel and Gerhard Friedrich. Translated by Geoffrey W. Bromiley. 10 vols. Eerdmans, 1964–1976

WBC Word Biblical Commentary

WUNT Wissenschaftliche Untersuchungen zum Neuen Testament

ZECNT Zondervan Exegetical Commentary on the New Testament

ZNW *Zeitschrift für die neutestamentliche Wissenschaft und die Kunde der älteren Kirche*

Introduction

But let us remember that we must have regard for justice even toward the humblest. Now the humblest status and the poorest fortune are those of slaves.

Cicero, *De officiis* 1.13.41 (Miller, LCL 21, 45)

A BLACK HOLE IS AN astronomical phenomenon with a gravitational pull so intense that even particles of light cannot escape it. An English clergyman and sometime naturalist, John Michell, first proposed the theory of black holes in 1784. At that time, not much attention was given to Michell's theory. It was not until 1971, almost 200 years later, that a black hole was discovered. Since the interior of a black hole is not observable, little is known about them. Instead, our understanding of black holes comes from data gathered from astronomical objects that surround them. Theoretical science is based on assumptions usually drawn from unobservable data rather than direct experimentation. Theoretical science uses inductive and abductive reasoning to draw the most likely conclusions from data in the field or related fields. In such instances, one cannot always draw conclusions with 100 percent certitude. Instead, inferences lead one to the most plausible explanation for the data.

Most of what has happened in the past has never been recorded. Writing systems developed at different times in different places, but the earliest writing occurred around 6,000 years ago. Prior to the invention of writing, we have what is known as the Prehistoric Age. Scant little is known about prehistoric life. Even written history can be difficult to understand. Documented history records nonrepeatable events, and what was documented is an edited version of past events from someone's perspective. All historical reports and details were selected from among a cluster of other accounts and details that could have been recorded but were not. Since actions are an interplay between causes and their effects, it is difficult to discern what actually happened and why it happened when most of the historical background and contributing causes are lost in the vacuum of unrecorded history. Research cannot verify historical events with 100 percent certitude. Even with ancient written sources, we cannot be sure that what was reported was true, partially true, biased, or completely fabricated.

Even today in our heavily politicized culture, with news organizations stocked with photographs and videos, we cannot be sure that news presentations accurately and fairly describe events. A report from the Pew Research Center indicates that only 56 percent of 18- to 29-year-old adults in America place "some or a lot of trust" in national news organizations. By comparison, 50 percent of the same group of 18- to 29-nine-year-old adults has "some or a lot of trust" in social media sites.[1] A report from the Gallup poll is even worse. According to their 2023 research, only 32 percent of those polled have a "great deal" or "fair amount" of trust in the media's reporting of news. Another 29 percent have "not very much" confidence in the media, and still another 39 percent "have no confidence at all." Altogether, 68 percent of those polled have "not very much or no confidence at all" in our media outlets.[2] Since we are on the topic, it might be appropriate to ask if we can even trust Pew and Gallup to poll the public on trust!

A public poll might offer a general sense of trust in the media, but our sense of trust is nuanced by several factors. Do we know (or believe) that the source was trustworthy or untrustworthy in the past? Do we know (and agree or disagree with) the biases of the source? Our trust also depends on the type of news. We are inclined to believe news regarding automobile accidents, deaths, and sports results. We are less inclined, however, to trust reporting on political and religious activities or the personal lives of popular personalities. It is safe to say that we tend to trust information that comes from what we perceive to be trusted sources in instances where there is no apparent bias on the part of the reporter and in cases that involve no political or religious activity.

For our recollection and understanding of ancient history, we depend on written and oral sources—but are these ancient literary sources trust-

---

1. "U.S. Adults Under 30 Now Trust Information from Social Media Almost as Much as from National News Outlets," Pew Research Center, October 27, 2022, https://www.pewresearch.org/topic/news-habits-media/media-society/media-attitudes/trust-in-media/.

2. Megan Brenan, "Media Confidence in U.S. Matches 2016 Record Low," Gallup, October 19, 2023, https://news.gallup.com/poll/512861/media-confidence-matches-2016-record-low.aspx.

worthy? In some instances, they are the only source available, so there is no other source to corroborate, supplement, or compare the data. For some ancient writers, we can discern a clear bias in their writings. This must be considered when utilizing their writings. This does not necessarily eliminate the information they provide, but it may require researchers to compensate for what they take away from the source. We realize that numbers are often exaggerated and that the consequences of actions are sometimes overblown. Yet even with biased writers, the information they record may be deemed trustworthy if it contradicts their biases.

The apostle Paul is one of the most studied individuals in human history. Yet there is a black hole, if you will, in his story. A few of his letters have been passed down to us, and the Acts of the Apostles details portions of his later life, but very little is known of Paul's early life. Like a black hole, there is no light from that period of his life.

Biblical research has seldom ventured into the dark and vacuous space of unwritten history. This is a realm with no parameters: No roads, no walls, and no solid ground, a realm where the lack of gravity offers no firm footing. This is a realm where the principles of quantum mechanics destabilize the assumptions we previously held as foundational tenets of research. We fear getting sucked into the vortex of the black hole that leads to the unknown. Still, the lure of the unknown bids us to proceed, yet with caution. So, we proceed to build a theory based on the corroborating evidence.

The Investigation

Studies indicate that somewhere between one-fifth and one-quarter of the population in the Mediterranean world during the first century were slaves or former slaves.[3] Several of the letters attributed to Paul addressed slaves who populated some of the churches he founded (1 Cor 7:21–24; Eph 6:5–9; Col 3:22–25; 1 Tim 6:1–2; Titus 2:9–10). However, of the scores of Christian disciples mentioned by name in the New Testament, only one, Onesimus,

3. The estimates vary. W. V. Harris, "Towards a Study of the Roman Slave Trade," in *The Seaborne Commerce of Ancient Rome: Studies in Archaeology*, ed. J. H. D'Arms and E. C. Kopff, Memoirs of the American Academy in Rome 36 (American Academy in Rome, 1980), 118, asserts that somewhere between a sixth to a fifth of the overall population were slaves. John Madden concurs with this estimate. "Slavery in the Roman Empire: Numbers and Origins," *Classics Ireland* 3 (1996): 109–28. Ramsay MacMullen supposes that the numbers in the countryside amounted to only a few percent but that the mid- and large-sized cities had slave populations of around 25 percent. "Late Roman Slavery," *Historia* 36 (1987): 359–82, 375.

was clearly identified as a slave. It was not prudent to identify someone as a "slave" or "freedman." Perhaps the negative connotations associated with such terms may have led scholars to underestimate the number of first-century Christians who were enslaved in ancient Rome. Still, the raw statistics should cause us to wonder if some of these rather familiar Christians were indeed slaves or persons freed from slavery. Here, I propose that one of them, Saul (later, the apostle Paul), was once a slave in Tarsus of Cilicia; that in time, he was freed from bondage and migrated to Jerusalem; and that it is in Jerusalem that we first encounter him.

Our biggest problem revolves around the desire for direct evidence, the so-called smoking gun. The smoking gun, however, has been thrown into the sea of history and can never be recovered. None of the New Testament writings, including Paul's letters, explicitly assert that he was enslaved. In general, we have practically nothing to say about Paul's past. We have testimony that he came from Tarsus, but not much more. What then? Are we to abandon any hope of peeling back the years and finding the apostle's early life?

There are dozens of questions and issues from the past that cannot be definitively resolved. Yet, like criminal cases today, there are generally clues that offer evidence. If enough of these clues can be found that fall in line with a given line of thought, then a hypothesis can be formed and investigated. This hypothesis is then tested as additional evidence is gathered. If enough evidence supports the hypothesis, then the hypothesis becomes a theory, and the theory is presented with the evidence before the court of public opinion.

How do we go about this investigation? Historical research involves the analysis of data that comes from sources. In many instances, the sources offer little data regarding the questions we are asking. But if the data from our sources are limited, where do we go? We label each piece of evidence and pack it away, thinking that it may be helpful later—that is, if we happen to find more pieces to the puzzle. Good research moves forward following the breadcrumbs of evidence in an attempt to trace the trajectory of the known details. Some may worry about venturing into a theory for fear of speculating about the past. Yet, what is better? To say nothing or to offer a calculated theory of events? A theory may never be proven to be true if we think that this proof has to be beyond the shadow of a doubt. Our courts do not require such certainty. Instead, juries are to convict or acquit on the basis of reasonable doubt. Research advances with the preponderance of evidence. Research progresses with hypotheses and theories.

Early Christianity is enshrouded in obscurity. There are numerous untold stories and histories about the work of unknown missionaries who rapidly spread the faith throughout the Mediterranean world. Even the histories of well-known figures of early Christianity, such as Peter, John, Timothy, Barnabas, and others, are not well documented. This book is an attempt to penetrate the darkness of time—into that black hole of history—and to propose theories about the earliest years of the apostle Paul.

Hearsay and Circumstantial Evidence

Hearsay is secondhand testimony and is generally considered inadmissible evidence in a court of law because the statement cannot be cross-examined. Hearsay, however, is not without merit and under certain conditions can be used in court. In our case, the one offering the secondhand testimony is not available, and the person described (Paul) is likewise not able to address the statements. In a later chapter, I will discuss the statements of the early church father Jerome, who relayed a tradition that Paul's family originally lived in Galilee. Jerome's brief comments lead us to believe that Paul was a slave during his younger years. Jerome had nothing to gain or lose by offering these statements; there was no discernible bias in sharing this information. Jerome attributed the comments to an unspecified predecessor of his. It is quite possible that the tradition came from Origen, the prolific Alexandrian scholar. Origen took up residence in Caesarea Maritima in Palestine from 231 until his death in 253. There, he established a Christian school where he taught and wrote most of his works. It was probably in Palestine that Origen received the tradition. While in Caesarea Maritima, he would have had access to a wealth of resources, both written and oral.[4]

In the absence of direct evidence, circumstantial evidence may be the only data to prove a point. Although circumstantial evidence can be questioned in court, it is often used to convict or exonerate persons accused of crimes. Fingerprints, for example, are circumstantial evidence that a person was present at the crime scene but not necessarily indicative that the owner of the fingerprints committed the crime. In court, most civil and criminal

4. The theological library at Caesarea Maritima reportedly contained more than 30,000 volumes. It was the largest theological library at that time. Jerome himself studied at that library, and it was probably there that he gained access to Origen's writings, many of which are lost today.

cases are built in part or in whole on circumstantial evidence. Based on the validity and preponderance of this evidence, individuals are acquitted, convicted, or found liable. It is commonly thought that circumstantial evidence is less valuable than direct evidence. In some cases, however, circumstantial evidence may be stronger and may override direct evidence. Even direct evidence, such as eyewitness testimony, is sometimes unreliable. Memories fade and the perceived facts change with time. We cannot always find that smoking gun.

I submit that there is enough trustworthy hearsay and circumstantial evidence for us to believe that Paul was formerly a slave.[5] Of course, in the texts that survive he never clearly claimed he was enslaved in his youth, nor do any of the writers of the New Testament say this. We have no direct evidence, no eyewitness testimony. But perhaps we should ask, why not? Why do we not have direct evidence of Paul's enslavement? I would suggest that the reason is that history seldom recalls the stories of those who lose. Instead, history tells the stories of those who prevail and thrive. History is recorded by the wealthy, the powerful, and the successful; we hear very little about the lives of the peasants, the slaves, or the defeated. Even with the story of the Christian faith as recorded in the New Testament, the writers do not dwell on failures. Instead, the biblical narrative relays the salvation history of progress despite opposition. It is the story of how Christianity overcame the odds and spread throughout the Mediterranean world. An account of Paul's distant past in slavery would not contribute to this broader narrative.

Honor, Shame, and Zeal in Galilee

It has been said that modern Western culture has lost a great deal of its sense of honor and shame. These concepts, however, still remain dominant factors in many cultures elsewhere in the world. Honor and shame were also powerful influences affecting the behaviors of people who lived 2,000 years ago in the Mediterranean world. The shame associated with the loss of fortune, status, social humiliation, or the prospect of exile sometimes led to suicide—something quite common in the Mediterranean. It was believed that suicide took great courage and was a way of restoring honor. Likewise,

---

5. A brief summary of this conclusion was published in Mark R. Fairchild and Jordan K. Monson, "Paul Unchained: What If the Apostle Grew Up a Slave? Would It Change the Way We Read Him?," *Christianity Today* 68.4 (2024): 34–47.

heroic acts of bravery and sacrifice for the benefit of others were considered the epitome of honor.

Jewish families living in Galilee at the end of the first century prior to the Common Era were faced with choices regarding the threat posed by the newly installed Roman authorities. Earlier, during the Hasmonean period, the Jews enjoyed a period of autonomy, free from the prior centuries of oppression under the Persian, Greek, and Seleucid rulers. Less than a hundred years later, the Romans expanded their dominions into the eastern Mediterranean. They took over Palestine and imposed their laws and taxes on the Jewish people. The collective shame of the Jewish people manifested itself in courageous attempts to expel the Romans. These rebel movements persisted in Galilee for decades. The Jewish historian Josephus described these groups with the term "Zealots." This term encompassed a number of Jewish rebel groups opposed to Roman rule.

Josephus stated that the primary dispute of the Zealot leaders was that Jews should have no master but God alone. Indeed, a Zealot mentality was the motivating factor that led to the success of the Maccabean Revolt against their Seleucid overlords in the second century BC. In the minds of these Zealots, serving the Romans and paying taxes to them was equivalent to slavery. In spite of the seemingly impossible odds, the chief goal of these Zealots was to remove the Romans from the land. Short of that, the Jewish Zealot resistance would at least restore honor to the Jewish people. Zealots were committed to maintaining the sanctity of the Torah and the honor of the Jewish nation, and they were willing to lay their lives on the line to oppose Roman oppression. Josephus recounted the demise of the Galilean town of Gamala at the beginning of the Jewish War with Rome. After a siege, the walls of the town were breached and the Roman troops rushed in.

Rather than surrender to the Romans, the fleeing residents flung themselves over the cliff on the far side of the town to their deaths. Rather than face a life of shame in slavery, the people of Gamala considered this act an honorable suicide. A few years later, the besieged Zealots who fled to Masada did the same rather than be subjected to the humiliation of slavery by the Romans.

This was the culture and context of Saul and his family in Galilee. The sack of their hometown, Gischala, was the consequence of Zealot opposition to Roman rule. Roman practices regarding their conquered territories prescribed the execution of male combatants and the sale of noncombatants, women, children, and the elderly in the slave markets. The Roman slave trade was massive and considered a necessary institution to fulfill the occupational needs of Roman citizens across the empire. Warfare was the primary contributor to supplying the number of slaves needed to meet the demand.

FIGURE 1. Gamala with the synagogue and breach in the city walls.

FIGURE 2. Synagogue at Gischala (modern Jish). A synagogue was built here as early as the 1st c. BC. It was later destroyed and rebuilt at the site in the 3rd c. AD.

Paul, in his letter to the Galatians, claimed that formerly he was "an extraordinary Zealot for his ancestral traditions" (1:14). This claim was also made in Acts 22:3 as Paul stood before the mob in Jerusalem.[6] His actions in persecuting the Christians prior to his conversion back up that claim. He used his words "I used to persecute the church of God beyond measure and tried to destroy it" (Gal 1:13) and "as to zeal, a persecutor of the church" (Phil 3:6) to demonstrate his willingness to shed blood as a Zealot.

It can be understood that Paul and his family were devout Jews from Galilee. Swept up in the rebellious mindset of Galilee near the turn of the century, his family radically opposed the presence of Rome in the region. Later, as captive slaves removed from the boiling cauldron of Galilee, the family settled into a life of servitude to a Roman master. After years of slavery, their Roman master manumitted them according to Roman custom and adopted them into the household. This conferred Roman citizenship on those adopted. Over those years, Paul realized that the Roman system of justice was fair. That realization, however, did not diminish his zeal for the Jewish faith or his determination to keep the sanctity of the Torah. While in Jerusalem, his zeal was once again stirred to such an extent that he felt compelled to attack the Christian "infidels" and drag them before the Sanhedrin for prosecution.

Following Paul's conversion, the apostle realized that his misdirected zeal had deflected his efforts and service away from God and his true mission. The Romans were not the problem. Likewise, the Christians were not the problem. The problem was sin, which had become the cruel master that enslaved humanity. Paul's zeal now took another turn and evolved into something new: a willingness to personally suffer persecution and death to defeat the powers of evil.

> Our struggle is not against flesh and blood, but against the rulers, against the powers, against the world forces of this darkness, against the spiritual forces of evil in the heavenly places. (Eph 6:12)

Perhaps this was Paul's penance. Instead of shedding the blood of others, Paul was willing to shed his own blood for the sake of the gospel. The sufferings that Paul experienced on his travels—the persecutions, beatings, harassment, and deprivations—were not worthy of being compared with the glory that would be revealed (Rom 8:18). Instead, he said, "*I will not be*

---

6. Mark R. Fairchild, "Paul's Pre-Christian Zealot Associations: A Re-examination of Gal 1:14 and Acts 22:3," *NTS* 45 (1999): 514–32.

put to shame in anything, but that with all boldness, Christ shall even now, as always, be exalted in my body, whether by life or by death. For to me, to live is Christ, and to die is gain" (Phil 1:20–21, emphasis added).

The Proposition

The research that stands behind this volume leads to the conclusion that the apostle Paul, one of the best-known figures of the New Testament, was formerly a slave. According to tradition, Paul wrote thirteen books that have been canonized, constituting 23.5 percent of the New Testament. A primary objection to the assertion that Paul was a slave could be the observation that he never referred to his past as a life of slavery. There are several reasons for this silence.

First, Paul seldom wrote anything about his past. He tells us nothing about his parents, siblings, childhood, youth, or life in Tarsus. There are a few autobiographical clues in Acts or Paul's letters, which we will deal with in short order. But there is not enough information to piece together a detailed narrative of Paul's distant past.

Second, the shame associated with slavery, not only in Mediterranean culture but particularly in Jewish culture, was enough for emancipated Jewish slaves to sweep the experience under the rug and to keep silent about the matter. Zealots taught that Jews were to serve no one except God alone.[7] It was difficult enough to reconstruct a life after slavery. Dwelling on the past would have made it all the more difficult to move forward.

Finally, Paul was always sensitive about how he might present the gospel in a manner that might be readily embraced. The sociological grid created by notions of status made it difficult for members of the lower class to persuade the nobility. The persuasive words of a former slave would not be as convincing as the words of a freeborn citizen.

In the chapters that follow, I will build the case for what I have suggested here. The first chapter will deal with the phenomenon of slavery in the first-century Roman world. This chapter will summarize what research has revealed about the widely embraced and deeply entrenched system of

---

7. Large numbers of Jews populated Rome during the imperial period. Many of them came to Rome as captured slaves following the Jewish War. Yet, Dale B. Martin notes that "among all the 500 or so Jewish funerary inscriptions from Rome, none explicitly names a Jewish slave or freedman." "Slavery and the Ancient Jewish Family," in *The Jewish Family in Antiquity*, ed. Shaye J. D. Cohen, BJS (Scholars Press, 2020), 120.

slavery in the Roman world. Although many other volumes have described first-century slavery in more depth than can be covered here, we will summarize the number and statistics of slaves, the causes of slavery, and the conditions of slaves in the Mediterranean area. Additionally, we will discuss the length of slavery and the process of manumission. Finally, the chapter will deal with the common practice of adoption, whereby the former slave was incorporated into the family of their former owner and received the conferral of Roman citizenship for those lucky enough to have a Roman citizen as their owner.

The second chapter will dig more deeply into an aspect of the sociological structure of Roman society: status, honor, and shame. All societies, both ancient and modern, have a sociological hierarchy, commonly known as a sociological grid. People are arranged on that grid on the basis of their perceived worth. Elements such as patrimony, race, wealth, gender, education, occupation, and power contribute to a community's estimate of one's worth and status. The upward mobility of individuals in terms of their status was limited. But the fall of one's status could entail a consequential impact on the fortunes and honor of the individual and their family. Slaves, with rare exception, fell at the bottom of the social grid, and the shame of enslavement hung like an albatross on the necks of those who experienced it.

Chapter 3 digs into Jerome's secondhand testimony. Jerome spent the latter part of his life in Judea and dwelled in a cave in Bethlehem. There, he no doubt heard much about the earliest Christians and received traditions that have long since passed away. One of those traditions pertained to Paul's family, which he claimed came from Gischala in the upper Galilee. The tradition was repeated twice in Jerome's writings in different contexts, so it does not appear to be a misunderstanding. When we conflate Jerome's observations with the writings of the first-century Jewish historian Josephus, we gain more clarity regarding what happened and how Paul's family was sold into slavery.

In chapter 4, we see that the Acts of the Apostles provides a sketch of Paul's life after his conversion in Acts 9, although it still does not offer a full description of Paul's activities during that time. In his letter to the Galatians, Paul revealed that he spent three years between his journey to Damascus and his return to Jerusalem. During that time, Paul journeyed to Arabia—the Roman term referring to the Nabataean Kingdom located south of present-day Jordan, with its capital at Petra. None of this was mentioned in Acts. After his brief fifteen-day return to Jerusalem (Gal 1:18), Paul was sent back to his hometown of Tarsus. He spent the next seven to nine years in Tarsus learning the gospel and preaching in nearby synagogues. Again, none of this was mentioned in Acts. Paul's letter to the Romans mentioned a trip to Illyricum (Rom 15:19), but Acts is silent on all these details.

Nevertheless, Acts does tell us a great deal about Paul and his travels. The narrative drops clues that suggest that Paul was a freedman. If it is conceded that the "we sections" of Acts come from Luke's personal travels with Paul, then it would make sense that Luke would know more about Paul's past. This fourth chapter examines these statements and draws out the implications of the text.

Chapters 5 through 8 are the most interpretive (exegetical) chapters in the book. We know from psychological studies that people look at life and express themselves from the perspective of their past experiences. We can therefore assume that Paul did the same. By studying repetitious patterns of symbols, word choices, phrases, and analogies, it is possible to uncover a writer's formative influences and background. Here, we examine passages in the apostle's letters to the churches in Galatia, Rome, Corinth, and his personal letter to Philemon. The expressions Paul used in these letters betray an involvement in slavery that goes beyond metaphors and figures of speech. In many instances, we see that the personal pronouns "we" and "I" are not just rhetorical devices but rather references to Paul's past history.

The ninth chapter deals with the theology of Paul's apocalyptic gospel. The term Paul used to describe his gospel and the manner in which he received it was "apocalypse," which means "revelation" or "unveiling" (Gal 1:12). Corresponding to this, while writing to the Corinthians, Paul relayed a curious story of someone (probably Paul) who fourteen years earlier was "taken up into the third heaven." There he received visions and revelations or apocalypses (2 Cor 12:1–2). Subtracting fourteen years from when Paul wrote 2 Corinthians, we can conclude that he had these apocalypses around AD 41, a few years after his conversion and sojourn in Arabia (Gal 1:17–18). At this time, Paul was in Tarsus and Cilicia (Gal 1:21). It was there that Paul came to a fuller understanding of the gospel. This was when he departed from the Judaizing tendencies of early Christianity (Acts 15) and understood the ramifications of doing ministry among the gentiles.

Related to our discussions in chapters 5 through 8, the content of chapter 10 focuses on a statistical analysis of the word choices Paul used in his writings. The words *slave*, *freedom*, *adoption*, and others, along with their cognate words, are used disproportionately in Paul's writings compared to the rest of the New Testament. It is hard to believe that such use is coincidental. Rather, the disproportionate use of these terms is what one would expect from a person whose life was marked by slavery during the most impressionable years of their youth.

The volume wraps up with a conclusion that brings together the secondhand testimony, the circumstantial evidence, and the evidence from Paul's own writings. These all lead us to conclude that the apostle and his family began their lives in Tarsus as the slaves of a Roman master. Once manumitted, Saul was adopted into his master's family, given a Roman name (Paul), and acquired Roman citizenship.

Seeing Paul in the light of his past offers us opportunities to look at his writings from a different perspective. Paul's impassioned appeal to Philemon to manumit Onesimus—"I have sent him back to you in person; that is, sending my very heart" (v. 12)—certainly takes on greater meaning. Also, Paul's association of slavery with sin and freedom with righteousness (Rom 6) reflects his conversion with enhanced meaning. Likewise, the apostle's claim to be a "slave of Christ" (Rom 1:1; Gal 1:10) echoes the transfer of his ownership to the Lord Jesus Christ. Perhaps now, we will even be able to answer the often-asked question of why Paul does not seem to condemn slavery.

| 1 |

Slavery in the First-Century Mediterranean World

Some things are under our control, while others are not under our control. . . . The things under our control are by nature free, unhindered, and unimpeded; while the things not under our control are weak, servile, subject to hindrance, and not our own.

Epictetus, *Enchiridion* 1 (Oldfather, LCL 218, 483)

Let us suppose a man had to throw part of his cargo overboard in a storm: Should he prefer to sacrifice a high-priced horse or a cheap and worthless slave? In this case, regard for his property interest inclines him one way, human feeling the other.

Cicero, *De officiis* 3.23.89 (Miller, LCL 21, 363, 365)

Evidence of slavery goes back to the earliest civilizations. In ancient Mesopotamia, for example, the Sumerians took slaves. In the earliest law code ever discovered, Ur-Nammu, six of the thirty-two surviving laws pertained to the treatment of slaves. The later Babylonian Code of Hammurabi contained at least thirty laws that concerned slaves. Egypt, likewise, took slaves.

Genesis relates the story of Joseph, who was sold to Midianite traders, who in turn sold him to the Egyptians (Gen 37). The book of Exodus continues the narrative and describes how Israel became enslaved to the Egyptians, some 400 years later. According to Exodus 1:11, these Hebrew slaves built the cities of Ramses and Pithom.

The walls of the Karnak Temple in ancient Thebes display several reliefs of the Egyptian overlords mistreating their slaves, including depictions of Semitic slaves. The Jews were again enslaved during the Assyrian and Babylonian conquests of Palestine.

Even the Hebrews themselves had slaves. Exodus 21:1–11 deals with the purchase of a Hebrew slave. After six years, the slave is to be set free; however, if the master gives the slave a wife, then the wife and children are to remain with the master. Leviticus 25:39–46 adds a somewhat different perspective.

FIGURE 3. *Top,* Sumerian box decorated with shell and lapis lazuli depicting the story of a Sumerian king. The top and middle registers show conquered nude prisoners on the right paraded as slaves before the king. From the royal tomb at Ur. 2500 BC. British Museum. See gallery for color version.

FIGURE 4. *Bottom left,* Mesopotamian inscription recording the sale of twelve slaves. Uruk, Sumer. 3100 BC. Oriental Institute Museum, University of Chicago.

FIGURE 5. *Bottom right,* Slave butchering a calf. Statue from tomb of Nykauinpu at Giza, Egypt. 24th c. BC. Oriental Institute Museum, University of Chicago.

FIGURE 6. *Left,* Slave preparing a meal. Statue from the tomb of Nykauinpu at Giza, Egypt. 24th c. BC. Oriental Institute Museum, University of Chicago.

FIGURE 7. *Right,* Mud brick with straw produced with slave labor. From the Ramesseum at Luxor, Egypt. 12th c. BC. Oriental Institute Museum, University of Chicago.

If a Hebrew sells himself to another Hebrew, he is to be treated as a hired man until the year of Jubilee, at which time he should be set free. The passage indicates that Hebrew slaves are to be fairly treated, since they are among those whom God brought out of Egypt. Slaves purchased from among the pagan nations, however, may become the master's permanent possessions (25:45–46).[8]

It should not be surprising that Christians also had slaves. Living in the first century at a time when scant few people questioned the institution, many of those who embraced the Christian faith had slaves at the time of their conversion. Jesus told the parable of the master who went on a trip and gave talents to his slaves (Matt 25:14–30), expecting them to invest the talents wisely. Upon returning, the master assessed the work of his slaves and treated them according to their work. In the parable of the prodigal son, Jesus referenced slaves who welcomed the prodigal's return (Luke 15:22–27). In Acts 12:12–13, John Mark's mother, Mary, had a slave named Rhoda. The recipient of Paul's letter to Philemon was a slave owner, and there were slaves who worshiped in the church at Corinth (1 Cor 7). Slaves were instructed to be obedient to their masters in the letter to the Ephesians (6:5–9), the letter to the Colossians (3:22), the First Epistle to Timothy (6:1–2) and

8. See E. E. Urbach, "The Laws Regarding Slavery as a Source for the Social History of the Period of the Second Temple, the Mishnah and Talmud," in *Papers of the Institute of Jewish Studies, London*, ed. J. G. Weiss (Magnes, 1964), 1–94.

FIGURE 8. *Top,* The sack of Lachish by the Assyrian Sennacherib with enslaved Jewish prisoners begging for mercy before the throne. From Southwest Palace, Nineveh. 695 BC. British Museum.

FIGURE 9. *Bottom left,* Votive relief of a family accompanied by slaves bringing animal sacrifices to a god. On the right, a nude slave pours wine. Athens, 4th c. BC. Athens National Archaeological Museum.

FIGURE 10. *Bottom right,* Funerary relief of Paramonos and Serapas erected for their parents and families. A slave seated with a scroll takes dictation as an amanuensis. AD 300–330. Thessaloniki Archaeological Museum. See gallery for color version.

the First Epistle of Peter (2:18). Likewise, masters were instructed to be kind to their slaves, knowing that the master of both the slave and master is in heaven and that there is no partiality with God (Eph 6:9).

In the Roman world, slaves could be treated quite harshly. Yet in Paul's letters, we begin to see a softened position with regard to slaves. Writing to the slaves at Corinth, Paul advised them to remain in their current condition, unless they were able to gain their freedom. Paul declared that the slave is the Lord's freedman (1 Cor 7:20–24), and he instructed the masters of slaves to grant them "justice and fairness, knowing that you too have a Master in heaven" (Col 4:1). In his letter to the Galatians, the apostle claimed,

"There is neither Jew nor Greek, there is neither slave nor free man, there is neither male nor female for you are all one in Christ Jesus" (3:28). And in his letter to Philemon, Paul urged Philemon to release his slave Onesimus, who was "no longer as a slave, but more than a slave, a beloved brother" (v. 16).

Slavery was ubiquitous throughout the ancient world and institutionalized in most, if not all, ancient cultures. The use of slaves supported the economy of civilizations and provided much of the labor needed for agricultural production. While the bulk of slaves were used for agriculture and herding, many were used for the construction of villas for the wealthy as well as for numerous household functions. Educated slaves or those with special skills could be appointed as financial managers, tutors, cooks, gardeners, entertainers, or couriers, or they could be assigned to household chores. Some were managers of other slaves, and many were engaged in the commercial endeavors of their masters. Slaves were trained to fight other slaves or animals in spectacles throughout the empire. Prized gladiators were much coveted by masters, and the *noxii* (the condemned) gladiators were fodder for entertainment in the arenas. The massive construction projects evident from existing ruins illustrate the large number of slaves tasked with the construction of temples, stadiums, theaters, libraries, roads, baths, basilicas, agoras, forums, shops, harbors, aqueducts, and bridges. Lacking the equipment we possess today, just the process of cutting stone blocks and transporting materials to the site of construction must have been monumental. None of this would have been possible without a large slave workforce.

The wealthy patrician families in Italy owned large tracts of land used for agricultural purposes, and large numbers of slaves were needed to work these farms. Pliny the Younger claimed that he held several estates throughout Italy. Yet he notes that his holdings were quite modest compared to the properties held by others.[9] It is not unusual to read about masters who owned hundreds of these slaves. Pliny the Elder claimed that Gaius Caecilius Isidorus had 4,116 slaves at his death, despite suffering heavy losses during their civil war.[10] Other slaves were used to deliver food and the raw materials needed to keep the legions supplied. Work in the mines and forests produced iron and timber, and the human labor involved was both difficult and dangerous.

---

9. Pliny the Younger, *Ep.* 2.4.
10. Pliny the Elder, *Nat.* 33.135.

The Magnitude of Slavery

FIGURE 11. African slave. Roman period. Bursa Archaeological Museum.

First-century slavery had little to do with race. There were no identifiable physical features that could indicate that someone was a slave. No discernible skin color, no hair or eye color, no shape for the eyes or nose, no height or clothing would suggest that an individual was a slave.[11] Walking on the streets of Rome, one might pass hundreds of people not knowing who was enslaved and who was free. "Slaves were, it would seem, indistinguishable from freemen, except so far as some enactments of late date slightly restricted their liberty of dress."[12]

In a highly structured society, though, it might be helpful to know the status of others. Seneca tells us that a proposal was put forward to the Roman Senate that slaves should be required to wear distinctive clothing. The proposal failed when it was noted that such a policy would make it clear that the slaves outnumbered the free and that this might endanger the citizens of Rome.[13] With the memory of slave revolts still fresh in the minds of the senators, no one wanted to make it easy for slaves to collaborate.

The failure of the proposal speaks volumes about the number of slaves in Rome. In terms of percentages, Rome had a larger slave population than the other cities of the Mediterranean. Jeffers refers to Rome as a "slave society" and cites three reasons why Rome had such large numbers: "the great increase in the landholdings of rich Romans, the depletion of the native workforce as its members were conscripted to fight its continual wars and the introduction of massive numbers of captured enemies in the slave market."[14] Appian asserts that "the race of slaves multiplied throughout the

---

11. "Most importantly, no single race was consigned to slavery by virtue of being part of that race." David A. deSilva, *Honor, Patronage, Kinship and Purity* (IVP Academic, 2000), 190.

12. William Warwick Buckland, *The Roman Law of Slavery: The Conditions of the Slave in Private Law from Augustus to Justinian* (Cambridge University Press, 1908), 5.

13. Seneca, *Clem.* 1.24.1.

14. James S. Jeffers, *The Greco-Roman World of the New Testament Era: Exploring the Background of Early Christianity* (IVP Academic, 1999), 221.

country while the Italian people dwindled in numbers and strength, being oppressed by penury, taxes and military service. If they had any respite from these evils they passed their time in idleness, because the land was held by the rich, who employed slaves instead of freemen as cultivators."[15]

Brunt maintains that 40 percent of Italy's population was enslaved by the second century (3 million of about 7.5 million total population).[16] Murphy-O'Connor believes a third of the population at Corinth were slaves and another third were freed slaves.[17] Scheidel suggests that 35 to 40 percent of the Italian population were slaves in the first century BC.[18] Barth and Blanke state: "In the great cities of Greece and Italy, as many as one-third of the inhabitants may have been slaves; in Corinth up to half. In Italy the number of slaves was drastically increased after the Punic Wars in the West and the conquest of Eastern territories; between about 200 and 150 B.C.E. 250,000 prisoners of war became slaves."[19] Earlier we mentioned the opinions of others who argue for smaller numbers of slaves across the Mediterranean region. Harris and Madden claim that the numbers ranged between 17 and 20 percent, while MacMullen opts for around 25 percent in the cities and only a few percent in the countryside.[20] Since large numbers of slaves worked in the fields in agricultural labor, I would tend to consider a higher percentage in the countryside. Even if we take the smaller numbers between 20 and 25 percent to be a safe estimate, the presence of slaves in the empire was extensive. These figures can be compounded by the number of freed slaves, which must have approximated the number of currently indentured slaves.

Roman Slave Revolts

Prior to the first century, the Romans experienced several slave revolts. These massive uprisings resulted in significant destruction of property and loss of life. In what has been considered the earliest slave revolt, Carthaginian slaves from the Second Punic War were moved to Setia, about forty

15. Appian, *Hist. rom.* 3.1.7.15–17 (McGing, LCL).

16. P. A. Brunt, *Italian Manpower 225 B.C.–A.D. 14* (Clarendon, 1987), 121–24.

17. Jerome Murphy-O'Connor, *1 Corinthians*, NTM 10 (Liturgical Press, 1979), xi.

18. Walter Scheidel, "Human Mobility in Roman Italy, II: The Slave Population," *JRS* 95 (2005): 64–79.

19. Markus Barth and Helmut Blanke, *The Letter to Philemon: A New Translation with Notes and Commentary*, ECC (Eerdmans, 2000), 8.

20. Harris, "Towards a Study," 118; Madden, "Slavery in the Roman Empire," 109–28; and MacMullen, "Late Roman Slavery," 359–82.

miles south of Rome. In 198 BC, the slaves rebelled. Rome sent troops with the city praetor, Lucius Cornelius Merula, and many of the rebels were captured, killed, or executed. Several fled to Praeneste, 20 miles east of Rome, where they were defeated, and another 500 slaves were executed.[21] Two slaves who revealed the plot were rewarded with their freedom and 25,000 asses each.[22] Two years later, in 196 BC, Manius Acilius Glabrio was sent to Etruria to quell a slave uprising. Accompanied by a legion of troops, Glabrio defeated the slaves, crucified the leaders, and sent the remaining slaves back to their masters.[23]

Livy describes a serious slave uprising in Apulia in 185 BC.[24] Reports emerged that slaves acting as shepherds were endangering the roads and countryside with robberies. Lucius Postumius, the praetor of Tarentum, seized around 7,000 of them and executed many, although a large number also escaped. The slave revolts that followed more than forty years later were much larger and more devastating to the region, the rich landowners, and the Roman sense of security.

The incomplete writings of Diodorus Siculus record a slave revolt in Sicily beginning around 141 BC and lasting about nine years. At the same time, revolts took place in the slave markets of Delos and Attica. Although the revolts at Delos and Attica were quickly suppressed, the Sicilian uprising was another matter. This revolt, which was precipitated by the harsh treatment of slaves by Damophilus, was led by a Syrian slave, Eunus, and the number of slaves involved was claimed to be 70,000 (according to Livy) or 200,000 (according to Diodorus). The rebellion lasted until 132 BC when the Roman consul, Publius Rupilius, ended the struggle.

Another outbreak began in 102 BC. This uprising was triggered by the manumission and then reversal of manumission of 800 slaves in Sicily by the propraetor Publius Licinius Nerva. Nerva sent soldiers to suppress the revolt, but they were slaughtered. Salvius Tryphon led the revolt with the Cilician Athenion. Together, they defeated another army assembled by Nerva. Salvius Tryphon's rebels numbered around 40,000.[25] It was not until 99 BC that the consul Manius Aquillius was able to assemble several cohorts to subdue the slaves.

---

21. Livy, *Ab urbe cond.* 32.26.4–18 (Conway and Walters, LCL).

22. "As" (plural "asses") was a Roman monetary unit that equaled about one-tenth of a denarius at this time.

23. Livy, *Ab urbe cond.* 33.36.1–3.

24. Livy, *Ab urbe cond.* 39.29.8–10.

25. Diodorus Siculus, *Bibliotheca historica* 36.8.

A final slave war began in 73 BC. The revolt began in Capua and soon grew to around 120,000 slaves. Many of them had been trained as gladiators, and the leaders took advantage of their training to defeat multiple Roman troops dispatched to suppress the revolt. This revolt was led by the famous Spartacus, and the slave army moved through southern and central Italy raiding the towns and countryside. Concerned with the security of Rome, the Senate sent eight legions led by Marcus Licinius Crassus to engage the rebel slaves. Crassus, aided by the legions of Pompey, defeated the slaves in 71 BC.[26]

Causes of Slavery

War

Rome's wars depleted the number of available laborers needed for agriculture. Rome had a hard enough time feeding its population without the loss of a significant portion of the workforce, and the enslavement of captives met the need for workers. As Rome's dominions grew and wealthy landowners acquired more property, the need for slaves intensified. Some have even suggested that an ancillary reason for the empire's expansion was to acquire more slaves. Wickham includes a valuable appendix listing examples from ancient sources of when the Romans captured prisoners of war from 502 BC through the first century AD.[27] The list contains 219 engagements where captives were taken. Several ancient sources do not offer specific numbers of prisoners. In a few instances, the captives were ransomed; in a small number of other instances, the captives were slaughtered; and in many cases, the outcome of the captives is not known. Yet in still many other instances, it is known that the captives were enslaved by the Romans or sold in slave markets elsewhere in the Mediterranean. Wickham's research concentrates on the years prior to 146 BC with the end of the Third Punic War, the sack of Corinth, and the end of the Achaean League. In a subsequent chapter, I will delve more deeply into developments in Galilee in the latter years of the first century BC when Rome tried to subdue the recalcitrant rebels of Galilee. In the paragraphs that follow, I highlight examples illustrating the massive enslavement of captives during the Roman Republican period.

---

26. Plutarch, *Crass.* 8.

27. Jason Paul Wickham, "The Enslavement of War Captives by the Romans to 146 BC" (PhD diss., University of Liverpool, 2014), 210–17.

During the First Punic War (264–241 BC), large numbers of slaves were taken and sold in the slave markets throughout the empire, many of whom were brought to Italy. In 262 BC, Roman troops surrounded, besieged, attacked, and conquered the Sicilian city of Agrigentum, capturing 25,000 as slaves.[28] Other victories at Mylae, Mytistratus, and Camarina, along with victories at the islands of Corsica and Sardinia, added smaller numbers of slaves. The fall of Aspis on the African mainland in 256 BC led to the capture of another 20,000 slaves seized from the African countryside.[29] When the Romans sacked Panormus in 254 BC, another 13,000 slaves were added to the tally. A final sea battle at the Aegates Islands in 241 BC produced another 10,000 slaves.[30] Overall, Frank estimates that at least 75,000 slaves were taken during the First Punic War.[31] Brunt asserts that there were perhaps as many as 500,000 slaves in Italy prior to the Second Punic War,[32] certainly not all from the war. Wickham argues for a smaller number, around 200,000.[33] Perhaps it is safe to assume that the actual numbers were somewhere in between. Scheidel posits a number between 311,000 and 351,000.[34]

FIGURE 12. Emperor Augustus and Nike (the goddess of victory) holding a trophy of conquest over the barbarians. The barbarian captive is depicted below with hands tied behind his back. Sebasteion, Aphrodisias. Early 1st c. AD. Aphrodisias Museum, Geyre, Türkiye.

Slaves were also sold to masters in other parts of the Mediterranean. Wickham further states that war supplied perhaps as little as a quarter of the overall slave population in Italy. "Whilst instances for the enslavement of war captives increased during the Second Punic War, it was still not the

28. Diodorus Siculus, *Bibliotheca historica* 23.9.1.

29. Livy, *Ab urbe cond.* 29.28.5.

30. Polybius, *Histories* 1.61.

31. Tenney Frank, *An Economic Survey of Ancient Rome*, vol. 1, *Rome and Italy of the Republic* (Johns Hopkins University Press, 1933), 67.

32. Brunt, *Italian Manpower*, 67.

33. Wickham, "Enslavement of War Captives," 146–47.

34. Walter Scheidel, "The Roman Slave Supply," in *The Cambridge World History of Slavery*, vol. 1, *The Ancient Mediterranean World*, ed. Keith Bradley and Paul Cartledge (Cambridge University Press, 2011), 297.

principal source of slaves considering the infrequent pattern of enslavements and the overall low figure for slaves realistically acquired in war and brought to Rome."[35]

The Second Punic War (218–201 BC) brought larger numbers of slaves to the Roman countryside. Wickham and Laroche claim that the number of slaves reported by Livy and Polybius is probably inflated.[36] Livy depended on Valerius Antias, who frequently exaggerated. Nevertheless, even discounting the inflated numbers, the number of slaves as a consequence of war clearly increased during the Second Punic War. The Third Punic War was a shorter affair, lasting from 149 to 146 BC. On the last day of battle, Carthage was destroyed, many of its inhabitants were killed, and 50,000 slaves were taken and sold in the slave markets.

During the Second Punic War, Philip V, king of Macedonia, allied with Hannibal and the Carthaginians. This was the beginning of four Macedonian wars with Rome. The first war was easily suppressed and ended with a treaty in 205 BC. The Second Macedonian War (200–196 BC) began after Rome's Second Punic War when Philip V attempted to conquer the Ptolemies in Egypt. Rome feared a growing Macedonian kingdom and intervened. In 196 BC, the Treaty of Tempea was signed, putting an end to hostilities. After Philip's death in 179 BC, his son Perseus again moved to acquire more territory. This was resolved in 168 BC when the Romans decisively defeated the Macedonians at the Battle of Pydna. At the conclusion of the Third Macedonian War in 167 BC, the Roman general L. Aemilius Paullus tore down the walls of seventy cities in Epirus, plundered a massive amount, and hauled 150,000 slaves of Epirus back to Rome.[37] A final Macedonian war was fought from 150 to 148 BC at the same time as the Third Punic War in Africa. This conflict quickly concluded with a second Roman victory at Pydna.

Meanwhile, trouble was brewing further south in Greece. The Achaean League, formerly allied with Rome, had expansionist ambitions and wanted to incorporate the southern Peloponnese, particularly Sparta, into the league. The Romans intervened and defeated the league's forces. In 146 BC,

---

35. Wickham, "Enslavement of War Captives," 147.

36. Wickham, 131; and Roland Laroche, "Valerius Antias and His Numerical Totals: A Reappraisal," *Historia* 26.3 (1977): 358–68.

37. Livy, *Ab urbe cond.* 45.34; Polybius, *Histories* 30.15; Adam Ziolkowski, "The Plundering of Epirus in 167 B.C.: Economic Considerations," *Papers of the British School at Rome* 54 (1986): 69; and Frank, *Economic Survey of Ancient Rome*, 1:188.

the same year Carthage fell, the Romans advanced to Corinth, the league's capital. They demolished the walls, plundered the city, and destroyed what was left. All the men of the city were executed, and the women and children were enslaved.[38]

The Romans were by no means the only ones taking slaves. Further to the east, the Greeks acquired slaves in large numbers. One distinctive feature of Greek enslavement is that the enslavement of Greeks by Greeks was, in most instances, prohibited or greatly discouraged.[39] The acquisition of slaves from wars outside Greece, however, was a common phenomenon. In 339 BC, the Macedonian King Philip II, the father of Alexander the Great, took 20,000 Scythian slaves. On his return to Macedonia, Philip's army was attacked by the Thracians and lost the entire company of slaves. His son, Alexander, took 30,000 slaves after his conquest of Tyre.[40] However, Alexander extended an olive branch to most cities during his conquests by not taking slaves. Exceptions were made at Gaza, where the obstinate men fought until

FIGURE 13. Broken funerary relief. Lost upper piece depicts Aulus Kapreilius reclining at a funerary banquet with the inscription: "Aulus Kapreilius, son Aulus, Freedman Timotheus, slavetrader." The surviving piece depicts his slaves producing wine. The bottom register shows shackled slaves following their master. 2nd or 1st c. BC. Amphipolis Archaeological Museum, Central Macedonia, Greece.

38. Pausanias, *Descr.* 7.16.2–9.

39. Kostas Vlassopoulos, "Slavery in Ancient Greece," in *The Palgrave Handbook of Global Slavery Throughout History*, ed. Damian Pargas and Juliane Schiel (Palgrave Macmillan, 2023), 70–71.

40. Arrian, *Anab.* 2.24.5.

the last,[41] and at the Bactrian city of Areia.[42] But these did not amount to large numbers of slaves. As Philip V tried to expand Macedonia's territories in the east, he enslaved the citizens of Cius and Thasos in 202 BC.[43] This and other military ventures precipitated the Second Macedonian War with Rome in 200 BC.

The Letter of Aristeas and Josephus relate that around 301 BC Ptolemy I came to Jerusalem and took over 100,000 Jewish slaves back to Egypt. Ptolemy II, his successor, freed these slaves and paid the Egyptian owners 20 drachmas for each slave released.[44] The subjugation of Palestine at the end of the first century BC and the subsequent uprisings brought more Jewish slaves to the slave markets. Less than a century later, Josephus claimed that Titus brought back 97,000 Jewish slaves from Galilee and Judea following the Jewish War with Rome.[45]

Even if, as some believe, the massive numbers of slaves captured from wars were inflated by ancient authors, the aggregate number of slaves still must have been enormous. One can add to this number unknown thousands more from battles, both large and small, where slaves were taken and not documented by our ancient sources. By far, the Roman war machine generated the vast bulk of slaves, but the battles and wars of other kingdoms and dominions contributed sizable numbers as well.

Piracy

The decline of the Seleucid and Ptolemaic Empires near the end of the second century BC created a power vacuum in the eastern Mediterranean, which was quickly filled with piracy. Diodotus Tryphon, a former Seleucid official, rose up against the Seleucid ruler Demetrius II Nicator, gathered an army, and utilized Cilician pirates to undermine Demetrius. Operating from a base in Coracesium in Rough Cilicia, Tryphon briefly seized the Seleucid throne but was killed in 138 BC. In the ensuing chaos, piracy proliferated in the far Mediterranean basin.[46]

41. Arrian, *Anab.* 2.27.

42. Arrian, *Anab.* 3.25.

43. Polybius, *Histories* 15.23–24.

44. Letter of Aristeas 12–25; Josephus, *Ant.* 12.1. Ernest L. Abel disputes the accounts by the unknown author of the Letter of Aristeas and by Josephus. "The Myth of Jewish Slavery in Ptolemaic Egypt," *REJ* 127 (1968): 253–58.

45. Josephus, *J.W.* 6.384, 420.

46. Strabo, *Geogr.* 14.5.2.

Crete and Cilicia emerged as major pirate havens. Crete's coastal cities and those on the southern shore of Anatolia were unable to fend off the pirates and fell under their control. The shoreline of Cilicia was particularly conducive to the needs of the pirates. With rich timber forests for building ships, hidden coves and sheltered water inlets along the coast, and an impenetrable mountainous interior a short distance inland, the Cilician coast was ideal for launching attacks on cargo-laden ships headed for Rome and the west.

FIGURE 14. Relief of a slave trader and three bound slaves. Miletus. 2nd–3rd c. AD. Istanbul Archaeological Museum. See gallery for color version.

The plunder of the pirates involved more than just the cargo onboard. A great deal of their income came from kidnapping and ransom. Sailors and passengers aboard captured ships were either ransomed or sold in the slave markets. Most of the southern port cities on the Anatolian coast were attacked and taken by pirates, with many residents captured and either sold in slave markets or ransomed by relatives. Many Syrian coastal cities were also sacked, and their residents sold. Strabo claimed that the large slave market at Delos could receive and sell as many as 10,000 slaves in a given day.[47] "With daily rates of up to one thousand persons, the islands of Chios and Delos, the Greek cities of Athens and Corinth, in the Near East Tyre

47. Strabo, *Geogr.* 14.5.2.

and Ephesus, in the West Rome and Syracuse were the most prosperous slave-trade centers. The majority of slaves sold on the market stemmed from the East."[48]

Initially, Rome did nothing to deal with the piracy. In fact, the Romans were pleased with the supply of slaves, which they gladly purchased in large numbers. Strabo places blame for the burgeoning market squarely on the Romans' shoulders: "The cause of this was the fact that the Romans, having become rich after the destruction of Carthage and Corinth, used many slaves; and the pirates, seeing the easy profit therein bloomed forth in great numbers, themselves not only going in quest of booty but also trafficking in slaves."[49] Westermann puts this in even stronger terms:

> The Roman state had been, for more than a half century, criminally negligent of its obligations in permitting the activities of the Cilician pirates to attain the scandalous proportions which they had assumed, rather than that Rome was incapable of meeting the military situation involved. The explanation of the Roman weakness is to be sought in the insistent and constantly growing demand for slaves in the West and the consequent development of an apathetic attitude among the ruling classes at Rome, perhaps amounting to conscious toleration of kidnapping as an occupation.[50]

Wealthy Romans increasingly depended on slaves to work the plantations and mines, and the slaves captured by pirates supplied this demand for labor. Additionally, the Romans were unconcerned about piracy in the eastern Mediterranean. The distance that separated Rome from Anatolia lent itself to a sense that the problem did not directly affect the lives of those in Rome.

The magnitude of the problem was illustrated by Diodorus Siculus around 104 BC. A Germanic tribe known as the Cimbri defeated the Roman army under Marcus Junius Silanus. This victory emboldened the recently subjugated Gauls, who began raiding the Gallic countryside and Hispania. The Senate sent Gaius Marius to deal with the problem. Marius tried to raise an army and sent envoys to Nicomedes, king of Bithynia. Nicomedes replied that most of the people of Bithynia had already been taken away as slaves and sold throughout the empire.[51]

---

48. Barth and Blanke, *Philemon*, 6.

49. Strabo, *Geogr.* 14.5.2, 329.

50. William L. Westermann, *The Slave Systems of Greek and Roman Antiquity* (American Philosophical Society, 1955), 65–66.

51. Diodorus Siculus, *Bibliotheca historica* 36.3.1.

In time, the piracy could no longer be ignored. The needed products from the east were choked off, and Rome had to deal with a problem that had gotten out of hand. The large grain ships navigating the Anatolian coast could no longer reach Rome. Italy's farms and estates were incapable of feeding Rome, leaving it heavily dependent on eastern provinces for food.

Roman Attempts to Deal with Piracy

To remedy the problem, Rome tried to annex Cilicia in 102 BC and sent the elder Marcus Antonius to Cilicia with military support. The Senate issued an edict, the *lex de provinciis praetoriis*, calling on the authorities of Anatolia, Cyprus, Syria, and Egypt to close their harbors to the pirates.[52] It is unlikely that Antonius received their full cooperation. The pirates were entrenched in several locations, making it difficult for the leaders of some ports to remove them. After fighting in a few skirmishes, Antonius purportedly returned victorious to Rome and was given a triumph in 101 BC. De Souza is probably right in suggesting that Antonius did not try to eradicate the pirate problem but was more interested in promoting himself with an exaggerated military campaign.[53] While pirates may have been driven out of some coastal cities, they retreated into the rugged mountainous interior of Rough Cilicia and returned to the coast shortly after the majority of the Roman troops departed. This action had little impact upon reducing pirate activity.

Predictably, the piracy continued after a short hiatus. Lucius Cornelius Sulla was assigned as governor of Cilicia in 96 BC. He was not only given the responsibility of subjugating the pirates, but he was also appointed to deal with a problem in Cappadocia.[54] The Pontic troublemaker Mithridates

52. Cicero, *De or.* 1.82; Livy, *Ab urbe cond.* 3.68. A copy of this edict was found at Delphi. In part, it reads: "The consul . . . shall order them to provide that Roman citizens and their Latin allies in Italy may conduct their business affairs, as is required, in the eastern cities and islands without danger and that they may be able to sail the seas in safety, and he shall remind them that Cilicia was occupied by the Roman people for these reasons and not from love of power or gain. . . . He shall make it clear that it is right for them to provide that no pirate shall proceed from their dominions, lands, or boundaries, that their magistrates and the commanders of garrisons whom they appoint shall not receive the pirates, and that they shall provide, so far as is in their power, that the Roman people shall have them as earnest cooperators for the common safety of all." Allan Chester Johnson, Paul Robinson Coleman-Norton, and Frank Card Bourne, *Ancient Roman Statutes: A Translation with Introduction, Commentary, Glossary, and Index* (University of Texas Press, 1961), 60.

53. Philip de Souza, *Piracy in the Graeco-Roman World* (Cambridge University Press, 1999), 104.

54. Lynda Telford, *Sulla: A Dictator Reconsidered* (Pen & Sword Military, 2014), 72.

VI had booted the Roman client king Ariobarzanes out of Cappadocia, and Sulla was given the task of restoring him to power. Sulla succeeded in restoring Ariobarzanes, but Mithridates continued to cause further problems for Rome. Sulla returned to Rome in 93 BC and was celebrated for his heroics, but he did little to address piracy in Cilicia.

Mithridates VI's aspirations to expand his kingdom soon brought him into conflict with Rome. In 88 BC, Rome had bigger problems than the pirates. Mithridates slaughtered 80,000 Roman citizens and associates in several cities throughout Asia and brought most of Anatolia under his control. Sulla was dispatched to Anatolia with several legions. There followed three Mithridatic wars from 88 BC until Mithridates's death in 63 BC. During that time, Mithridates collaborated with the pirates. In exchange for the pirates running supplies and attacking Roman forces, Mithridates allowed them to ravage the coasts. Appian relates that when Mithridates began the war, the pirates sailed in small fast ships, but as the war progressed, they acquired larger

> biremes and triremes, sailing in squadrons under pirate chiefs, who were like generals of an army. They fell upon unfortified towns. They undermined or battered down the walls of others or captured them by regular siege and plundered them. They carried off the wealthier citizens to their haven of refuge and held them for ransom. . . . They likened themselves to kings, tyrants, and great armies, and thought that if they should all come together in the same place, they would be invincible. They built ships and made all kinds of arms. Their chief seat was at a place called the Crags in Cilicia, which they had chosen as their common anchorage and encampment. They had castles and towers, and desert islands and retreats everywhere. They chose for their principal rendezvous the coast of Cilicia where it was rough and harborless and rose in high mountain peaks, for which reason they were all called by the common name of Cilicians.[55]

When the wars with Mithridates ended, the pirates continued to attack and plunder the coasts.

Publius Servilius Vatia was appointed governor of Cilicia in 78 BC, before the Third Mithridatic War. Vatia was given five legions and a large navy, partially composed of warships from Rhodes, which had an equal interest in eliminating the pirates. From his campaigns, it is evident that he did not want to tangle with the Cilician pirates. From 77 to 76 BC, Vatia attacked

55. Appian, *Hist. rom.* 12.92.

and captured pirate bases in the Lycian coastal cities of Phaselis, Corycus, and Olympus. At Olympus, Vatia's forces surrounded the region's pirate chief Zenicetes, who chose to set fire to his house and perish with his family rather than surrender to the Romans.[56] Vatia then ventured into western Pamphylia and then advanced northeast into the Taurus Mountains. From 76 to 75 BC, he conquered the rebellious Isaurian tribes and their allies, the Homonadeis and the Orondeis. Modern scholars follow Ormerod's conclusion that Vatia never fought further east in Cilicia.[57] Vatia's victories in Lycia and a portion of Pamphylia probably briefly reduced the piracy along the southern Anatolian coast, but nothing was done in Cilicia. Vatia returned to Rome in 74 BC, was given a triumph, and was honored with the title Isauricus, "Conqueror of the Isaurians." Isaurian prisoners, described as pirates, were paraded through Italy and Rome before being executed. But were they really pirates?[58] Roman authorities used propaganda to assure the people that the seas were safe, and Vatia was more interested in boasting of his achievements than in wiping out the pirate threats far away in Cilicia.

In 74 BC, Marcus Antonius Creticus (father of the better-known Mark Antony) was given unlimited imperium to deal with the pirates. He was the son of the orator Marcus Antonius, who earlier, in 102 BC, had tried unsuccessfully to eliminate the pirate threat. The grain supply for Rome and its legions was being disrupted to such a degree that something had to be done. To complicate matters, in 73 BC Mithridates emerged once again as a threat to Rome, and Rome was consumed with the Third Mithridatic War. For a long time, the island of Crete had been a haven for pirates, and at the outbreak of the war, Crete was supportive of Mithridates. In 72 BC, Antonius Creticus attacked Crete and was soundly defeated, in part because he was forced to requisition troops and money from cities throughout the Aegean. This went poorly, and in spite of the problem of piracy, the cities felt that his aggressive demands were extreme.[59] He was derisively given the title Creticus, "Conqueror of Crete," a contemptuous lampoon of Publius

56. Strabo, *Geogr.* 14.5.7.

57. "The only warrantable conclusion is that Servilius never penetrated into Cilicia Tracheia." H. A. Ormerod, "The Campaigns of Servilius Isauricus Against the Pirates," *JRS* 12 (1922): 42, 44.

58. De Souza thinks not. See *Piracy in the Graeco-Roman World*, 135.

59. Sallust claimed that Antonius was more malicious than the pirates. Pseudo-Asconius asserted that Antonius ravaged all the provinces that he was supposed to protect. Cf. T. V. Kudryavtseva, "Reconsidering the *imperium infinitum* of Marcus Antonius Creticus," *Vestnik of Saint Petersburg University* 64 (2019): 937–50.

Servilius Vatia's title of Isauricus. Antonius Creticus died in 71 BC of an unknown cause. His military campaign had no effect on the raging piracy in the Mediterranean.

The problem of piracy in the Mediterranean continued to grow, creating an increasing problem for Rome's grain supply because the massive city could not supply its needs locally. In 67 BC, the Senate gave Gnaeus Pompeius Magnus, known as Pompey, extensive powers and resources to deal with the problem. They gave him authority over the seas and coastal areas 50 miles inland.[60] This authority was unprecedented, yet it was indicative of Rome's perception of the problem. The topography along the southern Anatolian coast was shaped by the Taurus Mountains, which ran along the coast, creating an ideal terrain for the pirates. Pockmarked with coastal caves and hidden coves, the Cilician pirates could easily surprise cargo ships and retreat to their harbors. If pursued, the pirates had the surrounding high ground, cliffs, and rugged terrain for their defense and escape.

Pompey's objective was to invade and destroy the pirates' land bases. His tactics involved an ambitious land war over the rough territory of southern Anatolia. Incredibly, he and his legions finished the job in an astonishing 89 days.

The first part of the operation took 40 days.[61] The objective was to clear the western Mediterranean of pirates in order to secure the flow of grain to the city. De Souza comments, "The speed with which Pompey cleared the seas before heading for Cilicia makes it unlikely that a thorough operation was carried out."[62] The next phase of the operation was perhaps even more impressive. Cicero claimed that Pompey sacked all of Cilicia and that all of the pirates "were either taken prisoners and put to death or surrendered themselves voluntarily to the power and authority of this one man."[63] Again, de Souza is incredulous, maintaining that it was a rush job that had little lasting impact on the affairs of Cilicia.[64] Once the grain shipments returned to Rome, the people of Rome had little interest in what was transpiring in the far eastern reaches of the Mediterranean.

The conquest of the eastern Mediterranean pirates was impressive, not only for the speed at which it took place but also for the ease of the cam-

---

60. Cassius Dio, *Hist. rom.* 36.36.
61. Appian, *Hist. rom.* 12.95.
62. De Souza, *Piracy in the Graeco-Roman World*, 168.
63. Cicero, *Leg. man.* 12.35 (Hodge, LCL).
64. De Souza, *Piracy in the Graeco-Roman World*, 168–69.

paign. Roman propaganda attributed this to the power and benevolence of Pompey. According to the sources, the reputation of Pompey struck such fear into the pirates that many were willing to strike a deal. Pompey offered them land in exchange for abandoning their pirate activities. Cassius Dio and Appian both report that the cowering pirates realized the futility of fighting Pompey and knew that he would offer gracious terms for surrender.[65] According to the narrative, one after another, the pirate enclaves surrendered to Pompey. His decisive defeat of the pirates at Coracesium in western Cilicia (modern Alanya) resulted in the surrender of most of the pirates. They were then resettled further east to Soli (later renamed Pompeiopolis in honor of Pompey), Adana, Mallus, and Epiphaneia, where they were given land and encouraged to take up farming.

But did the pirates really abandon the seas and assume an agrarian lifestyle? Probably not.[66] All the communities in which pirates were resettled, with the exception of Adana (located on the Saros River, ten miles upstream from the sea), were seaside towns. Once Pompey's legions departed, piracy continued as in the past. Later Roman sources indicate that piracy persisted long after Pompey's campaigns. Meanwhile, slaves captured by pirates continued to flow into the markets.

Why was Pompey so hasty in his conquest and dealings with the pirates? Here again, it seems that the pesky problem with Mithridates VI was the bigger issue. Pompey needed to deal with the pirates in order to finish off Mithridates. In 66 BC, the Senate appointed Pompey to march north with his legions to battle Mithridates. There is no evidence that Pompey engaged any of the pirates east of Coracesium. He quickly concluded his campaigns against the pirates through a negotiated settlement and moved on to Pontus. This did not stop the piracy in Cilicia any more than his predecessors' efforts had. Pirates do not become placid tillers of the soil.

Debt Slavery

Poverty was a massive problem in antiquity. Estimates indicate that around 90 percent of the population in the Mediterranean lived in poverty, and

65. Cassius Dio, *Hist. rom.* 36.37.4; Appian, *Hist. rom.* 12.96.

66. In spite of Roman propaganda to the contrary, de Souza argues that the Romans never drove the pirates out of the region. He states, "It seems clear that piracy was still a major concern in the Mediterranean during the last few decades of the Republic and at the beginning of the Principate." *Piracy in the Graeco-Roman World*, 179.

around 67 percent of the population lived at or below subsistence level.[67] Steven J. Friesen breaks it down this way:

PS1. Imperial Elites	0.04%
PS2. Regional Elites	1.00%
PS3. Municipal Elites	1.76%
PS4. Moderate Surplus	7%
PS5. Stable near Subsistence	22%
PS6. At Subsistence	40%
PS7. Below Subsistence	28%[68]

The large gap between the very small, wealthy, and powerful minority and the huge, poor, peasant majority could potentially spell trouble. The gross inequity of wealth lent itself to instability and social upheaval. There was practically no middle class and few opportunities to overcome poverty. The problem was mitigated to some degree by a small retainer class. These retainers would be slaves or persons hired from the peasantry to assist the wealthy in controlling the peasants while enabling the wealthy to retain or increase their wealth. They commonly functioned as tax collectors and mid- or low-level administrators in cities and towns. Additionally, a strong patron-client structure in Roman culture kept peasants dependent on their wealthy patrons for food, employment, and other needs. Even at that, patrons were not able to alleviate the enormous burden of poverty for the majority of the people. This suggests that theft was common and that indebtedness was even more common. Jesus's parables in the Gospels commonly refer to individuals who have fallen deeply in debt and face the prospect of being sold into slavery.

There were three ways individuals could be enslaved for unpaid debts. First, they could voluntarily offer themselves as payment for their debts. This is known as debt bondage. Debt bondage was not permanent. The debtor could secure their freedom through labor or payment. Second, parents could offer one of their children as payment for the family's debts.

---

67. Steven J. Friesen, "Injustice or God's Will? Early Christian Explanations of Poverty," in *Wealth and Poverty in Early Church and Society*, ed. Susan R. Holman (Baker Academic, 2008), 19–20; and Walter Scheidel and Steven J. Friesen, "The Size of the Economy and the Distribution of Income in the Roman Empire," *JRS* 99 (2009): 61–91.

68. Friesen, "Injustice or God's Will?," 20.

Typically, the child could be redeemed later with a payment. Third, if the debtor was unable to repay a debt, the creditor could take them to court. The court could order the debtor to be sold as a slave if there was no feasible way for them to repay the debt.[69]

FIGURE 15. Sale of a baby. Titos, son of Lykos, buys from Amphotera the two-month-old slave girl, Nike. 3rd c. AD. Thessaloniki Archaeological Museum.

The number of debtor slaves was a problem as early as the sixth century BC. The *Athēnaīn politeia*, written by Aristotle or one of his students, asserts that all the land was in the hands of the rich and that the peasants were obliged to rent farmland. If anyone failed to pay the rent, then they, their wife, and their children were liable to be sold as slaves.[70] Solon's reforms in Athens in 594 BC overturned many of the draconian laws but also canceled debts, abolished the slavery of Athenians by fellow Athenians, and repatriated Athenian slaves who had been sold abroad. The reforms also forbade the use of the body as collateral for the repayment of a debt.[71]

Finley argues that chattel slavery became the dominant form of slavery, replacing debt bondage, after the Roman abolition of *nexum* in 326 BC.[72] *Nexum* was the Roman term for debt bondage. When the number of slaves obtained through debt bondage diminished, the need for slaves was filled by chattel slaves acquired through war. The Senate did away with bondage by

69. Westerman, *Slave Systems*, 4.

70. *Ath. pol.* 2.2–3.

71. *Ath. pol.* 6.1. Edward M. Harris, "Did Solon Abolish Debt-Bondage?," *ClQ* 52 (2002): 415–30, argues that Solon abolished only enslavement for debt but not debt bondage. The distinction that Harris makes is that in debt bondage, the debtor was able to work off his debt. Debt bondage was not a permanent condition. Harris claims that Solon's reforms forbade the permanent enslavement of a person for debt and that debt slavery continued after the reforms.

72. Moses I. Finley, *Ancient Slavery and Modern Ideology* (Chatto & Windus, 1980), 82–87.

nexum following the brutality of Lucius Papirius, who abused a boy given for debt bondage.[73] The Roman *nexus* debtor became the property of their creditor until the debt was paid through labor or payment from another person. The creditor could sell the debtor. Debtors retained their Roman citizenship and could serve as soldiers in the legions.[74] Challenging Finley's assertions, Kleijwegt suggests that debt slavery in some form continued after 326 BC:

> It seems that there is enough evidence to make the claim that enslavement for debt did not disappear after 326. The continuing enslavement of citizens for debt makes it very difficult to entertain the idea that an important pool of involuntary labour had become completely dried up, necessitating the introduction of other forms of involuntary labour.[75]

Westerman insists that enslavement for the refusal or inability to pay taxes was also common in the Seleucid and Ptolemaic kingdoms.[76] Egyptian laws make it clear that debt bondage and debt enslavement were prevalent in that land. However, similar to Solon's reforms in Greece, the laws in Alexandria prohibited the citizens of Alexandria from owning fellow Alexandrian citizens.

The arrest and enslavement of individuals for nonpayment of taxes was common in Palestine during the Roman period. This contributed to unrest in Galilee when the Romans occupied Palestine. Zealot leaders, such as Judas of Gamala and Saddok, asserted that the payment of taxes to the Romans was equivalent to slavery. They stirred up the people to refrain from paying taxes, which was a contributing factor leading to the war with Rome.[77] The refusal of Galilean villages to pay taxes to Rome actually preceded the actions of Judas and Saddok; at least a decade earlier, many towns and villages were sacked and their residents sold in the slave markets.

Abandoned Children

The economic hardships of peasants in the first-century Mediterranean world made it difficult to feed and clothe large families. With birth control

73. Livy, *Ab urbe cond.* 8.28.

74. Marc Kleijwegt, "Debt Bondage and Chattel Slavery in Early Rome," in *Debt and Slavery in the Mediterranean and Atlantic Worlds*, ed. Gwyn Campbell and Alessandro Stanziani (Routledge, 2013), 30.

75. Kleijwegt, 36.

76. Westerman, *Slave Systems*, 30.

77. Josephus, *Ant.* 18.1.1–2; *J.W.* 2.8.1.

unavailable, the prospect of rearing another child was often seen as impractical. Consequently, the exposure of children was a harsh reality of the time. Female infants were more commonly exposed, as male children were considered more valuable because they could generate more income for the family later in life. Although poverty was a major factor, it was not the only reason an infant might be exposed. An illegitimate child of a nobleman might be exposed, as could an infant with a physical defect. According to the Roman Twelve Tables (*lex duodecim tabularum*), it was mandated that a handicapped or deformed child be put to death.[78] Exposure was an ancient and common practice. As Bennett notes,

> In the mythology of ancient Greece, the exposure of infants is a very common phenomenon. . . . When, therefore, we learn that Zeus, Poseidon, Hephaistus, Asclepius, Ion and Oedipus were all exposed at their birth and left to die, we are justified in assuming that this method was employed by the primitive Greeks for disposing of their own unwelcome children.[79]

Bennett and Radin disagree on whether exposure was permitted and practiced during the Roman Republic, but they agree that the practice was clear during the imperial period. As Bennett notes: "Definitely attested cases of exposure begin to appear at the end of the republic."[80]

Among the letters of Pliny to Trajan, four of them mention people described as θρεπτοί (*threptoi*).[81] These are described as children exposed at birth and then reared by others.[82] Pliny's description makes it clear that they were born free, exposed, and raised as slaves. One letter mentions several such individuals who appeared before Pliny asking that their birthright as citizens be reestablished.[83] Pliny reported that the issue was an important one that affected the entire province. The practice affected more than just Bithynia. During the third century in North Africa, Tertullian criticized the

78. Max Radin, "The Exposure of Infants in Roman Law and Practice," *CJ* 20 (1925), 339; and H. Bennett, "The Exposure of Infants in Ancient Rome," *CJ* 18 (1923), 345.

79. Bennett, "Exposure of Infants," 344.

80. Bennett continues: "I venture to assert, however, that the exposure of a legitimate child of citizen parents was still a rare occurrence at the beginning of the empire." "Exposure of Infants," 347. W. V. Harris goes much further, claiming that "the evidence is after all, nearly overwhelming." "Child-Exposure in the Roman Empire," *JRS* 84 (1994): 1.

81. LSJ, s.v. θρεπτός.

82. Pliny the Younger, *Ep.* 10.65–66.

83. Pliny the Younger, *Ep.* 10.72–73. The correspondence implies that the original status of the exposed infant could be reclaimed later in life.

parricide of the Romans—both of the born and unborn. But he described the exposure of children to cold, hunger, and the dogs as most cruel.[84]

Parents would leave their infants outside the village or somewhere remote to die of hunger, thirst, hypothermia, or an animal attack. In some instances, children were dropped off at a location in Rome, and perhaps elsewhere, where infants were often left with hopes that they might be adopted. One might imagine that a friend of the mother would linger in the area to see if the child was taken and by whom.The parent might hope that the infant would be taken by someone who was barren and would raise the child as their own. In other cases, the infant would be raised in slavery or sold into slavery or prostitution.

The survival of an exposed infant depended on a number of factors. Foremost was the desire of the parents to keep the child alive. The father, as *paterfamilias*, held the right to determine the infant's fate. If the child was illegitimate, the mother made the decision. If the parent wanted the child to survive, the child might be abandoned but would be well fed to endure a long period without food and would be clothed to keep warm. Of course, the physical condition of the child after birth determined the length of survival and the desirability of the child to be rescued. Premature infants or those with respiratory problems might never get the chance to live. Gender was another important factor. Male children were more commonly rescued. Ultimately, the child's fate depended on being found by someone with the means and desire to feed and rear the child.

Slavery Due to Crime

Poverty drove others to crime. Some people in such desperate states stole money or goods to meet their families' needs. Those caught faced various penalties, including slavery. Criminals prosecuted for theft or other crimes might also be enslaved to the city or state. In Rome, Alexandria, and several Greek cities, such slaves could not be enslaved in their own city but rather had to be sold elsewhere. Some of these slaves were forced into the amphitheaters as condemned *noxii* to fight with beasts or armed gladiators. Ancient cites did not have prisons to hold criminals who needed to be removed from society for long terms. Thus, the arenas were where they met their end. *Noxii* in Rome's Colosseum were expected to greet the emperor

84. Tertullian, *Apol.* 9.

with the words: *Ave Imperator, morituri te salutant* ("Hail, Emperor, those who are about to die salute you"). Slaves and criminals were common fodder for the entertainment of the crowds in the "spectacles."

Birth to Slave Parents

Generally speaking, slaves were not permitted to be married.[85] However, there are known slave families. This can be accounted for by two reasons. First, a husband and wife may have been married before they were enslaved. This was often the case when slavery took place as a consequence of war. In slave markets, the married couple could be sold to separate owners, and if they had children, the family could be entirely separated and sold to whomever. Slave owners, however, recognized that a slave might better cooperate and work harder if allowed to keep their family. Thus married couples were sometimes purchased together and permitted to live together.[86]

Less frequently, unmarried slaves could choose a mate, or their master could assign them a spouse.[87] Such unions were on the periphery of Roman law, and they were given the name *contubernalis*, "companions." The term continued to be used even if the couple were freed. Children born to slave couples were not free; rather, they were owned by their parents' masters. Rarely, a slave was married to a free person. Treggiari examined 260 inscriptions of *contubernia* from Rome. Most were between slaves or freed slaves. But among the few that were between slaves and free persons, it was more common for a free female to marry a male slave than the other way around.[88] In such cases, children born to the free woman were considered free. Even more rarely, a free man might marry a female slave. In such cases, children born to the slave woman were considered slaves of her master. After Cato the Elder's wife passed away, he married his slave Salonia. Although technically she was a slave, Cato freed her prior to the marriage to make it legal.

---

85. "Legally, slave marriages were not recognized, and it was the owner's prerogative to sell off members of a slave's immediate family." Dale B. Martin, *Slavery as Salvation: The Metaphor of Slavery in Pauline Christianity* (Yale University Press, 1990), 2.

86. Martin refers to a large number of slave funerary inscriptions documenting family relations and suggests that "the evidence should dissuade us from assuming that a slave was automatically removed from the place and family of birth." Yet, as Martin notes, we need to be cautious about funerary inscriptions since only well-to-do slaves would have had permanent markers on their graves. *Slavery as Salvation*, 6.

87. Keith Bradley, *Slavery and Society at Rome* (Cambridge University Press, 1994), 50–51.

88. Susan Treggiari, "*Contubernales* in *CIL* 6," *Phoenix* 35 (1981): 45, 50.

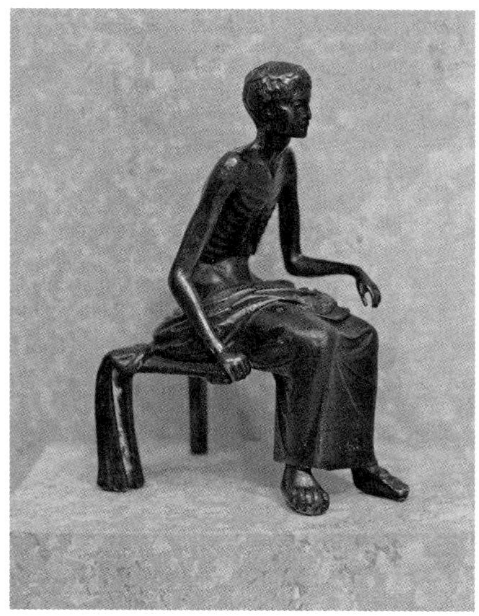

FIGURE 16. *Left,* Terracotta lamp with slaves carrying a barrel with poles. AD 175–225. Italy. British Museum.

FIGURE 17. *Right,* Small bronze emaciated slave with inscribed name "Eudamidas." 1st c. AD. Dumbarton Oaks, Washington, DC. See gallery for color versions.

Use and Conditions of Slavery

Most slaves were involved in common labor, with a massive number needed for agricultural tasks. Others worked in herding, mining, and construction. Monumental projects for roads, streets, theaters, stadiums, temples, civic buildings, baths, markets, and harbors required a multitude of slaves who were involved in stone cutting, transport, and construction. The welfare of these slaves was of little regard to their masters, and the dangers they faced were viewed as occupational hazards. Not much is known about the lives of slaves consigned to menial labor. Their labors were demanding, living conditions were poor, and their treatment by overlords could be fair, harsh, or brutal, as is known in some cases. Seen as disposable human property, their lives were unacknowledged even in death. They were thrown into paupers' graves without permanent markers, leaving their stories long forgotten.

In Apuleius's novel *Metamorphoses*, he illustrates the harsh life of slaves working at a mill. Although the work is a novel, Apuleius was drawing on the bleak, cruel, and abusive realities of slavery in the second century.

FIGURE 18. Funerary relief of relatives: Dionysios, Pammenos, Dionysios, and Theocritos. Three household slaves are depicted holding vessels. From Cyzicos, Hellenistic period. Istanbul Archaeological Museum.

FIGURE 19. Funerary stele of Ameinokleia leaning on her slave as she helps with a sandal. Found at Piraeus, 4th c. BC. Athens National Archaeological Museum. See gallery for color version.

> As to the human contingent—what a crew!—their whole bodies picked out with livid weals, their whip-scarred backs shaded rather than covered by their tattered rags, some with only a scanty loincloth by way of covering, and all of them showing through the rents in what clothes they had. There were branded foreheads, half-shaven heads, and fettered ankles, their faces were sallow, their eyes so bleared by the smoky heat of the furnaces that they were half blind; and like boxers, who sprinkle themselves with dust before fighting, they were dirty white all over with a floury powder.[89]

Masses of slaves destined for hard labor were cursed with exhausting toil in brutal conditions during the heat of the day, overseen by uncaring foremen who were tasked with demanding production quotas. Fettered and branded, the slaves had little prospect for relief or escape.

Many served as household slaves who supplied the personal needs of their masters. They acted as cleaners, cooks, tutors, gardeners, attendants, groomers, and personal guards. Skilled slaves could offer income opportunities for their masters, working as weavers, fullers, blacksmiths, butchers,

89. Apuleius, *Metam. 9.12, The Golden Ass, or Metamorphoses,* trans. E. J. Kenney (Penguin, 1998).

Clockwise from top left, FIGURE 20. Funerary inscription: "Here lies Italos. Chrestos buried his faithful steward." Iznik Archaeological Museum.

FIGURE 21. Funerary inscription: "The Steward [ΠΡΑΓΜΑΤΕΥΤΗΣ], a slave of God, while still alive built this tomb with the surrounding area to the wall for his children." Konya Museum.

FIGURE 22. Funerary relief. "Farewell, Kallikrite." Deceased woman with weeping daughter clinging to her tunic. Household slave looks up while holding burial spices. Hellenistic period. Izmir Archaeological Museum. See gallery for color version.

FIGURE 23. Funerary relief from Berea depicting two men and a slave. 1st c. BC, Thessaloniki Archaeological Museum.

bakers, leather workers, potters, carpenters, masons, writers, prostitutes, shopkeepers, and entertainers. Slaves often provided entertainment for their masters and their guests. Banquets were prominent social events, and the invited guests were amused by musicians, singers, dancers, jugglers, magicians, actors, and philosophers. Slaves could be rented to others in the community who could not afford to purchase one.

Managerial slaves (οἰκονόμοι) were highly valued. These trusted slaves operated agricultural plantations, vineyards, orchards, or other operations possessed by the slave owner.[90] They often acted as their master's agent in financial transactions and had managerial skills to oversee the work performed by other slaves. Merchants rarely traveled with goods to be sold, due to the dangers of robbers on the roads. Instead, these managerial slaves functioned as their master's representatives and completed the transactions. Jesus told parables about managerial stewards. In Luke 12:42–48 (the faithful steward) and 16:1–12 (the unrighteous steward), Jesus used managerial slaves as analogies for faithful and unfaithful disciples. Household slaves were generally well treated, respected, and loved by their owners. In death, they were usually honored with modest tombstones and sometimes represented on the funerary reliefs of their masters. On a larger, grand scale, wealthy citizens could sponsor blood events (*munera*) in amphitheaters (or theaters and stadiums modified to accommodate such events). These could include the spectacle (*spectacula gladiatorum*), as it was called, which pitted gladiators against one another, or featured animal hunts (*venationes*), or public executions of the condemned (*noxii*).[91]

Destined for execution, the *noxii* were slaves or criminals supplied with no weapons and no protection. They were slaughtered by animals or armed gladiators for the entertainment of the people. These *munera* were costly events that provided an opportunity for the host to advance his standing in the city. The gladiators in the spectacles were usually slaves trained in combat and equipped with various pieces of armor and weapons. Strong, agile, and well-trained gladiators who often won were hailed as heroes, much like sports figures. On the few occasions when they lost in the spectacle, they were usually spared death. The funerary inscriptions of several gladiators

---

90. Martin, citing Landvogt, asserts that by the early Roman period, all *oikonomoi* "were without exception taken from the slave population." Peter Vandvogt, *Epigraphische Untersuchung über den Oikonomos* (M. Dumont Schauberg, 1908), 8, 13 cited in Martin, *Slavery as Salvation*, 16.

91. Cf. Donald G. Kyle, *Spectacles of Death in Ancient Rome* (Routledge, 1998).

document their records, with both wins and losses. The corpses of the *noxii* and gladiators who performed poorly were mutilated and dragged out of the arena with hooks dug into their chests or necks as insults to the deceased. Victorious gladiator slaves were prized possessions of their owners and received public acclaim.

Highly skilled slaves could be employed as artists, philosophers, tutors, teachers, doctors, or lawyers. Almost any profession occupied by free persons could be occupations taken by slaves, whose profits were given to their masters. Some slaves, however, were able to keep a portion of their income, known as *peculium*. This was not unique to highly skilled slaves but rather a "slave wage" offered at the discretion of their owners. With the accumulation of *peculium*, it was possible for some slaves to purchase their freedom. As Martin states, "The price of freedom for an educated or managerial slave could be quite high."[92]

Some slaves were purchased for municipal, provincial, or imperial purposes. They might act as guards, constables, workers at the baths, functionaries at the temples, or clerks. Some were tasked with maintenance, work in the latrines, civic repairs, cleaning, garbage collection, and operational oversight in the agoras. Dockworkers were usually municipal slaves, as were attendants at the civic courts.

Contrary to popular notions of ancient slavery, many slaves in the first century enjoyed better health, living conditions, security, and sometimes even better financial standing than they had formerly. Slaves in positions above common labor usually lived under better conditions overall than they had as free persons. "Though the institution of slavery was severely oppressive, some slaves were able to manipulate it to become rather powerful persons with a certain degree of informal status in the society."[93]

FIGURE 24. *Top left*, Funerary relief of Gaius Popillus with his slave holding a scroll. Bilingual inscription: "Gaius Popillus, farewell, and with the many who pass by, farewell." 50 BC. Thessaloniki Archaeological Museum.

FIGURE 25. *Top right*, Roman terracotta lamp depicting a Murmillo gladiator standing over a defeated gladiator. Amphipolis Archaeological Museum. See gallery for color version.

FIGURE 26. *Middle right*, Venetio gladiator contest with the *noxii* (the condemned). Nysa, Roman period. Aydin Museum.

FIGURE 27. *Bottom right*, "Theodora made this for Lupercus, the courageous." Accompanied by his slave Apollonis. AD 150–200. Thessaloniki Archaeological Museum.

FIGURE 28. *Bottom left*, Murmillo gladiator, victorious nine times. Milas Museum.

92. Martin, *Slavery as Salvation*, 8.

93. Martin, xiii.

FIGURE 29. Funerary relief of Matrodoros, a writer. The slave lifting a scroll may have been his amanuensis. 1st c. BC. Istanbul Archaeological Museum.

Length of Slavery, Manumission, and Roman Citizenship

The types of slavery varied over time throughout the Mediterranean world. It is generally acknowledged that chattel slavery was the norm in Greece during the Archaic (700–500 BC) and Classical periods (500–300 BC).[94] Chattel slaves were regarded as the property of their owners and had little prospect of freedom. Aristotle justified slavery racially, believing that certain races were stupid and needed to be controlled.[95] During the Roman Republic, most slaves taken in war were chattel slaves.[96] However, by the time of the Roman Empire, most slaves were able to gain their freedom through payments or dutiful service to their masters. Lenski states, "Often loyal and productive slaves could expect manumission by a certain age, c. 25–

94. Niall McKeown, "Greek and Roman Slavery," in *The Routledge History of Slavery*, ed. Gad Heuman and Trevor Burnard (Routledge, 2011), 20–21.

95. Peter Garnsey, *Ideas of Slavery from Aristotle to Augustine* (Cambridge University Press, 1996), 107–27.

96. Westermann, *Slave Systems*, 80.

30, although this was never guaranteed."[97] He continues: "Attempting to assign numbers and percentages is difficult given the nature of our evidence, but careful analysis of the sources (especially inscriptions) points to remarkably high rates of manumission. Perhaps more than 30 percent of urban slaves above the age of 25 could have expected to be given freedom, and many have argued the numbers were even higher."[98] Thiselton asserts that "most domestic slaves could hope for manumissions by their early thirties. Cicero observed that many could expect freedom in seven years."[99] Jeffers adds, "We know of few urban slaves who reached old age before gaining their freedom."[100]

FIGURE 30. Bilingual funerary inscription of Lucius Cornelius Neon, erected by Poplios Tetrenios, freedman of Amphios. 50 BC. Thessaloniki Archaeological Museum.

The prospect of freedom added a stabilizing element to the massive number of slaves in the Mediterranean world. The earlier slave revolts in Italy and Sicily were prompted in large part by the mistreatment of slaves and the improbability of them ever achieving freedom. These concerns were somewhat mollified by Roman laws regarding the treatment of slaves and the broadening of manumission. In addition, these laws encouraged slaves to work harder and to buy into the system. The *peculium*, given for good work, was an incentive, and the accumulation of those assets could enable slaves to buy their freedom even earlier. This was a positive development for the Romans.

97. Noel Lenski, "Slavery in the Roman Empire," in *The Palgrave Handbook of Global Slavery Throughout History*, ed. Damian A. Pargas and Juliane Schiel (Palgrave Macmillan, 2023), 87–108, 103.

98. Lenski, 102.

99. Anthony C. Thiselton, *The First Epistle to the Corinthians: A Commentary on the Greek Text*, NIGTC (Eerdmans, 2000), 565.

100. Jeffers, *Greco-Roman World*, 229.

FIGURE 31. Latin funerary inscription: "Quintus Codicarius Florentinus and Codicaria Eutchia built this tomb for their relatives and their freedman and freedwomen." 2nd c. AD. Vatican Museum.

Freed slaves who were owned by Roman citizens were usually given Roman citizenship. This raised the status of former slaves, giving them rights and protections. "Manumission was both more common and more rewarding for the beneficiary in Rome than in Greece. Emancipated slaves belonging in certain categories—those manumitted formally in front of a magistrate . . . became Roman citizens automatically. This made a big difference to their lives."[101] "So long as slaves were acquired mainly by the conquest and capture of free peoples, *ingenuitas* [citizens born to Roman parents] would not be so obvious a criterion of social differentiation between the citizen by birth, the free born non-Roman admitted to citizenship, and the ex-slave, originally freeborn, restored to freedom and given citizenship."[102] In AD 4, Caesar Augustus, concerned that too many slaves were being freed and given citizenship, passed the *Lex Aelia Sentia*, a law proscribing the manumission of slaves until at least thirty years of age.[103] He also regulated how many slaves could be freed per year.[104]

101. Garnsey, *Ideas of Slavery*, 97.

102. Jane F. Gardner, "The Adoption of Roman Freedmen," *Phoenix* 43 (1989): 236–57, 240.

103. Kathleen M. T. Atkinson, "The Purpose of the Manumission Laws of Augustus," *Irish Jurist*, n.s. 1 (1966): 356–74.

104. Jeffers, *Greco-Roman World*, 230.

Patron-Client Relationships and Adoption

FIGURE 32. Bronze diploma granting citizenship to a retired soldier of the Praetorian Guard from Aelia Musa. AD 246. British Museum. See gallery for color version.

Patron-client relationships were ubiquitous throughout the Roman Empire. In a society where most were destitute and less than 1 percent were wealthy and empowered, patronage was necessary to control the masses. The society had a pyramidal structure, with the emperor at the top. He was the patron to governors and lower-level administrators, whose positions depended on the whims of the emperor, and their support for the emperor was required in return. These governors, in turn, were patrons who appointed local officials and civic leaders. These civic leaders likewise functioned as patrons to their clients, who were expected to offer support in return. This system extended all the way to the bottom of society with peasants and slaves.[105] At the base of society, peasants would search for patrons who would offer them a small dole of food, money, or work in exchange for their support.

Almost all freed slaves retained a relationship with their former master. This was an expectation of honor. Often, a freed slave would initially find it hard to find employment, although those with trade skills might find it somewhat easier. Some continued to work the same jobs as freedmen. Some could open shops owned or supported by their masters. Nevertheless, they continued to serve their former owners in patron-client relationships.[106] Clients commonly received money or food from their patrons. In a society and culture with little upward mobility, slavery in some cases benefited poor

105. DeSilva's *Honor, Patronage, Kinship and Purity* is excellent. See esp. chapter 3, "Patronage and Reciprocity: The Social Context of Grace," and chapter 4, "Patronage and Grace in the New Testament."

106. Thiselton, *First Epistle to the Corinthians*, 565.

peasants who otherwise would struggle for food and survival. Freed slaves likewise would struggle for life's essentials. Clients supported their patrons through social and political support as active and verbal advocates. Patrons could call on their clients for varied purposes as needs arose.

FIGURE 33. *Top*, Bronze diploma found at Laertes in Pamphylia granting citizenship and the right to marry to a retired soldier from Cyrrhos, Syria. AD 138. Alanya Museum. See gallery for color version.

FIGURE 34. *Left*, Bronze diploma granting citizenship and the right to marry to the retired Decurion Reburrus. Issued by Trajan, AD 103. British Museum. See gallery for color version.

FIGURE 35. *Right*, Bronze diploma granting citizenship and the right to marry to Dasmenus Azalus. Issued by Antonius Pius, AD 149. Metropolitan Museum of Art, New York.

In some cases, freed slaves were adopted into the household of their masters. As such, they acquired the status of their family,[107] and they were given the *praenomen* (personal name) and *nomen* (family name) of their master.[108] It appears that a master could also give a slave to someone else, who would manumit and adopt the former slave.[109] As Gardner concludes:

> In the early Republic, it appears that adoption by Roman citizens gave freedmen in all respects the same status as freeborn citizens. By the end of the Republic (for reasons probably connected with a change in the concept of citizenship itself), adoption no longer removed their public disabilities as freedmen or their obligations to their patrons. . . . There could also be direct economic advantages for the adopter and ultimately the adoptee.[110]

FIGURE 36. Marble funerary altar of Quintus Fabius Diogenes and Fabia Primigenia. The altar was erected by the freedmen and freedwomen of Diogenes, early 1st c. AD. Metropolitan Museum of Art, New York.

This may explain how the apostle Paul was given a Roman name. His Jewish name was Saul, but the Acts of the Apostles refers to him as Paul in the later chapters (13–28). Paul may have preferred the name Saul in the presence of Jews and the name Paul when in the presence of Greeks and Romans.

---

107. The first-century Roman jurist Masurius Sabinus (Aulus Gellius, *Noct. att.* 5, 19, 13) protested against a Roman law that allowed former slaves to be adopted and receive the status of their freeborn masters. "If that ancient law should be protected, even a slave can be given the rights of citizenship by his master in adoption." Hugh Lindsay, *Adoption in the Roman World* (Cambridge University Press, 2009), 76.

108. "Roman freedmen could be, and were, adopted by Roman citizens; there is legal and (perhaps) epigraphic evidence for the practice." Gardner, "Adoption of Roman Freed men," 236. Also, "The habit of a freedman taking on the *praenomen* and *nomen* of his patron could lead to ambiguities" (253).

109. "It appears that in Ancient Rome manumission by adoption took two forms: (1) Adoption of the slave by the master himself. (2) The giving of the slave by the master into adoption by a third party." Jacob J. Rabinowitz, "Manumission of Slaves in Roman Law and Oriental Law," *JNES* 19 (1960): 43. Rabinowitz claims that two fifth-century BC Aramaic papyrus manuscripts in the Brooklyn Museum document these methods of manumission and adoption.

110. Gardner, "Adoption of Roman Freedmen," 252–53.

| 2 |
Status, Honor, and Shame in First-Century Mediterranean Culture

Let not these reflections oppress you: "I shall live without honor and be a nobody anywhere." For, if lack of honor is an evil, you cannot be in evil through the instrumentality of some other person any more than you can be in shame, . . . how is it that you will be "a nobody anywhere," when you ought to be somebody only in these things which are under your control?

Epictetus, *Enchiridion* 24 (Oldfather, LCL 218, 499, 501)

Status

In every society, there exist social strata that determine one's place or rank. Typically, this stratification results from factors such as wealth, education, gender, race, family history, tribalism, employment, religion, physical strength, speaking abilities, and personal appearance. Societies arrange people on this scale according to what the community considers most important to least important. Those factors vary from one society to another, and the importance assigned to each one may differ in value. In every society, past and present, slaves occupy the lowest echelons of society. Regarding the first century, Martin states: "Slave terminology almost always carries negative connotations in Greco-Roman literature. Slaves are despised, and terms such as *doulos* and *servus* connote abuse or degradation. Other related terms derived from the institution of slavery are likewise devoid of positive meanings."[1]

Those individuals who rank on the higher levels of the social strata have a stronger voice in community decision-making, beliefs, and opinion for-

1. Martin, *Slavery as Salvation*, 46.

mation. The voices of those lower on the scale, if at odds with those higher, are often marginalized or ignored. More honor is given to those at the top of the scale and less to those at the bottom.

Roman dinners were important events for social posturing. They typically included nine or more invited guests who reclined on three or more couches arranged in a "U" shape. This arrangement, called a *triclinium*, was how Jesus celebrated the Last Supper. For most people, particularly peasants, an invitation to a dinner by a patron was an honor and an opportunity. Good food and entertainment or a lecture were standard fare. More important, however, was the opportunity to ascend, even marginally, the social ladder.

The Gospel of Luke records an incident when Jesus was invited to dine with a high-ranking Pharisee. After entering the house of a "leader of the Pharisees"—that is, a person near the pinnacle of Jewish influence—Jesus noticed the invited guests jockeying for the seats of honor at the table. Reacting to what he saw, Jesus told a parable:

> When you are invited by someone to a wedding feast, do not take the place of honor, for someone more distinguished than you may have been invited by him, and he who invited you both will come and say to you, "Give your place to this man," and then in disgrace you proceed to occupy the last place. But when you are invited, go and recline at the last place, so that when the one who has invited you comes, he may say to you, "Friend, move up higher"; then you will have honor in the sight of all who are at the table with you. For everyone who exalts himself will be humbled, and he who humbles himself will be exalted. And He also went on to say to the one who had invited Him, "When you give a luncheon or a dinner, do not invite your friends or your brothers or your relatives or rich neighbors, otherwise they may also invite you in return and that will be your repayment. But when you give a reception, invite the poor, the crippled, the lame, the blind, and you will be blessed, since they do not have the means to repay you; for you will be repaid at the resurrection of the righteous." (Luke 14:8–14)

In the parable, Jesus described the humiliation of an individual who was moved to a lower position at the table by the host. In contrast, Jesus instructed his listeners to take the least honorable position at the table so that they might be recognized for greater honor and moved to a higher position. He expanded on the parable by applying this teaching to those who were near the bottom of the social scale: the poor, the crippled, the lame, and the blind. Most of them were never invited to a nobleman's *triclinium*.

The parable is similar to the satires that Martial commonly wrote against wealthy people in Rome. One person, Phasis, relished his honorable seat in the theater, only to be moved later to the cheap seats for the peasants. As Phasis sat in the theater "praising the edict of our Lord and God [a reference to the emperor Domitian]," he exclaimed, "At last we can sit more comfortably. Equestrian dignity (*dignitas equestris*) is now restored, we are no longer pressed and soiled by the crowd."[2] Moments later, "Leitus [the attendant] ordered that resplendent and arrogant cloak to get up."[3] The best seats in the theater were reserved for those of the equestrian and senatorial ranks. Phasis's removal of one from these prestigious theater seats and the lowering of his status was an embarrassment, a huge blow to his dignity, and a cause for shame. Since this was such a common theme in Martial's satires, we conclude that he frequently witnessed arrogant wealthy people who overplayed their status and lost their dignity when that status was diminished. "Nanneius, who always used to sit in the first row in the days when squatting was allowed, was roused and moved camp twice and thrice." Finally, he positioned himself in a manner so as to appear to be sitting with those in the equestrian class.[4] "Loss of these ranks was a serious blow in a society where one's *dignitas* mattered almost as much as life itself."[5]

"The Romans evaluated a person's status based on whether the person was a citizen or foreigner, patron or client, free or slave, ethnic Roman/Latin or not, voluntary ally or conquered enemy, male or female, and married or unmarried."[6] Wealth and citizenship were preeminent. Those at the top of the social order were the senators. These were the old, established ruling families (patricians) who passed down their wealth and privilege to their descendants. Later, commoners (plebeians) were allowed into the Senate. Members of this class were required to possess assets of at least 400,000 sesterces. Later, Caesar Augustus raised the qualification to 1,000,000 sesterces. A second order, known as the equestrian order, had to maintain assets of at least 400,000 sesterces.[7]

---

2. Domitian restored the law (Roscian Law) that the places of honor in the stadiums and theaters be reserved exclusively for members of the equestrian order.

3. Martial, *Epigrams* 5.8 (Bailey, LCL).

4. Martial, *Epigrams* 5.14.

5. Albert A. Bell Jr., *Exploring the New Testament World: An Illustrated Guide to the World of Jesus and the First Christians* (Thomas Nelson, 1998), 187.

6. Jeffers, *Greco-Roman World*, 182.

7. Martial mentioned several people who fell somewhat below the 400,000-sesterce level who tried to borrow from friends in order to reach the threshold. Martial, *Epigrams* 5.23, 25.

The status of many people in the first century was evident from their name, title, clothing, wealth, or community recognition. Members of the senatorial class wore a toga with a broad purple stripe. Equestrians wore gold rings for identification along with togas with a thin purple stripe. These orders commanded respectful greetings on the streets and were usually accompanied by an entourage of clients, bodyguards, and friends. These two groups constituted less than 0.1 percent of the population and were the rulers of the empire and at the provincial levels of the Mediterranean world.

At the other end of the spectrum were the peasants and slaves, who made up around 95 percent of the population across the Mediterranean. Below the peasants, and in many ways indistinguishable from them, were the slaves. The clothing of the slaves was similar to that of most poor peasants, so it was not always easy to recognize slaves on the streets. However, many slaves were marked with a brand or tattoo, commonly called the stigma (στίγμα), somewhere on their bodies. Slaves were at the bottom of the social strata, and they were thought to be little more than living objects or talking possessions.

Perceptions of status, as well as estimates of honor and shame, exist at every level of society. Within each substratum, there are varying levels of status. And no matter how much or how little honor or dishonor is accorded to the strata above or below, honor and dishonor may be distributed differently within the substratum. As Garnsey and Saller convey:

> Since statuses reflect values and outlook rather than legal regulations, distinctions are less precise than in the case of orders. The principal ingredients of rank—birth and wealth—were not always in step with each other; a few of the very wealthiest came from very humble backgrounds, and some with the best pedigrees fell into poverty. Other factors, such as power, education and perceived moral stature, lent prestige to the holders and were not the exclusive possession of men of high rank.[8]

Because losing wealth would lower their status, many people of the senatorial and equestrian rank chose not to disclose their misfortunes and pretended to still retain their positions. Likewise, peasants might keep events of the past secret, inasmuch as possible, in order to preserve their personal dignity. The dishonor of one's former slave status was not evident to outsiders. Thus, in the company of strangers or while traveling in distant cities, a freedman could blend in with the free citizens of any town or city.

---

8. Peter Garnsey and Richard Saller, *The Roman Empire: Economy, Society and Culture* (University of California Press, 1987), 118.

However, among those who knew the former slave, the shame associated with slavery remained as a reproach or blot on their social standing. Jeffers states that almost 80 people were associated with the apostle Paul, and we are able to somewhat discern the social status of 30 of them.[9] Of those, only Onesimus is known to be a slave. However, based on their names and occupations, Jeffers suggests that Luke, Tertius, and Ampliatus may have been slaves (Rom 16:8). Yet, none of them were identified as such.

Martin has done much to illuminate the positive possibilities of being a slave. He observes:

> For some people—who, though a minority, were highly visible—slavery was a means of upward social mobility and was recognized as such throughout the society. Upper-class people bemoaned the fact; people originating from or caught in low-status positions celebrated it. Slavery did not mean the same thing to different people in the society. . . . The positive meaning of slavery, however, depended on certain factors. The lowest levels of slavery, and that may have been where most slaves served, knew few possibilities for improvement. Middle-level managerial slaves, educated slaves, and those trained in skills could nurse hopes more confidently. Furthermore, the wealth, position, and disposition of the owner were directly relevant for ascertaining a slave's own position in society and for predicting his or her future.[10]

The high-rank of senatorial or equestrian citizens elevated the status of those who served under them.

The authority of a senator's managerial slave or steward, although derivative, was directly related to the authority of the senator himself. This represented only a small fraction of the slaves in the Mediterranean world. However, as Martin's work has shown, for the many peasants who could barely feed their families, this was a significant movement, not only financially but also, for a few, an increase in status. Barrier, however, emphasizes the broader perspective and the experiences of the majority of the slaves: "Dale Martin attempts to create a positive gloss to the Christian designation of 'slave of Christ.' . . . While there is truth in this statement, one cannot overlook the fact that slavery is a form of severe subordination, no matter what society one might consider. In other words, slavery is social death."[11]

9. Jeffers, *Greco-Roman World*, 194.

10. Martin, *Slavery as Salvation*, 48–49.

11. Jeremy W. Barrier, "Paul and His Master: Defining and Applying a Postcolonial Definition to Galatians 6:17," *CSSRB* 35 (2006): 37.

FIGURE 37. Egyptian marble votive relief: "Epaphroditus, freedman [ΑΠΕΛΕΥΘΕΡΟΣ], dedicated this to Isis." Athens National Archaeological Museum.

Freed slaves, as well, could rise in status, but this depended on several factors, primarily their former master. Many freed slaves were reemployed by their former master, while others entered into patron-client relationships. If their former master was a Roman citizen, the freed slave might be granted Roman citizenship. In some cases, slaves were freed and then adopted into their master's family. However, many slaves were cut loose from their masters and left to fend for themselves, looking for food, shelter, clothing, and medical care. Even with their new freedom, freed slaves carried a negative social distinction that could not be erased.

It would not be surprising if Paul kept the matter of his own former slavery to himself because the reproach of having once been a slave might hinder some opportunities to share the gospel. Paul's mission strategy was to not place obstacles in the way of doing ministry. This was explained in the apostle's letter to the Corinthians, a city in which roughly a third of the population were slaves:

> For though I am free from all men, I have made myself a slave to all, so that I may win more. To the Jews I became as a Jew, so that I might win Jews; to those who are under the Law, as under the Law though not being myself under the Law, so that I might win those who are under the Law; to those who are without law, as without law, though not being without the law of God but under the law of Christ, so that I might win those who are without law. To the weak I became weak, that I might win the weak; I have become all things to all men, so that I may by all means save some. I do all things for the sake of the gospel. (1 Cor 9:19–23)

Paul adapted his message and actions to his audience. As a Jew, he could act in accordance with Jewish sensibilities and convey the gospel in ways that would not offend his listeners. Yet, as one who lived in Tarsus for a significant portion of his life, he knew Greco-Roman culture, literature, and social structures. Paul could share the gospel with gentiles in a way that made sense, bridging the chasm of status distinctions.

His status as a freedman added nothing to his message, but in some circles, it could have had a detrimental impact.

FIGURE 38. "Claudius Aristion made this tomb for his faithful and master-loving friend Maryllos." AD 117–18. Uşak Archaeological Museum.

Honor and Shame

Two thousand years ago, honor and shame were powerful factors guiding the lives and conduct of people in the Mediterranean world. People who were once free but, for reasons beyond their control, now found themselves enslaved were humiliated by the shame of slavery. For Aristotle, most slaves were thought to be subordinate beings from birth and thus fit for the service of others. The cultural differences that separate us today from the ancient world make it difficult for us to understand how this impacted the lives of slaves in the first century. The conditions and treatment of slaves varied, and their masters generally utilized the talents and skills of their slaves. Skilled slaves were highly valued, cost more at slave markets, and generally lived lives free of abuse. Others were consigned to harsh labor and suffered from austere living conditions. Nevertheless, the prevailing opinion was that slaves were subhuman "living property,"[12] and the shame of slavery lasted beyond the term of enslavement.

Honor and shame involve a sense of one's social standing and the community's perception of an individual's rank and value. Thus, the assessment of honor or shame is dependent on what a particular culture deems shameful or honorable. As Witherington notes: "What a society gives honor or homage to tells us a great deal about that society's major values. And if a culture loses its sense of shame, it also loses its sense of honor for these

12. The often-quoted belief of Aristotle, *Pol.* 1.4. Aristotle, on the basis of the natural created order, supported gender subordination, the superiority of Greeks over Barbarians, and the subjugation (perhaps even the dehumanization) of slaves. Aristotle believed that from the time of birth, some are created for subjection and others for rule (*Pol.* 1.5).

two concepts work in tandem."[13] Three dominant elements of honor and shame were the acquisition of wealth and power, and one's past failures. Failures and the loss of wealth or power were causes of humiliation and shame. Slaves were not the only people who experienced shame. Even the wealthy and powerful could be shamed due to inappropriate behavior or a community's shifting perception. Failure or cowardice in war, a humiliating loss in a public debate, demotion from a leadership position, or the failure of a financial venture could bring shame.

FIGURE 39. "Herein lies the slave of God, freedman Demetrios." Byzantine reliquary. Early Byzantine period. Silifke Museum.

Shame also has an introspective aspect. It is not just a matter of what one's culture may consider shameful. Shame also is an individual's personal assessment of their value or conduct. This may be largely influenced by the surrounding culture, but it is also a personal sense of one's measure. Has one lived up to their expectations? Has an individual failed to accomplish what was needed or desired? Chronic shame can lead to depression and suicide, particularly if there appears to be no way to gain honor.

Many people today might say we in America live in a shameless culture. Much of what used to be hidden has now come to light. The exposure of our private lives, however unseemly, now seems to be a cause for celebration for some. The shame that was formerly associated with certain behaviors has now evaporated in contemporary Western culture. Tamler Sommers's best-selling *Why Honor Matters* puts it this way: "Honor cultures probably rely too much on shame, but our modern alternative is an epidemic of shamelessness."[14] Perhaps some things are best left hidden.

Elsewhere in the world, many societies still have strong notions of honor and shame. Our Muslim neighbors, for instance, regard honor as among the highest virtues. Honesty, generosity, and loyalty contribute to a tightly committed community (the *ummah* in Arabic) in Muslim societies.

13. Ben Witherington III, *The Paul Quest: The Renewed Search for the Jew of Tarsus* (IVP Academic, 1998), 45.

14. Tamler Sommers, *Why Honor Matters* (Basic Books, 2018).

The welfare of the *ummah* over the individual is a distinguishing feature of Islamic culture. The honor of an individual is celebrated by the *ummah*, and the dishonor of an individual creates shame for the family and community.

FIGURE 40. The Roman emperor holding a victory trophy while being crowned by a personification of the Roman Senate. Below, a bound barbarian woman kneels and weeps. Sebasteion, Aphrodisias. Early 1st c. AD. Aphrodisias Museum.

I have traveled to Turkey every year for the past twenty-five years. My research has taken me to all parts of the land, from the Aegean Sea to the Mesopotamian rivers, the Tigris and Euphrates, from the Black Sea to the Mediterranean, and most places in between. I have met and befriended dozens of Turkish people. The population of Turkey is more than 99 percent Muslim. I often travel alone in the country. When I first began these journeys, I thought that I, an American, would not be welcomed by the people of the land. American political policy and its military presence in the Middle East are not favorably received by most of the Muslim world. I was surprised to discover the opposite to be true. The Turkish people have embraced me with more hospitality and trust than what I typically experience meeting strangers in my own country. I have been repeatedly welcomed by Turks who realized that I was an outsider. These kind people have fed me, housed me, traveled with me, and once even loaned me their automobile. I never asked for such courtesies.

On one occasion, I asked my new Turkish friend why they treated me so well. He responded that the welcoming of strangers brings honor to the home and that the neglect of strangers brings shame to the home and community. Those words hit home. I remembered the words of Jesus: "I was hungry, and you gave me something to eat. I was thirsty, and you gave me drink. I was a stranger, and you invited me in" (Matt 25:35). I do not welcome strangers like that, yet I was standing in the house of a Muslim who was doing what Jesus said. Hebrews 13:2 came to mind: "Do not neglect to show hospitality to strangers, for by this some have entertained angels without knowing it." I felt the shame that my Muslim host was wanting to avoid. Perhaps America needs a bit of that.

There is a darker side to honor and shame, particularly when it has to do with community shame. Insults directed at the Quran, Muhammad, or Muslim leaders are understood to be insults to all Muslims. The perception among some Muslims is that the shame must be alleviated by an act of honor, which sometimes is violent. The response to the publication of caricatures of Muhammad in the Danish *Jyllands-Posten* and the French *Charlie Hebdo* demonstrates the power of honor and shame in the Muslim world. These terroristic reactions in the modern Muslim world are by no means representative of Muslims worldwide. Opinion polls indicate that only a minority of Muslims believe that suicide bombings against civilians are sometimes or often justified.[15]

Sexual indiscretions also deeply shame not only the individual or family but also the community. Support for honor killings to uphold family honor is significantly higher in these Islamic communities than support for terrorism.[16] Additionally, support for honor killings of women is generally higher than the support for honor killings of men who have engaged in pre- or extramarital sex. In extreme cases, the rape of an innocent woman sometimes results in the victim and her family being isolated from the *ummah* and scorned. In some instances, the family feels compelled to publicly beat or kill the woman to requite the shame. These examples not only illustrate the radical nature of honor and shame cultures, but they also point to the tacit acknowledgment of honor and shame in the broader majority and the less radicalized communities.

Malina and Neyrey define honor as "the positive value of a person in his or her own eyes plus the positive appreciation of that person in the eyes of his or her social group. In this perspective honor is a claim to positive

15. Pew's 2013 poll indicates that support for such terroristic acts differs from region to region and country to country. The strongest support comes from the Middle East and North Africa, where support ranges between 7 percent in Iraq to 29 percent in Egypt and 40 percent in the Palestinian Territories. The weakest support comes from Southern and Eastern Europe, where support ranges between 3 percent in Bosnia-Herzegovina and 11 percent in Kosovo. The percentages in Central Asia, Southeast Asia, and South Asia fall somewhere between these numbers. Cf. Pew Research Center's Forum on Religion & Public Life, "The World's Muslims: Religion, Politics and Society" (Pew Research Center, 2013), 68–71.

16. "In 14 of the 23 countries where the question was asked, at least half say honor killings are never justified when a woman stands accused. Similarly, at least half in 15 of 23 countries say honor killings of accused men are never justified." Pew Research Center's Forum on Religion & Public Life, 89.

worth along with the social acknowledgment of that worth by others."[17] Regardless of how a person may consider their own honor, it is the honor or shame of the social group or surrounding community that weighs most heavily, and that group perception inspires or curtails the behavior of most people. DeSilva notes,

> While the powerful and the masses, the philosophers and the Jews, the pagans and the Christians all regarded honor and dishonor as their primary axis of value, each group would fill out the picture of what constituted honorable behavior or character in terms of its own distinctive set of beliefs and values and would evaluate people both inside and outside that group accordingly.[18]

Honor could be "ascribed" or "acquired."[19] Ascribed honor was not earned but rather attributed to a person via birth. Persons of noble birth or those born to wealthy or famous parents were considered honorable. On the other hand, persons born to dishonorable parents, poor parents, or those enslaved were considered without honor. It was possible, however, to acquire honor through one's actions. Bravery, physical prowess, victory in battle, eloquence, beneficence, and intellectual superiority were common ways to gain honor. The opposite of those attributes, however, brought shame and dishonor: cowardice, weakness, defeat, ignorance, and greed.

As with honor, shame could be "ascribed" or "acquired." Ascribed shame was associated with an ignoble birth, with membership in a shamed group, or with disease or physical disabilities. Ascribed shame was assigned to a person or group through no actions of their own. Acquired shame was attributed to those who acted contrary to the established values and behaviors of the group. Illegal or immoral behaviors brought about shame for the individual and for their associated family or group.

In the first century, slaves did not carry shame for their own misdeeds or for the dishonor brought on their families or people. The shame stemmed from the mythic stereotypes associated with slaves. "Contempt for slaves as a class abounds in the literature of antiquity from the fifth century BC, surfacing first in Greek tragedy. Slaves were idle, libidinous, greedy, bibulous, thieving, violent, treacherous and stupid—or if not stupid, scheming."[20] In addition, the shame of slavery was implicit in the very nature of being a

---

17. Bruce J. Malina and Jerome H. Neyrey, "Honor and Shame in Luke-Acts: Pivotal Values of the Mediterranean World," in *The Social World of Luke-Acts: Models for Interpretation*, ed. Jerome H. Neyrey (Hendrickson, 1991), 26.

18. DeSilva, *Honor, Patronage, Kinship and Purity*, 25.

19. This is well described by Malina and Neyrey, "Honor and Shame," 27–29.

20. Garnsey, *Ideas of Slavery*, 73.

slave: the loss of personal freedom and the humiliation of being the property of another. For a freed person, the shame might lie in the abuse suffered or the scars still evident on the person's skin.

Even after emancipation, the stigma of having been a slave hung ominously over the freed person.

> For all these status differences, the ultimate legal dependence of all slaves made them less difficult to accommodate in the Roman hierarchy than freedmen. Freedmen—as free, Roman citizens, able to accumulate great wealth in theory, and sometimes in practice, and yet tainted by their servile background—encapsulate the contradictions between rank and status that Roman society had to accommodate.[21]

Insults directed against freedmen by those of higher status lingered in conversations and written literature. Even the uncommon, freed slave who acquired wealth was not excluded from such scorn. "Freedom, citizenship and wealth, it was claimed, could not change the uncultured, servile spirit of a former slave."[22] In Petronius's *Satyricon*, Trimalchio's friend, a freedman, boasted of his accomplishments to overcome the shame of his former slavery: "And now I hope I live such a life that no one can jeer at me."[23]

For Jews whose national history was scarred by slavery in Egypt and Babylon, the prospect of slavery was a particularly sensitive issue. This is illustrated by Jewish funerary inscriptions in Rome. In the first century, there were thousands of Jewish slaves in Rome. The vast majority were slaves or former slaves (freedmen) brought there through the Roman conquests of Palestine. Yet, of the more than 500 Jewish funerary inscriptions that have been discovered, not one asserts that the deceased was a slave or freedman.[24] It can be understood that Paul followed this train of thought. He realized that his ministry in the synagogues and streets of the Mediterranean would be hampered if his slave past was well known.

Paul's Understanding of Status, Honor, and Shame

Honor and shame were dominant in the Mediterranean world, but the perceptions of what was honorable or shameful differed from one culture to another. Those of high status looked down on the occupations of the poor

---

21. Garnsey and Saller, *Roman Empire: Economy, Society and Culture*, 120.
22. Garnsey and Saller, 120.
23. Petronius, *Satyricon*, trans. P. G. Walsh, Oxford World's Classics (Oxford University Press, 1997), 57.
24. Martin, "Slavery and the Ancient Jewish Family," 120.

and considered manual labor a servile task of peasants. Cicero, for instance, asserted: "Unbecoming to a gentleman, too, and vulgar are the means of livelihood of all hired workmen whom we pay for mere manual labor, not for artistic skill; for in their case the very wage they received is a pledge of their slavery."[25] Cicero claimed that reputable occupations for freemen involved a higher degree of intelligence or professions that benefitted society, such as teaching, medicine, and architecture. At the other end of the scale, Cicero despised those who labored in workshops of various sorts, as well as fishermen, butchers, and cooks.

Hock has raised the issue of Paul's work as a tentmaker. Since Paul was trained by the famed rabbi Gamaliel, possessed a command of the Greek language, gained Roman citizenship, and was well acquainted with Greco-Roman literature and culture, it is often assumed that he came from a wealthy, high-class Jewish family.[26] However, Hock recognizes that Paul's work as a tentmaker calls this assumption into question: "Paul's working at a trade had, on the one hand, allowed him to be self-supporting and so free, but his very trade had, on the other hand, also made him appear slavish. By entering the workshop, he had brought about a considerable loss of status, since, as Cicero put it, a workshop can in no way be an appropriate place for a free man."[27] This notion falls in line with the views of early Christians such as John Chrysostom, Gregory of Nyssa, and Theodoret who believed that Paul and his family were peasants.[28]

Ultimately, Hock concludes that Paul did come from the Jewish upper class:

> When Paul's use of status terms is taken into consideration, it becomes clear that the attitude toward work expressed in those terms corresponds more closely to that of the upper classes than to that of the lower. . . . By working at

---

25. Cicero, *On Duties.* 1.150.

26. Bruce Chilton seems unaware of this difficulty: "Families of wealthy men such as Paul's father could afford real mansions with courtyards, space for the extended family, and servants' quarters" (p. 13), and "Paul's family enjoyed the services of slaves and had contacts with many other Jewish families who owned slaves. They could easily afford to detail one or several of them to teach the children their letters and numbers and higher subjects" (p. 20). *Rabbi Paul: An Intellectual Biography* (Doubleday, 2004).

27. Ronald F. Hock, "Paul's Tentmaking and the Problem of His Social Class," *JBL* 97 (1978): 559–60.

28. According to Chrysostom, Paul "was not from a distinguished family. For how is that possible, if he had such an occupation?" Hock, "Paul's Tentmaking," 556. John Chrysostom, *De laud. S. Pauli* 4.494 (PG 50:491); Gregory, *Ep.17* (PG46:1061B); Theodoret, *De grace. aff. curat.* 5, 9 (PG 83:945B, 948C and 1053B).

> a slavish and demeaning trade Paul sensed a considerable loss of status, a loss that makes sense only if he were from a relatively high social class.[29]

The term "tentmaker" described the occupation of Aquila, Priscilla, and Paul in Acts 18:3. The Greek σκηνοποιοὶ is commonly translated "tentmakers," but the word could simply refer to leathermakers, since most tents were made of leather. However, if tentmaking is the intended understanding of the word, they may have made tents of *cilicium*, goat's hair.[30] Goat's hair had excellent water-repellent qualities. The word *cilicium* was so named because many of these tents were made in Cilicia, the province of Paul's home. One might resolve Hock's conundrum by speculating that Paul's family was indeed a family of high status as the evidence suggests, but that after being cast into slavery, they were forced to work in an "unbecoming, slavish" trade (as Cicero would describe it) in Cilicia, producing tents, some of *cilicium*, for which Cilicia was known, and some of leather.

The Christian subculture differed in many respects from the Greco-Roman notions of honor and shame. The support or violation of common moral principles by acts such as theft, murder, adultery, deception, and betrayal was universally acknowledged as honorable or shameful. But Christians took a different view of the honors bestowed on the rich and the shame associated with the poor. The Christian virtue of humility was viewed as a weakness in the surrounding culture of pride. Paul laid out this contrast in his letter to the Corinthians:

> Who regards you as superior? . . . We are fools for Christ's sake, but you are prudent in Christ; we are weak, but you are strong; you are distinguished, but we are without honor. To this present hour we are both hungry and thirsty, and are poorly clothed, and are roughly treated, and are homeless; and we toil, working with our own hands; when we are reviled, we bless; when we are persecuted, we endure; when we are slandered, we try to conciliate; we have become as the scum of the world, the dregs of all things, even until now. I do not write these things to shame you, but to admonish you as my beloved children. (1 Cor 4:7, 10–14)

Here, Paul was challenging the established categories of honor and shame. The ironic dissimilarity between the church's notions of honor and Paul's humble state caused the Corinthians to disrespect Paul and question his apostolic authority and teachings. Could someone with such dishonor

29. Hock, 564.
30. Wilhelm Michaelis, "σκηνοποιός," *TDNT* 7:393–94.

and shame really be a spokesperson for God? The contrasts between the Corinthians' expectations for an apostle and Paul's ministerial approach were stark.

Paul	**Corinthian Expectations**
Fools	Prudent
Weak	Strong
Without honor	Distinguished (4:10)
Hungry and thirsty	Implied [well-fed]
Poorly clothed	Implied [well-dressed]
Roughly treated	Implied [pampered]
Homeless	Implied [housed] (4:11)
Toiling in work	Implied [nobility do not work]
We bless	When reviled
We endure	When persecuted (4:12)
We conciliate	When slandered
The scum of the world	Implied [esteemed]
The dregs of all things	Implied [respected]

Fee comments: "The Corinthians' pride in spiritual status apparently included a degree of embarrassment for them over Paul's lack thereof, not to mention his lack of wisdom and eloquence. It was perhaps doubtful from their perspective whether he was an apostle with much standing."[31]

The Corinthian expectations were common for community leaders, politicians, teachers, philosophers, and lawyers. But the qualifications expected of Paul may have been inflated by Corinth's proximity to Athens, a short 54 miles away. Even though the golden age of Athens was past, the glow of Athens's reputation for rhetoric and philosophy still spilled over into Corinth. The best and brightest philosophers still came to Athens. Luke observed: "All the Athenians and the strangers visiting there used to spend their time in nothing other than telling or hearing something new" (Acts 17:21). Contrary to what we have been conditioned to think, Paul was not a great speaker. After conversing with the Epicurean and Stoic philosophers, their reaction was: "What would this idle babbler wish to say?" (17:18). When given the chance to address the people at the Areopagus, Paul was unconvincing, leading to ridicule and a prompt dismissal (17:32). When

31. Gordon D. Fee, *The First Epistle to the Corinthians*, rev. ed., NICNT (Eerdmans, 2014), 191.

Corinth superseded Athens in population and became the administrative capital of Achaea, many of the leading philosophers and teachings made their way to Corinth. By comparison, Paul was not in the same league with the dynamic and persuasive speakers of Corinth.

Criticism of Paul continued to grow in the church at Corinth. By the time the apostle wrote 2 Corinthians, he was forced to defend his ministry despite his weaknesses. His detractors particularly attacked his speech and lack of personal charisma. "For they say, 'His letters are weighty and strong, but his personal presence is unimpressive and his speech contemptible" (2 Cor 10:10). In response, the apostle stated, "You are looking at things as they are outwardly" (2 Cor 10:7). "But even if I am unskilled in speech, yet I am not so in knowledge; in fact, in every way we have made this evident to you in all things" (2 Cor 11:6). The Corinthians' categories of honor and shame reflected the Roman culture prevalent throughout the empire. But Paul's standard of honor derived from an honor bereft of worldly notions.

> I was with you in weakness and in fear and in much trembling, and my message and my preaching were not in persuasive words of wisdom, but in demonstration of the Spirit and of power, so that your faith would not rest on the wisdom of men, but on the power of God. Yet we do speak wisdom among those who are mature; a wisdom, however, not of this age nor of the rulers of this age, who are passing away; but we speak God's wisdom in a mystery. (1 Cor 2:3–7)

Thus Paul could say, "Therefore I am well content with weaknesses, with insults, with distresses, with persecutions, with difficulties, for Christ's sake; for when I am weak, then I am strong" (2 Cor 12:10). In short, the honorific notions and status roles established through money, power, and manipulation mean nothing in God's eyes. Such illusions detract from the message and messengers of the gospel.

The honored and privileged status of Jews as the elect and chosen people likewise is disregarded in God's eyes. Paul made this point repeatedly in his letter to the Romans. In chapter 2, Paul claims that God's anger and wrath, as well as his glory and honor, are administered equally to both Jews and gentiles.

> God who will render to each person according to his works. (2:6)

> For those who steadfastly pursue good works, glory, honor, immortality, eternal life. (2:7)

> But to those who . . . obey unrighteousness, wrath and indignation. (2:8)

> Tribulation and distress for every soul of man who does evil, of the Jew first and also of the Greek. (2:9)
>
> But glory, honor and peace to all who perform good works, to the Jew first and also to the Greek. (2:10)
>
> For there is no partiality with God. (2:11)

Many Jews felt that they had a privileged position with God and that their birth status provided them with guarantees of salvation. But Paul makes it clear that God plays no favorites. The actions of their ancestors are not a factor in God's consideration of individuals. God weighs the actions of each person according to their deeds. Paul emphasized this by the repetitions in these verses.

> God who will render to each person according to his *works* [ἔργον]. (2:6)
>
> *Glory and honor* and immortality . . . for those who steadfastly pursue *good works* [ἔργον ἀγαθόν]. (2:7)
>
> Tribulation and distress for everyone who does evil, *for the Jew first and also for the Greek.* (2:9)
>
> But *glory and honor* and peace to all who perform *good works* [ἐργάζομαι ἀγαθόν], *to the Jew first and also to the Greek.* (2:10)

There is no partiality with God. For God, glory and honor rest on the good works of the person, not on the special privileges of ancestry. Dunn comments:

> So far as judgment is concerned the Jew is not in a privileged position. As Paul points out with the devastating simplicity of a generalization whose breadth of application has come home with something of a shock, "God has no favorites" (v 11); he shows none of the partiality between Jew and Gentile that Jewish self-confidence in divine election had come to assume.[32]

Even within the Christian community, Paul regarded fellow Christians deemed worthy of high honor as having no greater status than anyone else. Writing to the Galatians, Paul claimed that God showed no partiality to the Jerusalem church leaders, despite their high reputation: "But from those considered to be someone important, what sort of persons they were makes no difference to me, God shows no partiality" (2:6). Paul's opponents ap-

32. James D. G. Dunn, *Romans 1–8*, WBC 38A (Word, 1988), 93.

pealed to the status of the Jerusalem leaders to denigrate Paul's teachings. As Witherington notes, "Paul does not wish to discredit these Jerusalem leaders, indeed he has admitted he sought and desired their approval and cooperation with his ministry work, but he does wish to discredit those who are touting them, and he wishes to make clear that the normal sort of criteria used to determine human honor ratings do not and should not apply in the church."[33] Betz adds that Paul's "evaluation includes a statement on the nature of their status, the present argumentative value of their status, and the theological reason for Paul's evaluation."[34] Betz continues: "At present a theological question is to be decided, and for this decision one must not be unduly influenced by considerations of external status. It is, however, proper to render judgment upon the existing status of people, past or present, while applying the rule of God's impartiality."[35]

Jesus repeatedly emphasized the eschatological reversal of honor and shame. Those who are esteemed greatest are, in fact, the least in God's kingdom. When James and John approached Jesus on the road to Jerusalem, they asked for places of honor and power in the coming kingdom. "Grant that we may sit in your glory, one on your right and one on your left" (Mark 10:37). Jesus's response was countercultural. Those who are the least, in the manner of this world's reckoning, are the greatest in God's kingdom. "Whoever wishes to become great among you shall be your servant; and whoever wishes to be first among you shall be a slave [δοῦλος] of all" (Matt 20:26–27; Mark 10:43–44). Jesus's answer was more about status than it was about power. Those who wish to climb to the top must be willing and humble enough to serve from the bottom.

Some of Paul's teachings on honor, shame, and status probably came from Jesus's teachings. But it is hard to escape the conclusion that Paul weaves a great deal of personal rumination into his teachings. The apostle had gone through the highs and lows of status. From the shame of slavery to the pinnacle of prestige as a student of the highly esteemed Gamaliel—Saul, a freed Jew, was being groomed for leadership "advancing in Judaism beyond many of [his] contemporaries" (Gal 1:14).

Yet, Paul was willing to give it all up for the sake of the gospel. The Damascus Road experience convinced Paul that earthly status was not all

33. Ben Witherington III, *Grace in Galatia: A Commentary on Paul's Letter to the Galatians* (Eerdmans, 1998), 139.

34. Hans Dieter Betz, *Galatians: A Commentary on Paul's Letter to the Churches in Galatia*, Hermeneia (Fortress, 1979), 93.

35. Betz, 95.

it was cracked up to be. He was willing to be maligned, humiliated, and persecuted for what he knew to be true. So, once again the apostle suffered the shame of the cross. When he was criticized, debased, and humiliated by opponents in Corinth, Paul acknowledged "to my shame I must say that we have been weak by comparison" (2 Cor 11:21). In response, Paul offered his so-called boast consisting of imprisonments, beatings by Jews and Romans, dangers throughout his travels, hunger, thirst, exposure, sleepless nights, and various other hardships (2 Cor 11:23–27). Yet, he also realized that the present shame would become an honor in the days to come. While in prison in Rome, the apostle wrote of his "earnest expectation and hope, that I shall not be put to shame in anything, but that with all boldness, Christ shall even now, as always, be exalted in my body, whether by life or by death" (Phil 1:20).

Although some may look on the humble state of the Christian as a demeaning loss of status, the early Christians took pride in their dishonor. The anonymous author of the Letter to Diognetus (ca. AD 170) wrote of Christians:

> They are "in the flesh," but they do not live "according to the flesh." They live on earth, but their citizenship is in heaven. . . . They love everyone, and by everyone they are persecuted. . . . They are dishonored, yet they are glorified in their dishonor; they are slandered, yet they are vindicated. They are cursed, yet they bless; they are insulted, yet they honor others.[36]

Epictetus: The Freedman and Philosopher

The Greek Stoic philosopher Epictetus lived in the first century and had much in common with Paul. Both were freed Roman slaves. In the introduction to his translation of Epictetus's works, Oldfather remarked:

> Epictetus was a slave woman's son, and for many years a slave himself. The tone and temper of his whole life were determined thereby. An all-engulfing passion for independence and freedom so preoccupied him in his youth, that throughout his life he was obsessed with the fear of restraint, and tended to regard mere liberty, even in its negative aspect alone, as almost the highest conceivable good.[37]

---

36. Diogn. 5.8–15 (Lightfoot and Harmer).

37. W. A. Oldfather, *Epictetus: The Discourses as Reported by Arrian, Books 1–2*, LCL 131 (Harvard University Press, 1925), vii-viii.

The experience would indelibly impact a young man, and it is not surprising that Epictetus's writings reflect that period of his life.

One can assume that Paul, like Epictetus, who underwent a similar experience in his youth, would echo those experiences in his writings. Paul's writings, like Epictetus's, are disproportionately salted with slave and freedom terminology compared to other New Testament writings. We will explore Paul's use of these terms in a later chapter.

Born into slavery in Hierapolis of Phrygia around AD 50, Epictetus was granted permission to study philosophy by his master. He studied under Gaius Musonius Rufus, a Stoic philosopher who taught in Rome. Epictetus was freed sometime in the late 60s and continued to teach philosophy in Rome and Nicopolis (Greece) until his death in AD 135. With his philosophic training, Epictetus enjoyed benefits that many other slaves did not experience. However, he was not shielded from the abuse that slaves commonly experienced. Origen relayed information from Celsus that Epictetus was handicapped when his master intentionally broke his leg.[38] With his personal experiences, Epictetus was able to address both the negative and the positive aspects of slavery.

Epictetus began his chapter "On Freedom" with a succinct definition of freedom: "He is free who lives as he wills, who is subject neither to compulsion, nor hindrance, nor force, whose choices are unhampered, whose desires attain their end."[39]

In the discussion that follows, Epictetus clarified that his understanding of freedom goes far beyond the emancipation or manumission of slaves. Epictetus asserted that any compulsion to act contrary to one's desire is an act of slavery. Unwanted obedience to an employer, actions taken to satisfy the wishes of another person, and untrue flattery to advance one's standing are all considered acts of slavery. Likewise, uncontrolled desires for power or material gain are vices that indicate that a "free" person is enslaved to their passions.

> It is the slave's prayer that he be set free immediately. Why? Do you think it is because he is eager to pay his money to the men who collect the five per cent tax? No, it is because he fancies that up till now he is hampered and uncomfortable, because he has not obtained his freedom from slavery. "If I am set free,"

---

38. That Epictetus was crippled, there is no doubt. Some, however, doubt that it was caused by abuse. Oldfather supports that claim, noting that Celsus may have been a contemporary of Epictetus, and as a philosopher he was likely familiar with the report. Gregory of Nazianzus likewise accepted the account.

39. Epictetus, *Diatr.* 4.1.1 (Oldfather, LCL).

> he says, "immediately it is all happiness, I shall pay no attention to anybody, I talk to everybody as an equal and as one in the same station in life, I go where I please, I come whence I please, and where I please." Then he is emancipated, and forthwith, having no place to which to go and eat, he looks for someone to flatter, for someone at whose house to dine. Next he either earns a living by prostitution, and so endures the most dreadful things, and if he gets a manger at which to eat he has fallen into a slavery much more severe than the first; or even if he grows rich, being a vulgarian he has fallen in love with a chit of a girl, and is miserable, and laments, and yearns for his slavery again. "Why, what was wrong with me? Someone else kept me in clothes, and shoes, and supplied me with food, and nursed me when I was sick; I served him in only a few matters. But now, miserable man that I am, what suffering is mine, who am a slave to several instead of one![40]

Epictetus was greatly influenced by the Cynic philosopher Diogenes, who was captured by pirates, sold into slavery, and settled in Corinth. In Epictetus's mind, Diogenes was the only truly free person. Diogenes's disdain for society's cultural mores and his utter detachment from material possessions made him free in his actions and desires. Epictetus never followed the austerity of Diogenes's lifestyle, but Diogenes deeply influenced his Stoic apathy and his worldview. On Diogenes's refusal to be enslaved, Epictetus wrote:

> Diogenes says somewhere: "The one sure way to secure freedom is to die cheerfully. . . . Diogenes was set free by Antisthenes, and afterwards said that he could never be enslaved again by any man. How, in consequence, did he behave when he was captured! How he treated the pirates! He called none of them master, did he? . . . How he censures them because they gave bad food to their captives! How he behaved when he was sold! Did he look for a master? No, but for a slave. And how he behaved toward his master after he had been sold? He began immediately to argue with him, telling him that he ought not to dress that way, or have his hair cut that way, and about his sons, how they ought to live."[41]

Again, regarding Diogenes's freedom from desire and society's expectations, he noted:

> Diogenes was free. How was he free? It was not because he was born of free parents, for he was not, but because he himself was free, because he had cast

40. Epictetus, *Diatr.* 4.1.33–37.
41. Epictetus, *Diatr.* 4.1.30, 114–15.

> off all the handles of slavery, and there was no way in which a person could get close and lay hold of him to enslave him. Everything he had was easily loosed, everything was merely tied on. If you had laid hold of his property, he would have let it go rather than follow you for its sake; if you had laid hold of his leg he would have let his leg go. . . . "I do not regard my paltry body as my own; because I need nothing; because this and nothing else is a law to me." This it was which allowed him to be a free man.[42]

Epictetus recognized that the practicalities of life make it necessary to be subject to others and to attend to the physical needs of sustaining life. Although Diogenes was held up as a paragon of the free person, Epictetus did not follow his example. Instead, Epictetus submitted his will to God and, in true Stoic fashion, apathetically aligned his will with whatever God decreed.

> I have never been hindered in the exercise of my will, nor have I ever been subjected to compulsion against my will. And how is this possible? I have submitted my freedom of choice unto God. . . . He wills that I should choose something; it is my will too. He wills that I should desire something; it is my will too. . . . My body that is made of clay, how could He make that unhindered? Accordingly, He has made it subject to the revolution of the universe—my property, my furniture, my house, my children, my wife. Why, then, shall I strive against God?[43]

In many ways, Epictetus echoed Paul's submission to God, saying, "For freedom is not acquired by satisfying yourself with what you desire, but by destroying your desire."[44] This resonates with the apostle's words: "Our old self was crucified with Him, that our body of sin might be done away with, that we should no longer be slaves to sin" (Rom 6:6). Similarly, Epictetus's words, "I have submitted my freedom of choice unto God," may recall Paul's words to the Galatians: "I have been crucified with Christ; and it is no longer I who live, but Christ lives in me" (2:20), and "those who belong to Christ Jesus have crucified the flesh with its passions and desires" (5:24). It is plausible that while in Rome and Greece, Epictetus had read some of Paul's writings.

42. Epictetus, *Diatr.* 4.1.152–53, 158.
43. Epictetus, *Diatr.* 4.1.89–90, 101–2.
44. Epictetus, *Diatr.* 4.1.175.

| 3 |
Josephus and Jerome: Early Accounts

But, to mix rashly in the fray and to fight hand to hand with the enemy is but a barbarous and brutish kind of business. Yet when the stress of circumstances demands it, we must gird on the sword and prefer death to slavery and disgrace.

Cicero, *De officiis* 1.23.81 (Miller, LCL 21, 83)

For the sake of what is called freedom some men hang themselves, other leap over precipices, sometimes whole cities perish; for true freedom, which cannot be plotted against and is secure, will you not yield up to God, at His demand, what He has given?

Epictetus, *Diatribai* 4.1.171–72 (Oldfather, LCL 218, 303)

Josephus's Account of Hostilities in Palestine

Josephus was born into and raised by a wealthy and prestigious Jewish family in Jerusalem in the AD 30s. At the outbreak of the First Jewish War with Rome, Josephus was assigned to Galilee to lead the resistance. He was captured when Yodfat (Jotapata) fell to the Romans. Josephus deftly talked his way out of execution and was spared. He traveled with the legions and acted as a negotiator when Vespasian assaulted Jerusalem. After the fall of Jerusalem, he was given Roman citizenship, taken to Rome, and became a client of the Flavian emperors. He was given the name Flavius Josephus. While in Rome, he wrote *Jewish War*, finishing in AD 78, and *Jewish Antiquities*, completed in AD 94. Josephus's histories are the most valuable collection of Jewish history and culture available to scholars today. He had his biases and a tendency to exaggerate, but without his works, much of the history of ancient Judaism would have been lost.

Turmoil in Judea Prior to the First Century

The civil war that ended the Hasmonean dynasty created an ideal opportunity for a Roman intrusion into Palestine. Sectarian squabbles between Jewish parties, coupled with power struggles among leading families, created chaos and a weakened Jewish state that Rome quickly exploited.

The end of the third century and the beginning of the second century BC saw the transfer of control over Palestine from the Ptolemies in Egypt to the Seleucids in Syria. The Ptolemies pursued a *laissez-faire* policy, allowing the Jews to live freely and practice their faith. The Seleucids, on the other hand, wished to impose a Hellenistic lifestyle on their territories. At the time of this transition the house of Onias, the high priestly family, generally favored the Egyptians. The house of Tobias favored the Seleucids and their Hellenistic policies. When Menelaus, a member of the house of Tobias, paid a large bribe to the Seleucids, he was appointed high priest (2 Macc 4:23ff.). Menelaus was not a member of the high priestly family, and fighting broke out in Jerusalem. The vast majority of the population was conservative and supported the Oniads, but the Tobiads, smaller in number, had the support of the Seleucids. The Tobiads, with the support of the Seleucids, instituted a policy of Hellenization in Palestine, a policy that greatly incensed the broader population. The intensification of Hellenization during the reign of Antiochus IV, who took the name *Theos Epiphanes* (God Manifest) and demanded to be worshiped, was the tipping point.[1] These

FIGURE 41. Tetradrachma. Antiochus IV Epiphanes seated, holding the goddess Nike. "King Antiochus, the manifestation of god, Victorious." 175–164 BC. From https://www.coinarchives.com.

1. Antiochus IV had numerous tetradrachma coins minted that depicted the king seated upon his throne, holding Nike, the goddess of victory. The coins were inscribed: "King Antiochus, God manifest, bearing victory."

developments resulted in the Maccabean Revolt, culminating in the independence of the Jewish people under the Hasmonean dynasty.

The freedom and independence of the Jewish people did not resolve the tensions between the conservative and devout factions of the people and the wealthy, aristocratic leaders of the nation who supported Hellenistic practices. After almost eighty years of independence, still shaken by internal struggles, this rift within Judaism resulted in civil war. In 63 BC, Pompey attacked Jerusalem, entered the temple's holy of holies, and added Judea to Rome's dominions. Hyrcanus II, a Hasmonean, was set up as a governor, but the Romans were in control and demanded taxes.

In the years that followed, Jewish resistance, sparked by the successes of the Maccabees and inspired by messianic aspirations, broke out in Palestine. Most of these were in Galilee. In 57 BC, Alexander, the son of Aristobolus, assembled rebels and gained control of fortresses at Alexandreion, Hycania, and Machaerus. Alexander gathered 10,000 troops and 1,500 horsemen. The newly appointed governor of Syria, Gabinius, was dispatched to suppress the revolt and, with the help of Mark Antony, defeated Alexander.[2] A year later, Aristobolus and his son Antigonus rose up against the Romans, who had little trouble suppressing this uprising as well.[3] A short time later, Alexander rebelled again, this time with 30,000 men. They began killing all the Romans throughout Galilee. Gabinius destroyed 10,000 rebels at Mount Tabor, ending the rebellion.[4] It is not known if captives were taken and enslaved in these conflicts.

A larger uprising emerged in Galilee three years later. Gabinius was replaced by Crassus, who was tasked with dealing with the emerging threat of the Parthians. To finance the operation, Crassus raided the temple in Jerusalem and stole its treasures. The temple was similar to a bank, a place where the wealthy stored their money for safekeeping. Crassus was killed in the engagement with the Parthians, and his army was defeated. The new Syrian governor, Cassius, was left to deal with the Parthians and the Jewish outrage at what was transpiring. In 51 BC, Cassius brutally suppressed the Jewish uprising, crushing the rebels at Tarichaea, killing one of the leaders, Peitholaus, and selling 30,000 Jewish rebels as slaves.[5]

---

2. Josephus, *Ant.* 14.5.2–4; *J.W.* 1.8.2–7.
3. Josephus, *Ant.* 14.6.1.
4. Josephus, *Ant.* 14.6.3–4.
5. Josephus, *Ant.* 14.7.1–3.

Judea fell into the hands of Antipater, who had curried favor with Julius Caesar. Antipater appointed his son Herod as governor of Galilee in 46 BC at the young age of 15. Around 45 BC, a Jewish rebel named Hezekiah had a large number of associates who were raiding the regions to the north of Galilee in Syria. Herod assembled troops and promptly killed Hezekiah and his robbers.[6] A short time later, around 42 BC, Antigonus, the son of Aristobulus, invaded Galilee with the aid of Ptolemy, the son of Mennaeus, and Marion, the tyrant of Tyre.[7] Herod again rose to the occasion, defeated them, and recaptured three Galilean strongholds that had fallen to Marion. Around 39–38 BC, Herod moved into Galilee to retake some strongholds still controlled by Antigonus's men. There, Herod confronted robbers who had taken refuge in caves on precipitous cliffs near Arbela. The Roman troops constructed cages and lowered them over the cliffs to combat the robbers, who were there with their families.[8] Those not killed by the sword and fire jumped to their deaths rather than submit to Roman slavery.[9]

In 39 BC, Herod was elected King of Judea by the Roman Senate. But it took another two years before he was able to secure that position with Roman support. Josephus explained that Herod departed to Samosata to seek the assistance of Antony. Antony gave two legions to Herod to secure Judea. While Herod was away, his brother Joseph was killed with his forces near Jericho. This defeat inspired unknown numbers of Galileans to rise up. They seized Herod's leaders and drowned them in the lake. When Herod arrived with the full force of the Roman troops, the Galilean rebels were defeated, and Herod proceeded to Jericho, where he avenged the slaughter of his brother.[10] After the winter, Herod surrounded Jerusalem with Sosius, Antony's general. After a three-month siege, Jerusalem fell, and a vast number of the residents were slaughtered. Herod, the new client king, ruled Palestine for more than three decades, but that did not quell the unrest in Galilee. As Freyne notes, the "opposition to Herod in Galilee was not totally eradicated, no matter how much it had to go underground or swallow its pride during his long reign."[11]

---

6. Josephus, *Ant.* 14.9.2.
7. Josephus, *Ant.* 14.12.1; *J.W.* 1.12.2.
8. Josephus, *Ant.* 14.15.4–5.
9. Josephus, *J.W.* 1.16.1–5.
10. Josephus, *Ant.* 14.15.9–11.
11. Sean Freyne, *Galilee: From Alexander the Great to Hadrian 323 BCE to 135 CE* (T&T Clark, 1980), 67.

After Herod's death in 4 BC, his son Archelaus rose to power. A seditious movement emerged in Jerusalem, demanding concessions from Archelaus. Archelaus acquiesced to several demands, but protests increased. He sent troops to the temple where protestors had gathered, and they slew 3,000 men. Shortly afterward, Archelaus sailed for Rome to argue for his rule of Judea. Caesar Augustus appointed him ethnarch of Judea. While he was absent from Judea, Sabinus was sent to Jerusalem from Syria to keep the peace. His heavy-handed approach to suppressing uprisings, along with his attempts to seize the temple treasury, had the opposite effect.

At this time, according to Josephus, there were 10,000 disturbances in Judea.[12] Josephus mentioned only a few. In Galilee, Judas, the son of the aforementioned Hezekiah, rose up and attacked the armory at Sepphoris, seizing the weapons and money.[13] Herod sent troops and dispatched him and his insurgents. At this time another rebel, Simon, a slave of Herod, proclaimed himself king, gathered a number of associates, and burned the palace at Jericho. They began plundering the countryside. Gratus, a leader of Roman troops, defeated Simon and his rebels, a great many of whom came from Perea.[14] Additionally, a shepherd named Athrongeus proclaimed himself as king and, with the support of his four brothers, assembled an army. They raided the countryside and surrounded a Roman garrison at Emmaus, killing the centurion and forty of the soldiers. After they had terrorized the region for some time, Gratus and Archelaus were able to subdue them.[15]

In response to these developments, Varus, the governor of Syria, brought two legions to Judea to join a legion he had sent earlier. These were joined by 1,500 troops from Berytus and forces from Petra. They converged on Galilee and sacked the city of Sepphoris, the largest in Galilee, enslaving the population.[16] They plunged further to the south, destroying cities and villages along the way. When Varus arrived in Jerusalem, most of the rebels had departed. He granted amnesty to those who remained and turned to the countryside to find the culprits. Two thousand of those caught were crucified.

---

12. Josephus, *Ant.* 17.10.4. This was, no doubt, a gross exaggeration, but exaggeration or not, Josephus's rhetoric suggests that the region was overrun with turmoil.

13. Josephus, *Ant.* 17.10.5; *J.W.* 2.4.1.

14. Josephus, *Ant.* 17.10.6; *J.W.* 2.4.2.

15. Josephus, *Ant.* 17.10.7; *J.W.* 2.4.3.

16. Josephus, *Ant.* 17.10.9.

According to Josephus, approximately ten years later in AD 6, another pair of rebels, Judas and Saddok, stirred up a rebellion in Galilee.[17] Judas, who was from Gamala, was joined by Saddok, who was described as a Pharisee. They claimed that paying taxes to the Romans was tantamount to slavery, and they rose in rebellion. They persuaded the people that God would assist in the fight to gain their freedom. The movement gained a great deal of momentum as the nation was "infected with this doctrine to an incredible degree." Josephus never described the outcome of these events. Rather, he suggested that the movement persisted and ultimately resulted in the Jewish War with Rome, the devastation of the land, and the destruction of the temple (AD 70). Acts 5:37 provides more detail: "Judas of Galilee rose up in the days of the census and drew away some people after him; he perished, and all those who followed him were scattered." Even though Judas's rebellion fizzled, Josephus makes it clear that the Zealot movement did not end with Judas.

Josephus's references to the names and examples of Jewish resistance movements from the end of the first century BC to the first half of the first century AD are primarily anecdotal and certainly not comprehensive. His terminology suggests that his examples are only the tip of the iceberg. According to Freyne, "The silence of our sources is in this case no evidence that such a movement did not continue to exist, even flourish, given the harsh realities of political life in procuratorial Judaea."[18]

Although Josephus referred to all these rebel groups collectively as "Zealots," some of these movements had different motivations. Under the burden of heavy taxation imposed by the Romans and Herod himself, some of the resistance was financially motivated, an attempt to relieve peasants of a tax that was not attainable. In other cases, the resistance was politically motivated. Freshly freed from centuries of pagan overlords during the Hasmonean monarchy, the Jewish people wished to plot their own national destiny. In some instances, the rebels were religiously motivated, believing that it was their religious duty to serve God alone rather than Caesar and the emperor cult. Some of these groups were led by messianic claimants who rallied the people by representing themselves as God's appointed, long-awaited Messiah. A common thread among all these groups was their leaders' appeal to people's zeal to take up arms and uphold Jewish ancestral traditions.

17. Josephus, *Ant.* 18.1.1; *J.W.* 2.8.1.

18. Freyne, *Galilee: From Alexander the Great*, 219.

Jerome, Origen, and Paul's Origins

Jerome (AD 345–420) was born in Dalmatia. At a young age, he moved to Rome, where he studied philosophy and rhetoric. In AD 386, he moved to Palestine and lived in a cave next to the Church of the Nativity in Bethlehem for the last thirty-four years of his life. Jerome was one of Christianity's most noted writers. However, Jerome paid the highest respect to an earlier writer, Origen, whose commentaries Jerome frequently used. Jerome believed that Origen surpassed all other Greek and Latin writers.

Not only was Origen the most prolific writer in the ancient church, but his writings also exhibited a depth of scholarship and erudition that exceeded others. Born in Alexandria, Egypt, around AD 184, Origen was the son of Christian parents who provided him with an excellent education. At that time, Alexandria had a large Jewish and Christian population, and the renowned library at Alexandria was reputed to be the largest in the ancient world. Although the library was burned prior to the time of Origen, it was restored, and the city was one of the intellectual centers of the Mediterranean world. Origen's father was martyred during the persecutions of Septimius Severus in AD 202, and according to Eusebius, Origen himself would have followed his father to martyrdom if his mother had not hidden his clothes.

Origen was one of the early church's most esteemed scholars and its earliest textual critic. He was an astute scholar who carefully evaluated claims of canonicity and demonstrated keen insight and discerning judgment in his works. As the author of numerous exegetical commentaries, treatises on philosophies, and works of theology, Origen was respected by Christians and pagans alike. Many of Origen's writings have survived, but many more have been lost. Snippets of the lost writings can be culled from the writings of the later church fathers, who continued to utilize his scholarship years after his death.

Jerome related a tradition that suggests Paul's parents were former residents of Gischala (Gush Ḥalav) in upper Galilee and that they were sold as slaves when the city was taken by the Romans.[19] Murphy-O'Connor is correct in arguing that the tradition has solid grounds for historical credibility, and he believes that Paul's ancestors were taken to Cilicia in one of the deportations mentioned by Josephus.[20] Josephus reported that this area

19. Jerome Murphy-O'Connor, *Paul: A Critical Life* (Oxford University Press, 1996), 37.

20. Murphy-O'Connor thinks the tradition came from Origen's commentary on Philemon. Since Gischala is not mentioned in the Bible, had no connection with Benjamin, and

of Galilee was rife with insurrection during the early Roman period,[21] and on several occasions the Romans sacked a town and sold the insurgents in order to stabilize the area.[22] Although members of a family could be sold separately, Bradley has shown from literary sources, legal sources, and sepulchre inscriptions that family units were often preserved in servitude.[23]

This tradition about Paul is found in Jerome's commentary on Philemon:

> We have heard this account. They say that the parents of the Apostle Paul were from Gischala, a place in Judaea and that, when the whole province was destroyed by the hand of Rome and the Jews were dispersed throughout the world, they were taken to Tarsus a town of Cilicia and the adolescent Paul inherited the personal status of his parents.[24]

The initial sentence clearly indicates that Jerome was repeating a preceding tradition, and since Jerome was using Origen's commentaries, it is likely that the tradition was preserved in Origen's lost commentary on Philemon. Jerome commonly used Origen as a source. From the last half of the first century BC into the first century AD, Galilee was known as a hotbed of rebellion against Roman rule in Palestine. The Romans responded to these uprisings in a harsh manner, destroying the cities of Galilee and enslaving

---

had no Christian residents during the Byzantine period, there is little chance that the tradition was invented (38). Josephus mentioned such deportations in *J. W.* 1.157–58, 177, 180; 2.68.

21. Gischala was located in an area with frequent disturbances. It was a fortified Jewish city on the Syrian border and seems to have engaged in constant skirmishes with its Syrian neighbors. Josephus (*J. W.* 4.105) claims that the Syrians in Kadasa (eight miles to the north) were continually feuding with their Galilean neighbors to the south. Herod was successful in doing away with Hezekiah around 47 BC to the great relief of the Syrians. Peter Richardson offers a playful account in *Herod: King of the Jews and Friend of the Romans* (University of South Carolina Press, 1996), 10.

The Syrian leader Marion invaded northern Galilee around 42 BC and captured three fortresses on the border (*J. W.* 1.238; *Ant.* 14.297–98). No doubt Gischala was one of these. Herod intervened and seized the fortresses. Later, Josephus described how Antigonus rallied anti-Roman forces in this area and occupied the fortresses. On several more occasions Herod sent troops to quell the uprisings (*J. W.* 1.303, 316, 329–34; *Ant.* 14.413, 432–33, 450–61). Continued troubles are evident in Josephus's mention of Judas, the son of Hezekiah (*Ant.* 17.271–72, 286–89) around 4 BC.

22. Murphy-O'Connor dates these slave deportations to 61, 55, 52, and 4 BC and AD 6. However, given the number of disturbances and conquests reported by Josephus at this place and time, it is likely that there were even more slave deportations, particularly in the second half of the first century BC. *Paul: A Critical Life*, 39.

23. Keith R. Bradley, *Slaves and Masters in the Roman Empire: A Study in Social Control* (Oxford University Press, 1987), 47–80. Likewise, Martin, *Slavery as Salvation*, 2–7.

24. Jerome, *Commentariorum in Epistolam ad Philemonem liber*, Patrologia Latina 26.617.

the residents. Another phrase in Jerome's comment is important: "They were taken to Tarsus, a town of Cilicia." The passive voice is used here, suggesting that Paul's family was sold to people in Tarsus. We will discuss this further in the next chapter.

This tradition was repeated in Jerome's *On Illustrious Men*: "Paul, previously known as Saul, an apostle not numbered with the twelve apostles, was from the tribe of Benjamin and from the town of Gischala in Judaea. When the town was sacked by the Romans, he moved with his parents to Tarsus in Cilicia."[25]

In both of these passages, Jerome asserted that Paul's origins were in Gischala of Galilee and that he and his family relocated to Tarsus. The first comment used the passive voice, "they were taken," and the second one used the active voice, "he moved with his parents." There is little difference in these statements since slaves who were forced to relocate would naturally be actively involved in the move. It was a matter of perspective: From the slave owner's point of view, they were taken to Tarsus. From Paul's perspective, he moved to Tarsus with his parents. Likewise, not much should be made of the difference between "the whole province was destroyed by the Romans" and "the town was sacked by the Romans." As we know from Josephus's writings, many of the cities and towns of Galilee were destroyed during this period. The second statement simply focused on Paul's hometown, Gischala.

A third difference in these statements of Jerome is somewhat more interesting. The subject of the first statement is Paul's parents, while the subject of the second account is Paul. The second account claimed that Paul moved with his parents to Tarsus, while the first statement only mentioned his parents being taken to Tarsus. This raises the question: Was Paul born in Gischala and then taken to Tarsus with his parents, or was he born in Tarsus? Perhaps Jerome's words, "he moved with his parents to Tarsus," refer corporately to the family, not indicating that Paul was born and moved with them at that time. Since the first statement focuses on Paul's parents, the expression "they were taken to Tarsus" applies only to them and not necessarily to Paul. In Acts 22:3, Luke recollected Paul's words to the people at the temple in Jerusalem: "I am a Jew, having been born in Tarsus of Cilicia, but brought up in this city." This also can be understood differently. Paul may have been born at Gischala and then moved to Tarsus with his family shortly thereafter. In the Acts speech, he could have been associating him-

25. Jerome, *De Viris Illustribus* 5.

self with Tarsus since it was the only boyhood home he had ever known. Also, we must bear in mind that this statement may be Luke's rewording of Paul's words, since it is clear that the speeches in Acts were recast when Luke included them in Acts. Thus, it is hard to say where Paul was born. He may have been born in Gischala and then moved to Tarsus with his family at an early age. Or he may have been born in Tarsus.

Jerome's statement may also be construed to suggest that Paul received his Roman citizenship through slavery. The assertion "When they were moved to Tarsus . . . the adolescent Paul inherited the personal status of his parents" indicates that the move to Tarsus resulted in a status change for Paul and his parents. The status change suggested by this statement would be either the lowering of his status to that of a slave or (more likely) the reception of Roman citizenship on his manumission.[26] Slaves who gained manumission from Roman citizens were commonly granted citizenship along with their freedom. Philo refers to Jews who were former captives, who lived across the Tiber in Rome and were emancipated Roman citizens.[27] Likewise, Tacitus tells of 4,000 Jewish freedmen.[28] As Légasse explains, "The most common origin of this status for Jews outside Palestine was the manumission of Jewish slaves by masters who were themselves Roman citizens."[29] Thus, as Lüdemann suggests, "It seems worth considering the possibility that Paul had citizenship as the descendant of a freedman."[30]

Jerome's reference to Paul inheriting the status of his parents makes no sense unless it involved a status change. If Paul's parents moved to Tarsus as a free family, they would have remained free in Tarsus, and there would have been no status change. It would be unnecessary to mention status at

---

26. Klaus Haacker, "Zum Werdegang des Apostels Paulus: Biographische Daten und ihre theologische Relevanz," *ANRW* 26.2:833–40, rightly maintains the historicity of Paul's Roman citizenship in spite of Wolfgang Stegemann's insistence to the contrary ("War der Apostel Paulus ein römischer Bürger?," *ZNW* 78 [1987]: 200–229). Skepticism arises because Paul never claimed Roman citizenship in his letters. However, Luke reported Paul's claim of citizenship in Acts 16.37; 22:25–28; 23:27; 25:10–12. Most scholars agree that Paul was a Roman citizen. See Brian Rapske, *Paul in Roman Custody*, vol. 3 of *The Book of Acts in Its First Century Setting* (Eerdmans, 1994), 72–83; and Simon Légasse, "Paul's Pre-Christian Career According to Acts," in *Palestinian Setting*, ed. Richard Bauckham, vol. 4 of *The Book of Acts in Its First Century Setting* (Eerdmans, 1995), 366–72.

27. Philo, *Legat.* 23.155.

28. Tacitus, *Ann.* 2.85.

29. Légasse, "Paul's Pre-Christian Career," 372. So also Murphy-O'Connor, *Paul: A Critical Life*, 39.

30. Gerd Lüdemann, *The Acts of the Apostles: What Really Happened in the Earliest Days of the Church* (Prometheus, 2005), 302–3.

FIGURE 42. Basalt city street with curbs and sewer in Tarsus. 1st c. AD.

all. Why would Jerome (or perhaps Origen) even mention this? The fact that Paul inherited the status of his parents can only mean that the status of Paul (and his family) changed—either as slaves or as Roman citizens, which would most likely be due to manumission.

Though the pre-Augustan period witnessed the indiscriminate endowment of citizenship with manumission, Augustan reforms restricted not the number but the type of slaves who received citizenship.[31] The Augustan reforms were designed to reward good behavior and award citizenship to those who had been successfully integrated into Roman society.[32] Roman prisoners of war would naturally have a measure of animosity toward Rome. Cooperation while a slave, and the gradual appreciation of Roman rule, were prerequisites to receiving freedom and citizenship.[33] If it is true that

31. Bradley, *Slaves and Masters in the Roman Empire*, 81–112. Prior to the Augustan reforms, political aspirants offered manumission to slaves in order to enlist their aid in coups. This contributed to the instability of the empire. "The revolutionary period had created a climate in which slaves in Rome and Italy could be and were offered their freedom, randomly and opportunistically, by men immersed in war and politics who needed all possible support to further their public ambitions" (84).

32. "Thus, the potential reward of Roman citizenship conferred by free society became, from the slaves' point of view, an inducement to sound moral behaviour during the period of enslavement or, in other words, to assimilating themselves within the existing social status quo. This preempted, at least in theory, their participation in acts of rebellion, escape by flight, or any other means of securing freedom not condoned by free society." Bradley, 93.

33. "By A.D. 4 war captives who had earlier been enslaved for periods of twenty or thirty years would be nearing the time when manumission may have been becoming a real possibility for those who had survived. Yet it is perfectly credible that the Roman au-

Paul's family had gained Roman citizenship (as suggested by Acts 22:27–28), this would indicate that they successfully integrated into Roman culture. This is supported by Paul's positive posture toward the Roman government in Romans 13:1–7.[34]

FIGURE 43. Bronze diploma granting citizenship to Gemellus of Pannonia. AD 122. British Museum.

From what little information Paul provided, it seems that his family was a pious Jewish family. In his letter to the Philippians Paul stated that he was circumcised on the eighth day, asserted that he came from the tribe of Benjamin, and contended that he was a "Hebrew of Hebrews" (Phil 3:5). The expression "Hebrew of Hebrews" should probably be taken as testimony that both of his parents were Hebrews. Some Jews, particularly in the diaspora, had taken gentile wives, but here Paul affirmed that he was a purebred Jew. With the reference to the tribe of Benjamin, Paul not only maintained an understanding of his genealogy, but he also stressed that he came from one of the faithful tribes that survived the Assyrian deportation and dispersal. Circumcision on the eighth day was a requirement of devout Jewish families (Lev 12:3).

Jews and Gentiles in Galilee

Studies of Galilee suggest that its demographics were tilted toward a predominantly Jewish population. Archaeologists excavating the towns and villages of Galilee point to the presence of stone vessels (considered to be kosher), the absence of pork (the consumption of which was banned in the Torah) in the refuse dumps of cities, and the presence of *mikva'ot* (Jewish ritual baths) to determine the proportion of Jews in Galilee. Additionally,

thorities still felt the need to guard against admission to the *ciuitas* [*sic*] of elements which had not yet achieved a demonstrable degree of commitment towards Rome and its values." Bradley, 95.

34. Klaus Haacker develops this in much more detail and also looks to Philemon 3:20 as another text that reflects Paul's biographical retrospection. *Paulus: Der Werdegang eines Apostels*, SBS 171 (Katholisches Bibelwerk, 1997), 38–44.

the relative lack of gentile structures, such as Roman baths, leads us to the same conclusion.

However, the preponderance of Greek inscriptions in Galilee leads us to believe that there was a significant gentile population in the land. Likewise, coins and pottery indicate that Galilee had trade associations with pagan neighbors. Of course, the populations varied from town to town, and it seems that the largest cities of Galilee (Tiberias and Sepphoris) had somewhat larger gentile populations. Yet synagogues have also been discovered in both Tiberias and Sepphoris.

Some scholars have argued that the depopulation of the Jews in Galilee following the Assyrian deportation created a vacuum that was slowly filled by gentiles. After Aristobulus I conquered the territory, the residents were forcibly converted to Judaism, and Galilee was colonized by Jews from elsewhere. These Galilean Jews were stigmatized by those in Judea because they were viewed as mixed-blood Jews.

Poverty in Galilee is another factor to consider. Scholars today recognize that during the first century, approximately 95 percent of the population in the Mediterranean world lived in poverty. Moreover, about half of these people lived at or below the level of subsistence, resulting in a significant proportion of the population not receiving enough calories to sustain life. In order to control the desperate masses, the wealthy in cities and towns supported the poor through patron-client relationships. In exchange for favors, patrons usually supplied clients with a small amount of food or money. To meet their needs, many people were forced to borrow with little prospect of repaying their debts. The Gospels record several parables of people who had spiraled so far into debt that they were unable to repay it. In such instances, the debtor could be taken into debt slavery.

The Roman Presence in Galilee and the Rise of the Zealots

When the Romans seized Palestine in the first century BC, Jewish hopes for independence were dashed. After centuries of oppression at the hands of pagan conquerors, the Jewish Maccabean Revolt during the second century BC resulted in a Hasmonean dynasty that lasted little more than one hundred years until the Romans intervened. Nonetheless, the taste of independence inspired the Jewish people to fight to overthrow Roman dominion in Palestine and establish a Jewish theocratic state. The resistance that shortly arose in Galilee stemmed from three causes: economic deprivation, political frustration, and religious aspirations.

The severe economic hardships were exacerbated by Roman taxes, which were a heavy burden for the impoverished people of Galilee. When the Romans imposed these taxes on the struggling Galileans, most realized that there was no feasible way for them to pay these taxes and support their families. These Roman taxes were compounded by additional taxes that Herod imposed on the people. They chose to feed their families and refused to pay the Roman taxes, which brought consequences. Tax collectors were empowered to seize property, and in some instances, they sold tax debtors and their children into slavery. It is not hard to imagine that when many Jews rose up against the Romans and their collaborators, violence would follow.

The political frustrations experienced by the Jews during this period stemmed from the resentment that had been building during the Jews' long history of oppression by pagan nations. They were keenly aware of their history, which extended back to their enslavement in Egypt and God's mighty deliverance during the exodus. The events of the exodus were often repeated in the written and oral traditions of the Jewish people as evidence that they were God's chosen people. However, in the centuries that followed, the Jewish people experienced catastrophic destruction and subjugation by the Assyrians, Babylonians, Persians, Seleucids, and finally, the Romans. Many Jews were asking questions of theodicy: If we are God's covenant people, why does he not raise up his righteous nation and install the Jewish people in power? The thought that polytheistic pagans could control the world challenged the assumption that God was omnipotent and benevolent. Perhaps God was waiting for his faithful people to take matters into their own hands. It was time for the devout men of Israel to rise up against Rome.

More than a hundred years earlier, the Seleucid ruler Antiochus IV demanded that the Jews offer sacrifices to him. At that time, the elderly Jewish priest Mattathias "burned with zeal for the law" (1 Macc 2:26), rose up, and killed the officer who was enforcing the apostasy. He then supposedly turned to the townspeople and cried out, "Let everyone who is zealous for the law and supports the covenant come out with me!" (1 Macc 2:27). With these words, the Maccabean Revolt began against the Seleucid rulers. The revolt was inspired by the belief that God would reward the efforts of those willing to lay down their lives for the God of Israel. Utilizing guerrilla warfare tactics, the revolt was remarkably successful. It might have helped that the Seleucid Empire was in turmoil during this time, but the Maccabees were ultimately able to achieve political independence. In the minds of many Jews, this achievement solidified the belief that God was keeping covenant with his people and that he would honor the efforts of those who zealously defended the Jewish way of life. "Zeal was more than just a fervent commitment to the Torah; it denoted a willingness to use violence against any—Jews, Gentiles, or the wicked in general—who were contravening, opposing, or subverting the Torah. Further, zealots were willing to suffer and die for the sake of the Torah, even to die at their own hand."[35]

This frame of mind persisted in the middle of the first century BC. Many Jews believed that the fall of the Hasmonean dynasty and its replacement by the illegitimate Herodian clan was a course that could be reversed if the devout followers of Yahweh rose up against the Roman powers. Rather than appointing a Jew to rule over Judea, Julius Caesar appointed an Idumean, Antipater, to govern the territory. After Antipater's death, his son Herod was appointed king of the Jews by the Roman Senate. Under his father's authority, Herod had been given administration of Galilee, and Herod brutally suppressed Jewish uprisings during that time. Later, when he assumed power, Herod married Mariamne, a descendant of Hasmonean rulers, in order to enhance his legitimacy as ruler of the Jews, but to no avail. Most Jews continued to view him as a Roman crony and opposed his rule.

Josephus claimed that during this time, many Jews rose up against Roman authorities. He described these people as a fourth sect of the Jews in addition to the Pharisees, Sadducees, and Essenes. We previously mentioned the uprisings that began in the early 50s BC with Alexander, the son of Aristobolus. This event cannot be seen as an isolated incident. Certainly, there were additional revolutionary currents circulating in Judea and Galilee that Josephus was not aware of. Even if he knew of other seditious activity, he edited or limited his account to a few of the more notable events. These revolts continued into the 40s BC with Hezekiah and into the 30s with the brigands in the cliffside caves at Arbela. Josephus mentioned nothing of insurgent activity during the next two decades, but this is probably due to a lack of source material more than anything else.

When Josephus noted the movement in the first decade BC, he mentioned ten thousand disturbances in Judea. It is hard to believe that this exaggerated number represents an outbreak of rebellions due to Archelaus's

35. Terence L. Donaldson, *Paul and the Gentiles: Remapping the Apostle's Convictional World* (Fortress, 1997), 286.

FIGURE 44. Caves of the Galilean Zealot rebels. Arbela, Galilee.

ineptitude. The transition of power from Herod to Archelaus may have provided an opportunity for rebels to step forward, but Archelaus made several concessions to the Jews. Rather, we should view this number like a volcano that had been continually erupting for almost sixty years. Continuity with the earlier movements is clear with Josephus's identification of Judas in 4 BC as the son of the earlier Hezekiah.

Despite its lack of success, the movement persisted until the war with Rome. In AD 6, another Judas, identified as being from Galilee, teamed up with the Pharisee Saddok.[36] There is a gap in Josephus's description of the movement until closer to the Jewish-Roman War. However, three of the sons of Judas the Galilean emerged around AD 47. Josephus identified James and Simon as two of these sons. They were crucified by the procurator Tiberius Julius Alexander, presumably for stirring up revolt.[37] The third son, Menahem, became one of the leaders in the war with Rome.[38] More likely, he was the grandson of Judas. At the outbreak of the war with Rome, he took Masada and equipped his men with the weapons from its armory. He then proceeded to the Antonia Fortress in Jerusalem and captured it.

Thus, we see a movement that Josephus later called "Zealots," which persevered for more than a century until Rome put an end to it with the

36. Some scholars have proffered the unlikely suggestion that Judas the son of Hezekiah was the same as Judas the Galilean. Judas was a common name among Jews of the day, and Josephus never connected the two, as he usually did when describing someone he previously mentioned. Compare Judas the son of Hezekiah (Josephus, *Ant.* 17.10.5; *J.W.* 2.4.1) with Judas the Galilean (Josephus, *Ant.* 18.1.1; *J.W.* 2.8.1). Although Josephus never mentioned Judas the son of Hezekiah's death, this can be assumed by Varus's conquest of Sepphoris and the countryside when he brought two legions to subdue the area. Josephus, *Ant.* 17.10.9.

37. Josephus, *Ant.* 20.5.2.

38. Josephus, *J.W.* 2.17.8.

final war that devastated the land and enslaved vast numbers who were taken back to Rome for Titus's triumph. Josephus explained that followers of this sect (which he called a philosophy) "have a passion for liberty that is almost unconquerable, since they are convinced that God alone is their leader and master."[39] Judas the Galilean asserted that the payment of taxes to the Romans amounted to slavery and that the Jewish people should have no master other than God. Thus, the movement had a religious and an economic appeal. Most Galileans could not afford to pay Roman taxes, and if the Zealot theology was to be believed, it was sinful to do so. Many joined the movement with the hopes that God would reward their pious efforts, just as God had earlier rewarded the Maccabees in their uprising against the Seleucids.

Of course, the refusal to pay taxes was a serious matter and entailed dire consequences. Residents of the Galilean cities of Gophna and Emmaus, as well as two other unmentioned towns, were sold into slavery for failing to pay the tribute.[40] Josephus notes that these deportations into slavery were particularly odious to the Jews. As it was with the Zealots, many refused and fought, dying as "free men."

Even among the Jews who chose not to resist, the Zealot ideology was still widely embraced, though concrete actions to support the ideology were infrequently expressed. Few people would publicly profess adherence to the Zealot sect, but privately the movement still retained a great deal of appeal to the Jewish people, not only in Galilee but also in Judea. Palestine was a powder keg of frustrations and hatred, but the Roman procurators managed to maintain control until the time of Gessius Florus. In AD 66, Procurator Florus's boneheaded moves and provocations provided the spark for the regeneration of an active Zealot uprising. Seizing the moment, John of Gischala persuasively spearheaded a revolt that ultimately led to the Jewish-Roman War and the destruction of Galilee, Jerusalem, and most of Palestine by AD 73.

The Subjugation of Gischala (Gush Ḥalav)

What do we know about the town of Gischala, from which Jerome claims Paul's family originated? It was located in upper Galilee about four miles

39. Josephus, *Ant.* 18.6.

40. Josephus, *J.W.* 1.222; *Ant.* 14.275.

north of Meron and three miles southeast of Bar'am. Early sources indicate that Gischala was known for the production of olive oil, which was prized for its excellent quality. The Talmud also claims that the town was involved in the production of silk. Archaeological evidence at the site shows it was occupied continuously from the eighth century BC to the Roman period, and it was predominantly an Israelite settlement. Literary evidence indicates that Herod the Great and perhaps the Hasmoneans used the site as a fortress to guard the north. The Mishnah refers to several old fortresses that date back to the days of Joshua: "the old castle of Sepphoris, the fortress of Gush Ḥalav, old Yodpat, Gamala, Gadwad, Hadid, Ono, Jerusalem and the like" (m. ʿArak. 9.6). It is doubtful that all these fortresses date to the time of Joshua; however, the reference does indicate the existence of a fortress at Gush Ḥalav in the early Roman period or earlier.

According to Josephus, when Herod the Great came to power, he took back some of the fortresses of Galilee from Marion, the king of Tyre, who had invaded the region in the latter half of the first century BC. Though the villages were unnamed, Josephus claimed that Marion captured three fortified villages of Galilee that "lay in his neighborhood."[41] Herod drove Marion out of Galilee and repossessed the three fortresses.[42] Gush Ḥalav, close to the border of Tyre, was probably one of these. Later, Josephus claimed to have assisted John of Gischala in rebuilding the fortress at Gischala.[43] The fortification was formidable enough that Titus ordered the walls to be torn down after the town surrendered in AD 67.[44]

Archaeological work at Gischala has identified two synagogues at the site. One lies on the summit of the city hill. The remains are poorly preserved, and the few pieces that exist suggest a date in the second to fourth century AD. The lower synagogue was located in the valley to the east of the current city and was built in the late Roman period (around AD 250, although some scholars argue that it was built in the second half of the fifth century).

The lower synagogue was destroyed by an earthquake in AD 551. This synagogue was almost square, measuring 46 feet by 50 feet on the inside. It

41. Josephus, *Ant.* 14.298. Richard A. Horsley is confident that Gischala was one of those, along with Meiron and Nabratein. He claims Gischala and Meiron were the largest villages, with an estimated 500 residents. *Galilee: History, Politics, People* (Trinity Press International, 1995), 194–95. Synagogues have been found at each of those sites.

42. Josephus, *Ant.* 14.298; *J.W.* 1.238.

43. Josephus, *J.W.* 2.590; *Life* 45.

44. Josephus, *J.W.* 4.11.

had columns on three sides of the hall and stone benches along the walls. A large, monumental tomb dating to the late Roman period was found on the western side of the town, and two rock-cut tombs were found on the southern slope of the hill. These contained several ossuaries (stone burial boxes). A network of more than a dozen underground hidden passageways also has been found in Gischala. These were probably used as escape routes when the city was attacked. These have not yet been adequately studied, and it is presently not possible to date these underground tunnels.

FIGURE 45. Synagogue at Gischala (Modern Jish), home village of Paul's parents in Galilee. See gallery for color version.

During the early Roman conquests, the residents of Gischala and Galilee had ample cause to build up resentment toward the Romans. First, taxation was greatly increased to support Roman imperialism, and Herod, eager to win favor and position with the Romans, ambitiously pursued its collection. Three taxation schemes were imposed on the people of Galilee: Roman imperial taxes, Herod's taxes for his building projects, and Jewish taxes for the temple, high priests, and Jewish institutions. The Jews felt compelled to supply the temple tax, but the Roman imperial tax was greatly hated. Also, Herod's taxes were excessive and incensed the population. Herod used tax revenue to support his vast building projects not only in Galilee, Samaria, and Judea but also elsewhere in the Mediterranean world. His building projects included the extensively renovated and enlarged temple in Jerusalem, as well as royal palaces at Caesarea Maritima, Jericho, Hyrcania, Herodium, Masada, Machaerus, and Jerusalem. An artificial harbor was constructed on the coast at Caesarea Maritima, which became the Roman capital of Palestine. The city was lavishly laid out with a theater, hippodrome, amphitheater, temples, an aqueduct, and fortified walls. Elsewhere, Herod built theaters, stadiums, aqueducts, baths, and various other projects that benefited cities throughout Palestine. He also funded additional structures and benefactions in Tyre, Damascus, Syrian Antioch, Lycia, Rhodes, Samos, Chios, Cos, Pergamon, Athens, and other locations. Taxes paid by the Jewish people supported all these projects.

A second reason that residents of Gischala and Galilee resented the Romans is that nationalistic Galileans supported Antigonus, a Hasmonean, rather than the Roman crony Herod. Herod was a sycophant to Caesar, building temples and cities dedicated to the emperor throughout the land. Josephus claimed that there was no place throughout the land that did not have something honoring Caesar.[45] Additionally, Herod divested the high priests of any meaningful power and appointed his own supporters as high priests. Even after Antigonus's defeat, pockets of resistance continued for almost a century. Josephus experienced this firsthand since many of these rebels stubbornly resisted Josephus's leadership as a Roman sympathizer sent by the Sanhedrin to maintain peace and to keep the tribute flowing.

Third, Josephus noted that under Roman dominion many Jews were deported from Galilee to other lands, where they were sold as slaves. Murphy-O'Connor dates these deportations to 61, 55, 52, and 4 BC and AD 6.[46] If the people of Galilee were unable to pay the tribute, they would be sold to generate the necessary revenue.[47]

Around AD 66, Gischala became the centerpiece of resistance against the Romans. A resident of the city, John ben Levi, fomented rebellion not only in Gischala but also throughout Galilee. John of Gischala, as he was known, quickly gathered a following of almost 5,000 men and seized the storehouses holding grain taken by Roman authorities in lieu of tax payments. Realizing the likely consequences of his actions, John rebuilt the walls of Gischala in anticipation of Roman reprisals. Roman legions led by Vespasian and Titus descended on Galilee and destroyed all the rebel cities and towns. The last city to fall was Gischala. John escaped from Gischala and retreated to Jerusalem, where he continued his resistance against Rome.

---

45. Josephus, *J.W.* 1.407.

46. Murphy-O'Connor, *Paul: A Critical Life*, 39. Without doubt, there were deportations throughout this period to quell the rebels and to generate tribute.

47. Josephus, *J.W.* 1.222; *Ant.* 14.275. Josephus noted that the deportations into slavery were abhorrent to the Jews. In *Ant.* 16.1–5, he reports that Herod instituted a law whereby thieves would be sold into slavery to foreigners, contrary to Jewish law. Josephus commented that this aroused the hatred of the Jews.

It is hard to determine how involved Paul's family was with the earlier uprisings. Were they actively involved in the insurgency, or were they passively supportive of the actions of others in the Gischala community? It is impossible to say. Nevertheless, the fact that Paul identified himself with this movement in his early years provides a clue to his upbringing and ideological inclinations. If Paul was born in Gischala, he was far too young to participate in these revolts or even to remember them. However, his family's history and heritage were wrapped up in this ideology, and this would have been inherited by Paul himself.

4
The Book of Acts and the Pre-Christian Paul

Anyone who thinks that people put up for sale by kidnappers thereby become slaves goes utterly astray from the truth. Selling does not make the purchaser a master, nor the purchased a slave.

Philo, *Every Good Man Is Free* 37 (Colson, LCL 363, 31)

THE TÜBINGEN SCHOOL CHALLENGED THE historicity of the Acts of the Apostles about two hundred years ago. Influential scholars in the school asserted that Luke's recollection of the early years following Christ's crucifixion was more the creation of Luke's imagination than a chronicle of actual events. The publication of Ernst Haenchen's commentary on Acts in 1971 was a more recent product of the movement.[1] Haenchen, followed by Conzelmann, Debelius, and others, denigrated Luke's historical narrative, claiming that Luke created history to fit his theological agenda. Haenchen's volume set the course for Acts research some sixty years ago. Discoveries in Turkey over the last thirty years, however, have done much to redeem Luke's credibility, and some scholars are now recognizing that Acts contains valuable information for compiling an account of the earliest Christian history.[2] Still, it is important to recognize what Acts lacks.

1. Ernst Haenchen, *The Acts of the Apostles: A Commentary* (Westminster John Knox, 1971).

2. Earlier research by William Ramsay and J. B. Lightfoot, along with later works by Ward Gasque, F. F. Bruce, I. H. Marshall, and others, did little to move the needle for the majority of scholars.

Most people familiar with the story of the apostle Paul—from his remarkable conversion on the road to Damascus, through his epic journeys and missions, to his arrest and imprisonment—assume they know much of his history from the Acts of the Apostles. Those acquainted with the apostle through his epistles, which have become the bedrock of the Christian faith and have framed the theological discourse for Christians over the last two thousand years, possess various notions of Paul's theological convictions. Yet, however much we have absorbed from these scriptures, much is missing from Paul's story. Little is known about his birth, childhood, education, and early career prior to his Christian conversion. Even following his conversion (Acts 9), very little is known about the next twelve or thirteen years until Barnabas sought him in Tarsus and brought him to Syrian Antioch to minister with him (Acts 11).

Acts, which preserved most of the biographical information we have about Paul's life, left out a great deal of information regarding the apostle and abbreviated many of the accounts of his work and ministry. Paul traveled hundreds of miles on foot during each of his missions and visited dozens of cities along the way. But Luke selected only a few narratives from a few cities on the route to describe the journeys. Brief details from Paul's letters, such as his trip to Illyricum (Rom 15:19), are missing in Acts. Paul's dispute with Peter (Gal 2:11ff.) is also omitted from Acts. Although Luke spent a great deal of time describing Paul's imprisonment in Jerusalem, Caesarea, and Rome, he never mentioned a word about Paul's trial or death.

Without depreciating Luke's work, we realize that he depended on other sources for much of the information he recorded. As with his Gospel, he compiled and thoroughly investigated the information that he received (Luke 1:1–4). Yet, if the "we sections" of Acts (Acts 16–28) represent instances when Luke traveled with the apostle, then we might assume that Luke knew more than he wrote. Are there any other resources that would enable us to recover Paul's past?

Just as there were numerous oral traditions regarding Jesus, so also there must have been a number of traditions regarding Paul, his travels, and the spread of the gospel throughout the Roman world. Some of these traditions were included in the writings of the second-generation Christians (the patristic writings). Other stories were incorporated into apocryphal gospels and acts, along with legends that developed alongside these traditions. Unfortunately, time fades memories and washes away the recollection of history. Oral traditions and written records are helpful means of slowing the process, but the claws of time slowly scratch away the details of antiquity, leaving historians with an indistinct puzzle to unscramble. Fortunately, however, the untangling of history is aided today by tools that have been sharpened over the years. In particular, advances in literary research, archaeology, and cultural anthropology have greatly improved our ability to do historical research on the ancient world. These tools offer us a measure of hope that some details of the past may be brought to light.

The legacy of the Christian faith is due in large part to the remarkable tenacity with which the early Christians preserved their scriptures. The text of the twenty-seven books of the New Testament has been preserved extremely well compared to other ancient writings. Unfortunately, many historical and theological questions still remain unresolved despite an examination of the New Testament. Other early Christian writings provide some insights. However, many of these traditions and noncanonical writings of the early church have deteriorated over time. An untold number of early traditions and writings have been lost or damaged. Further complicating the task of historical recovery is the occasional creation of legends by well-intentioned church fathers to fill in historical gaps. Thus, historians of early Christianity must reconstruct early traditions as accurately as possible, assess their value, and piece together the most plausible interpretation of the evidence.

When one turns to a high-profile figure of the Christian faith such as Paul, one is struck by the utter paucity of information regarding his early life and background. To adequately understand the writings of the apostle Paul (or any other person, for that matter) one must understand his social and historical background. Unfortunately, Paul provided little autobiographical information in his writings, and the other New Testament writings offer scant testimony to his origins. One can imagine that reliable traditions about the apostle existed in the early church, yet few of them survive today.

Why did neither Paul nor his followers preserve more detailed information about his family and his formative influences? Let me suggest two reasons for this deficiency. First, the Gospels and the early Christian writings revolve around Jesus and God's work in the early church rather than around the followers of the Lord. Written accounts of the disciples were secondary elements of the Christian message. Second, I would suggest that Paul's background was thought to be ill-suited for one who was to become the church's leading proponent of the faith. Paul's dishonorable past could hinder the propagation of the gospel. At the very least, it was thought that such information was irrelevant to Paul's current role. Thus, the information was ignored or suppressed.

The Synagogue of the Freedmen (Acts 6:9; 7:58)

Paul first appears in the narrative of Acts at the end of Stephen's trial. When Stephen was being stoned, the witnesses laid their robes at the feet of "a young man named Saul" (Acts 7:58). This statement is highly suggestive. First, the reference to Saul as a young man (νεανίας) gives us an approximate age for Saul. The term describes a man prior to the age of marriage. Young men in the first century typically married between the ages of 20 and 30.[3] This would suggest that the apostle was born sometime in the first decade AD. Second, this statement implicates Saul in the arguments with Stephen. Bock observes: "That witnesses have a key role in the execution is also according to Jewish custom (Deut. 17:7; 13:9–10)."[4] Paul's ambitious persecution of the church immediately after this event (Acts 8:1–3) demonstrates that he had much to do with Stephen's arrest.

This subdued introduction to Paul was a skillful way for Luke to ease Paul into the narrative. Witherington notes: "Luke regularly uses this deft technique of briefly mentioning a figure who will later become important in narrative."[5] In fact, this brief introduction is preceded by a more subtle reference in Acts 6:9.

When Stephen was first introduced as one of the so-called deacons, he began to preach in Jerusalem. He was quickly confronted by members of a synagogue called the Synagogue of the Freedmen (Acts 6:9). It consisted of men from Cyrene, Alexandria, Cilicia, and Asia. The connection with Saul is overt. Witherington comments:

> It is plausible to conjecture, since Saul from Cilicia was the ringleader of this persecution, even going from house (church) to house (church) and dragging both men and women off to prison, that he had been a part of the synagogue that Stephen had been a member of and had been one of those disputing with him there. . . . It is thus plausible that Saul and other Zionistic conservative Jews from the Diaspora led the persecution.[6]

---

3. Schnabel reckons Paul's age at this time between 18 and 30. Eckhard J. Schnabel, *Acts*, ZECNT (Zondervan, 2012), 392. Joseph A. Fitzmyer believes the term designates someone between 24 and 40. *The Acts of the Apostles*, AB 31 (Doubleday, 1998), 394.

4. Darrell L. Bock, *Acts*, BECNT (Baker Academic, 2007), 315.

5. Ben Witherington III, *The Acts of the Apostles: A Socio-Rhetorical Commentary* (Eerdmans, 1998), 278n322.

6. Witherington, 278.

Fitzmyer adds, "Witnesses probably piled their cloaks at the feet of Saul, because he was known to them personally and probably attended the synagogue of the Freedmen (6:9), and because he was a Roman citizen."[7]

The implications of this are huge. If Saul was a member of the Synagogue of the Freedmen, then Paul was a freedman. If this is true, Paul was formerly enslaved and was manumitted, probably sometime in his youth. As has been detailed in the previous chapters, numerous Galilean Jews were taken captive during the turbulent years of unrest decades earlier. These captives were sold in the slave markets across the Mediterranean world. Many were freed over the years. Sometime after gaining his freedom, Paul migrated from Cilicia to Jerusalem, perhaps with his sister, who is mentioned in Acts 23:16.

While the historicity of the speeches in Acts 6:1–8:3 is often questioned,[8] the narrative portions of this section are generally acknowledged as credible and were probably part of a united pre-Lukan tradition.[9] As a traveling companion of Paul's, Luke may have received this information from the apostle himself. The details of this narrative[10] suggest that Paul was a member of the Synagogue of the Freedmen,[11] which strengthens the thesis that he was a former slave.

---

7. Fitzmyer, *Acts of the Apostles*, 394.

8. Cf. Marion L. Soards, *The Speeches in Acts: Their Content, Context, and Concerns* (Westminster John Knox, 1994), 1–17.

9. Gerd Lüdemann, *Early Christianity According to the Traditions in Acts: A Commentary* (Fortress, 1987), 82–83, 93, believes that the narrative portions of 6:1–8:3 substantially derive from traditions received by Luke and that these narrative sections were a connected unit in the tradition. More specifically, Lüdemann states that the reference to the opponents of Stephen ("those from the so-called Synagogue of the Freedmen") is traditional. So also Fitzmyer, *Acts of the Apostles*, 355, who cites a pre-Lucan Antiochene tradition; Charles Kingsley Barrett,

The Acts of the Apostles, vol. 1, ICC (T&T Clark, 1994), 1:319; Hans Conzelmann, *Acts of the Apostles*, Hermeneia (Fortress, 1987), 47–48; and Haenchen, *Acts of the Apostles*, 266.

10. The reference to those from Cilicia among those in the Synagogue of the Freedmen may be Luke's way of slowly drawing Paul into the picture. He was first anonymously referenced (6:9), later explicitly mentioned (7:58; 8:1), then grew in narrative significance (9:1–31), and gradually came to occupy center stage (chaps. 13–28).

11. So Witherington, *Acts of the Apostles*, 254; Fitzmyer, *Acts of the Apostles*, 394; Martin Hengel, *The Pre-Christian Paul*, trans. John Bowden (SCM, 1991), 69; Haacker, *Paulus*, 22; and evidently Rainer Riesner, "Synagogues in Jerusalem," in *The Book of Acts in Its First Century Setting*, vol. 4, *Palestinian Setting*, ed. Richard Bauckman (Eerdmans, 1995), 206. Riesner states: "It is tempting to conclude that both Stephen and Paul belonged originally to the hellenistic synagogue of the Freedmen. . . . The Jewish hellenists may have feared that the new messianic belief could be spread through converted members to the whole Diaspora. This may further explain the zeal of Saul to persecute the Christian hellenists" (206).

An inscription from the city of David in Jerusalem, dating to the first century or earlier, may refer to the Synagogue of the Freedmen. It indicates that a synagogue was built (or rebuilt) by Theodotus, son of Vettenus, who was a son and grandson of chief synagogue officials.[12] The inscription indicates that the synagogue was used for instruction in the law and also as a boardinghouse for Hellenistic Jewish pilgrims to the city (literally, εἰς κατάλυμα τοῖς χρήζουσιν ἀπὸ τῆς ξένης). The name Vettenus is Roman. It seems that Vettenus was taken as a family name after Theodotus's father was granted freedom from his Roman overlord, which attests to the use of the synagogue by former freed slaves.[13]

FIGURE 46. Theodotus inscription. Early 1st c. AD. Israeli Museum. Theodotus, son of Vettenus, was a freed slave and functioned as the head of the synagogue, which was repaired as described in the inscription. This was probably the "Synagogue of the Freedmen" mentioned in Acts 6:9. It appears that Paul was a member of this synagogue.

This synagogue may also be mentioned in the rabbinic writings.[14] In the Tosefta (t. Meg. 3.6) it is reported that Rabbi Eleazar, the son of Rabbi Zadok, bought the synagogue of the Alexandrians, which was in Jerusalem.[15]

---

12. Riesner, 192–200, offers a detailed analysis of the inscription.

13. This is followed by Reisner, 198; Lüdemann, *Traditions in Acts*, 83; Barrett, *Acts*, 324; Witherington, *Acts of the Apostles*, 254; and Martin Hengel, *Between Jesus and Paul: Studies in the Earliest History of Christianity*, trans. John Bowden (Fortress, 1983), 18.

14. See Riesner, "Synagogues in Jerusalem," 188–89.

15. Riesner argues for the antiquity of this tradition since the Mishnah prohibits the selling of a synagogue for personal interest. Moreover, he notes that Rabbi Eleazar, who lived around AD 100, could only have purchased the synagogue if it lay in ruins after the destruction of Jerusalem during the war and only if its congregation had been dispersed. The concoction of this story is not plausible during the later rabbinic period.

This tradition is also reported in the Jerusalem Talmud (y. Meg. 73d) and the Babylonian Talmud (b. Meg. 26a). The parallel version in the Babylonian Talmud designates this as the synagogue of those from Tarsus. These variations support identifying this reference with the synagogue mentioned in Acts 6:9, and the reference to Tarsus is particularly interesting.

Saul and Paul: Jewish and Roman Names (Acts 13:9)

By the imperial period, the typical Roman name had three parts. The *praenomen* was the personal name given to a child to differentiate them from others in the family. The *nomen* was the surname, the family name, passed down from one's ancestors. Since only one or two dozen praenomina were used in the first two centuries AD, many people had the same praenomen and nomen. A third name, the *cognomen*, was added as a second personal name. The cognomen was often passed down to an individual's descendants, so it sometimes became a second family name. It was not uncommon for people to have a second cognomen as a kind of nickname.

In Acts, Paul is introduced as Saul. Jews of the Second Temple period commonly named their children after relatives. Sons would commonly be given the name of their grandfather. Reumann believes that Saul was named after Israel's first king, who was a Benjaminite like Paul (Phil 3:5).[16] A second name would be attached, indicating one's father (e.g., Jesus ben Joseph). Due to the influence of Greek culture, several Greek names became popular among Jewish families, such as Alexander and Jason.

Saul is mentioned with his Jewish name in Acts 7:58; 8:1, 3; 9:1, 8, 11, 22, 24; 11:25, 30; 12:25; 13:1, 2, 7, 9—a total of fifteen times. After 13:9, he is never called Saul again. In Acts 13, Barnabas, Saul, and John Mark began a mission to Cyprus. After passing through the island, they came to the capital city, Paphos. There they met the proconsul, Sergius Paulus, who converted to Christianity, and thereafter, Saul is called Paul (Παῦλος). Paul was possibly the apostle's cognomen, a family name handed down from an adoptive father.[17] Schnabel observes:

---

16. "Paul's letters never use 'Saul,' but he was of the tribe of Benjamin (Phil 3:6) and could have had the name of the tribe's greatest king as *signum*." John Reumann, *Philippians: A New Translation with Introduction and Commentary*, AB 33B (Yale University Press, 2008), 53, 513.

17. "Paul[l]us was a well-known Lat. *Cognomen*. . . . Saul, his 'synagogue name,' from birth; Paul, his name in the Gentile world. Harrer: Paul's father, a freed slave, took the *praenomen* and *nomen* of his former master plus his own slave name as *cognomen*." Reumann, 53. So also Rapske, *Paul in Roman Custody*, 86.

> The name Paulos or "Paul" was either the cognomen of his family, that is, the official element of his name as a Roman citizen, which his family received after manumission from the Roman owner who had released an ancestor (his father?) from slavery. Or "Paul" was the *signum* or *supernomen*, that is, the Roman, Latin-sounding surname that the family used. Since we have no information about the history of Paul's family, there is no certainty in this matter. It is possible, however, that Paul's father received Roman citizenship through manumission. Several church fathers claim to know that Paul's father, living in Gischala in Galilee, had been sold as a slave as a prisoner of war.[18]

It was common for manumitted slaves to maintain a relationship with their former masters. Some worked as hired hands, while in many cases, freed slaves were adopted into the family of their former masters and given their master's Roman nomen and cognomen. Slaves formerly owned by Roman citizens, who were adopted and integrated into the Roman way of life, were given not only their master's names but also Roman citizenship. This is how most non-Romans received Roman citizenship, which may account for how Paul acquired Roman citizenship. Murphy-O'Connor notes, "The simplest possibility, as already noted, is that Paul's father had been a slave who was set free by a Roman citizen of Tarsus, and who thereby acquired a degree of Roman citizenship which improved with each succeeding generation."[19]

Paul the Zealot, Slave, and Roman Citizen (Acts 22)

The previous chapter discussed the state of affairs in Judea and Galilee during the decades following Rome's takeover of Palestine. Judea was a hotbed of insurrection during that period, but Galilee was even more unstable, with revolts breaking out seemingly unabated. The Romans harshly put down these rebellions, killing the combatants and often selling the survivors in the slave markets. Enslaving rebel populations served the Romans in three ways: It became a strong deterrent to rebellion, it supplied slaves for the empire's great need for labor, and it provided funds for the Romans to carry on their military endeavors.

---

18. Eckhard J. Schnabel, *Paul the Missionary: Realities, Strategies and Methods* (IVP Academic, 2008), 42.

19. Murphy-O'Connor, *Paul: A Critical Life*, 41.

In two separate writings, Jerome referenced a tradition he received, claiming that Paul's family originally came from a village called Gischala in Galilee. The information from Jerome, coupled with Josephus's history of Galilee during that period, indicates that Gischala and a number of other villages were sacked and enslaved. As I have previously written, Paul and his family were among those Josephus described as Zealots.[20]

In Acts 21, after Paul's so-called third mission he arrived in Jerusalem, where he anticipated encountering a hostile environment. True to his expectations, Paul was attacked in the temple. His life was saved by a Roman cohort who responded to the disturbance and arrested him. In the questioning that followed, the crowd was shouting accusations against Paul. This led the tribune to assume that Paul was a leader of one of the revolutionary groups. He asked, "So you are not the Egyptian who some time ago stirred up a revolt and led the four thousand men of the Sicarii (σικαρίων) out into the wilderness?" (v. 38). The Sicarii were one of the rebel groups that Josephus categorized as Zealots. Josephus mentioned this incident, which occurred around AD 55 when Felix was procurator of Judea.[21] Felix dispatched soldiers who killed 400 rebels and took 200 prisoners. The Egyptian escaped and was never found.

When Paul was given an opportunity to speak, he claimed that he was from Tarsus, an important city of Cilicia. Paul addressed the tribune in the Greek language. He then spoke to the mob in Hebrew (or Aramaic), probably so the tribune would not understand. Addressing the Jews (22:1ff.), Paul again claimed that he was a Jew "having been born in Tarsus of Cilicia." The word translated "having been born" is γεγεννημένος, a perfect passive participle. The same word is used again in Acts 22:28, where Paul claimed he was *born* a Roman citizen.

It can be questioned whether Paul's assertion that he was a Roman citizen was a literary fiction created by Luke.[22] Paul never mentioned it in his letters, and the fact that he was thrice beaten with rods (2 Cor 11:25), a Roman form of punishment forbidden for citizens, raises questions for

20. Fairchild, "Paul's Pre-Christian Zealot Associations," 514–32.

21. Josephus, *Ant.* 20.8.6.

22. "The story nevertheless appears in quite another light if we recall that Luke himself devised the speech and the scene preparing for it. . . . Here it serves to bring Paul's Roman rights of citizenship to light. As a good narrator, who allows the suspense to reach its highest point, Luke has his hero speak the liberating word only at the last moment." Haenchen, *Acts of the Apostles*, 635. See also Calvin Roetzel, *Paul: The Man and the Myth* (Fortress, 1999), 2; and Helmut Koester, *Introduction to the New Testament* (Fortress, 1982), 2:98–99.

some interpreters.[23] In spite of these concerns, most commentators believe the apostle was a Roman citizen.[24] Even Lüdemann, who generally distrusts the historicity of Acts, defends this point.[25]

It could be objected that since Acts 22:28 claims that Paul was born a Roman citizen, he could not have been a slave. However, that may be reading too much into the statement.[26] In fact, Lüdemann proposes that this might be the means by which Paul received citizenship: "Here it seems worth considering the possibility that Paul had citizenship as the descendant of a freedman, for the legal freeing of a slave by a Roman citizen secured his citizenship without further ado, and without state consent."[27] We need to back up a bit to consider the context of the discussion.

In 22:25 Paul revealed that he was a Roman citizen. When this was brought to the attention of the tribune, the tribune asserted that he purchased his citizenship with money. To the tribune's statement, "I acquired this citizenship with much money" (ἐγὼ πολλοῦ κεφαλαίου τὴν πολιτείαν ταύτην ἐκτησάμην—an *emphatic* statement), Paul countered with a stronger assertion: ἐγὼ δὲ καὶ γεγέννημαι (likewise an *emphatic* statement). One could not buy Roman citizenship. The tribune bribed an official to obtain citizenship.[28] Paul's response was to say that he was "born" a Roman citizen.[29] The contrast in this dialogue is that the tribune obtained citizenship illegally, while Paul asserted that he received citizenship legally.

The verb γεγένναμαι does not necessarily refer to birth. The middle voice of γεννάω is commonly translated as "to produce from oneself" or "to create."[30] The term can refer to birth, but it equally can refer to one's

---

23. Yet, as Francis Lyall observed: "It seems obvious and natural that it is Paul, the Roman citizen, who makes the plainest use of the citizenship metaphor, while his fellow writers, aliens, speak of alienage." *Slaves, Citizens, Sons: Legal Metaphors in the Epistles* (Academie Books, 1984), 60.

24. Bock, *Acts*, 665; Witherington, *Acts of the Apostles*; Schnabel, *Acts*, 923; Fitzmyer, *Acts of the Apostles*, 712; Carl Holladay, *Acts: A Commentary*, NTL (Westminster John Knox, 2016), 430; and David G. Peterson, *The Acts of the Apostles*, PNTC (Eerdmans, 2009), 609.

25. Lüdemann, *Acts of the Apostles*, 302–3.

26. Most scholars follow Cadbury's suggestion that Paul was asserting his *ingenuus*, his birthright citizenship, although Cadbury conceded that the Greek word did not match the Latin technical term. Henry J. Cadbury, *The Book of Acts in History* (Black, 1955), 68.

27. Lüdemann, *Acts of the Apostles*, 302–3.

28. "The tribune's claim that he became a Roman citizen by paying a 'heavy price' (*pollou kephalaiou*, Acts 22:28) doubtlessly refers to the widespread practice of bribery." Holladay, *Acts*, 429–30.

29. Fitzmyer, *Acts of the Apostles*, 712; and Witherington, *Acts of the Apostles*, 681.

30. LSJ, 344.

heredity. Büchsel notes that γεννάω and its cognates were never used in the mystery religions to refer to birth but rather to adoption.[31] Paul himself used the word to refer to his converts (1 Cor 4:15; Phlm 10), indicating that they were adopted into a new household. Good Roman slaves were not only granted citizenship upon manumission but were also often adopted into their patron's household and given their patron's *nomen* and cog*nomen*. Thus, the statement in Acts 22:28 may be taken as a reference to citizenship by adoption.

Returning to 22:3, Paul had more to offer. His statement "being brought up in this city" could suggest that he moved to Jerusalem at an early age.[32] However, no age is specified, so it is impossible to determine when he moved to Jerusalem.[33] Paul's fluency in Greek, his intimate knowledge of Greco-Roman culture and literature, and his command of rhetoric suggest that the move may have occurred after his bar mitzvah.[34] He also claimed that he was educated in Jerusalem under Gamaliel. This was quite an achievement. Gamaliel was considered the preeminent Jewish scholar at the time.[35]

Paul asserted that he was a Zealot. Our English translations have modified the statement in translations ("being zealous for God" in NRSV, NASB, ESV, NIV), but the word is a noun (ζηλωτής). Perhaps translators do not want to portray Paul as a radical, bloodthirsty Zealot. But this is what Paul was saying. He was willing to shed blood in order to protect the sanctity of the Torah. His response to the mob, "just as you all are today" (22:3),

---

31. Friedrich Büchsel, "γεννάω," *TDNT* 1:669.

32. The participle could refer to either Tarsus or Jerusalem. I think it is more likely the latter. Cf. W. C. van Unnik, *Tarsus or Jerusalem: The City of Paul's Youth*, trans. George Ogg (Epworth, 1962).

33. Schnabel, *Acts*, 900.

34. Tarsus was an intellectual center with well-known philosophic schools and schools of rhetoric. Strabo declared: "The people at Tarsus have devoted themselves so eagerly, not only to philosophy, but also the whole round of education in general, that they have surpassed Athens, Alexandria, or any other place that can be named where there have been schools and lectures of philosophers. . . . Further, the city of Tarsus has all kinds of schools of rhetoric, and in general it not only has a flourishing population but also is the most powerful, this keeping up the reputation of the mother-city." *Geogr.* 14.5.13.

35. Gamaliel was the son (or perhaps grandson) of Hillel, the founder of one of the chief rabbinic schools in Judaism (the other being the school of Shammai). Later rabbinic tradition eulogized Gamaliel: "When Rabbi Gamaliel the elder died, the glory of the law ceased and purity and abstinence died" (m. Sotah 9.15). Gamaliel was a member of the Sanhedrin (Acts 5:34ff.). The Sanhedrin was chiefly populated with priests and members of the Sadducees. Gamaliel's presence in the Sanhedrin suggests that he was respected by other Pharisees as well as Sadducees.

suggests that those attacking him were likewise acting as Zealots. The mob was trying to kill Paul, just as Paul formerly tried to kill Christians in Jerusalem. Recall Acts 9:1: "Saul still breathing threats and murder against the disciples of the Lord." The phrase in 22:3 is better translated as "being a Zealot for God, just as you are today."

Paul makes the same statement in his letter to the Galatians: "For you have heard of my former manner of life in Judaism, how I used to persecute the church of God beyond measure and tried to destroy it; and I was advancing in Judaism beyond many of my contemporaries among my countrymen, *being an extraordinary Zealot* for my ancestral traditions" (Gal 1:13–14).[36] Once again, the word used is the noun ζηλωτής, though our English translations soften the expression ("being more extremely zealous"). The point is that Paul was identifying with the well-known Zealot movement that was common during the first century.

One could object that Paul was a Pharisee, so he could not have been a Zealot. Not so. Earlier we described a Pharisee named Saddok, who, along with Judas the Galilean, was identified by Josephus as a leader of the Zealot movement.[37] Hippolytus associated some of the Essenes with the Zealots. Describing the Essenes, Hippolytus wrote:

> If a member of the second party hears that someone has been speaking about God and his laws, but is not circumcised, he lies in wait for him and when he finds him alone threatens him with death if he does not let himself be circumcised. If he does not obey, he is not spared, but is killed. It is for this reason that they have received the name Zealots (ζηλωται). But some call them Sicarii (σικαριοι). The members of another tendency call no one Lord other than God, even if they are tortured or killed.[38]

The radical ideology of shedding blood in order to maintain the Jewish ancestral traditions and the sanctity of the Torah was not isolated to the group Josephus loosely described as Zealots. It had broad appeal across the Jewish population. The "Zealot" philosophy spanned several groups within Judaism.[39]

---

36. Fairchild, "Paul's Pre-Christian Zealot Associations," 526–28. This will be discussed in more detail in the next chapter.

37. Josephus, *Ant.* 18.1.1–6; *J.W.* 2.8.1.

38. Hippolytus, *Haer.* 9.21.

39. "That they were not merely a religious 'philosophy' appears to be precisely why Josephus and others found them problematic in Roman-dominated Jewish society." Richard

Paul expressed himself similarly in his letter to the Philippians. There, he used the cognate term "zeal" (ζῆλος) rather than ζηλωτής. Defending himself against the "false circumcision" (3:2), the apostle touted his superior Jewish credentials. In ascending order, he claimed that he was circumcised on the eighth day (Phil 3:5). This squared with the practice of a devout Jewish family (Lev 12:3). He was of the nation of Israel and could trace his ancestry back to the tribe of Benjamin. Paul was "a Hebrew of Hebrews," claiming that he was a purebred Jew. Paul came from Tarsus, a city in the diaspora. Perceptions were that diaspora Jews (or Hellenistic Jews) were not as devout or pure as Palestinian Jews. Paul maintained that he was fully Hebrew in both heredity and culture. This phrase may suggest that Paul spoke Hebrew, whereas most Hellenistic Jews spoke Greek.[40] Further, perhaps the apostle insinuated that he spoke Hebrew at a time when most Jews spoke Aramaic.

Building on these claims, Paul declared that he was a Pharisee (Phil 3:5). The climax of Paul's pedigree was expressed with his actions: "as to zeal, a persecutor of the church." In this instance, Paul did not use the term ζηλωτής but rather the less politically charged cognate ζῆλος. Why? When Paul wrote this letter, he was in prison in Rome (1:7, 12–14, 17). It is probable that Paul's correspondence in prison was read by Roman officials. If Paul had described himself as a Zealot, he would only have complicated his chances for release. Roman struggles with Zealots over the preceding one hundred years created an atmosphere where the term was incendiary. Anyone described as a Zealot was subversive. It can be understood that the apostle tempered his language and used the more circumspect term "zeal."[41]

What Was a Zealot?

Josephus used "Zealot" somewhat loosely to describe a variety of pious Jewish groups motivated by religious convictions, a desire to protect ancient Jewish traditions, or a commitment to addressing the physical needs of thousands of people struggling to put food on the table. When the Romans

---

A. Horsley, *Jesus and the Spiral of Violence: Popular Jewish Resistance in Roman Palestine* (Fortress, 1993), 82.

40. Marvin R. Vincent, *A Critical and Exegetical Commentary on the Epistles to the Philippians and to Philemon*, ICC (T&T Clark, 1972), 97.

41. Reumann, *Philippians*, 514, notes that the word *zeal* had positive connotations associated with it.

first intruded into Palestine, following a brief period of Jewish independence under the Hasmoneans, the Zealots triggered the nationalistic sentiments of the people. The heavy burden of Roman taxation, compounded by Herod's additional taxes, placed an intolerable financial load on the shoulders of Jewish peasants. Harsh measures to suppress dissent among the Jews exacerbated the situation. The harvesting of slaves from those who could not pay taxes or who took up arms against Roman injustices fueled hatred against the Romans and contributed to growing unrest in the land. When the religious leaders lent support to the cause, the fuse was lit that set the Zealot movement ablaze. In reality, the religious leaders were there at the outset. But when these other factors coalesced, the rebel wildfires spread throughout the land, especially in Galilee, and Rome was unable to extinguish them until the great war of AD 67 to 73. Inspired by the improbable success of the Maccabees a hundred years earlier, the insurgency lingered for more than 100 years before the land was destroyed and thousands of Jews were paraded back to Rome as slaves.

Horsley has carefully subdivided the so-called Zealots into a number of groups with diverse motivations.[42] Horsley begins with the protests of intellectuals: "Intellectuals such as teachers and priests, either as individuals or as leaders of larger groups of people, have often been in the forefront of resistance against oppression and the exercise of violence by illegitimate authority."[43] The Hasidim (pious ones) were instrumental in the Maccabean Revolt. Josephus's reference to the Zealots as a "philosophy" can also be understood as indicating an intellectual foundation for the protest movements in the first century AD. These intellectuals spawned a number of resistance movements. Horsley believes these movements in the first century were mostly nonviolent reactions of peasants opposing the Jewish social elite who supported Roman policies.[44]

---

42. Horsley, *Jesus and the Spiral of Violence*; Richard A. Horsley and John S. Hanson, *Bandits, Prophets and Messiahs: Popular Movements in the Time of Jesus* (Winston, 1985); Richard A. Horsley, "The Sicarii: Ancient Jewish 'Terrorists,'" *JR* 59 (1979): 435–58; Richard A. Horsley, "Ancient Jewish Banditry and the Revolt Against Rome, A.D. 66–70," *CBQ* 43 (1981): 409–32; and Richard A. Horsley, "Popular Messianic Movements Around the Time of Jesus," *CBQ* 46 (1984): 471–95.

43. Horsley, *Jesus and the Spiral of Violence*, 62.

44. Horsley insists that the first-century protest movements were primarily nonviolent. "Far from there having been any 'Zealots' around, there was apparently no indication of the propensity toward violence that has often been projected upon first-century Jewish society. . . . Far from being the organized expression of a nation united in its religious and/or political concerns, these Jewish anti-Roman protests were spontaneous demonstrations generated

One of the chief problems with Horsley's theory is that Josephus connected the violent rebel movements during the Hellenistic Roman occupation with the later developments in the first century. According to Josephus, Judas the Zealot (d. AD 6) was the son of the arch-rebel Hezekiah (d. 47 BC). Hezekiah was also the father of James and Simon, who were crucified for insurrection by procurator Tiberius Julius Alexander in AD 47, and the grandfather of Menahem ben Judah, who was a leader of the revolt against Rome in AD 66. In between, Josephus weaves in the stories of the rebellious activities of several others.[45]

The motives of rebels are generally complex, and those involved in revolts typically have more than one agenda. These agendas may differ from others in the revolt and may not entirely align with the underlying motives of others. Mass protests have many moving parts, with people participating for various causes. What unifies a revolt is a sense of violation. Perhaps justice or religious convictions have been violated. In many cases, intolerable social or economic conditions exist, and people feel that their ability to live in a viable or feasible manner has been violated.

Notwithstanding, Horsley differentiates between several of these rebel groups and their motives. Thieves (λῃσταί) were active to alleviate poverty and heavy taxation. Assassins (σικάριοι) emerged to deal with prominent Jewish-Roman collaborators. Messianic leaders arose to persuade and inspire the people to fight a holy war against Rome. These categorizations are helpful. However, I am not confident that these movements can be completely isolated from one another. To assume that these groups had no connection with one another is, in itself, an assumption with no proof.

Paul's Sister (Acts 23:16)

Earlier, we briefly mentioned Paul's sister, the only member of his immediate family with any historical trace. Acts 23:16 contains the singular reference to her, although her name is not given. After Paul's arrest, while he

---

and, apparently, organized in remarkably self-disciplined fashion by the ordinary people." *Jesus and the Spiral of Violence*, 117. Josephus, contrary to Horsley's portrayal, blames this movement for the escalating rebellious sentiment that culminated in the Jewish War with Rome.

45. It is widely acknowledged that Josephus had biases, but it is hard to imagine that his *Jewish Antiquities* and *Jewish War* are wholesale fabrications of developments. Josephus is our most valuable source for these periods of Jewish history, and other ancient historians who used Josephus did not discount his details.

awaited a hearing or trial in Jerusalem, a plot to assassinate him was formed by about forty Jews. The son of Paul's sister heard of the plot and reported it to Paul, who in turn reported it to the centurion and tribune. The presence of Paul's sister and her family in Jerusalem, and Paul's awareness of their presence, indicates that the family unit was preserved throughout the period of slavery. Paul may have stayed with his sister when he migrated to Jerusalem.

It was not unusual for families to be separated from one another at the slave markets. Husbands, wives, and children could be sold separately. However, families were sometimes preserved and purchased as a whole. It is possible that Paul and his sister were born in Tarsus after their parents were enslaved. In any case, after gaining their freedom, Paul and his sister made their way to Jerusalem. Nothing is mentioned about their parents. Jürgen Roloff has suggested that Paul's nephew had some sort of connection with a Zealot group in Jerusalem, which accounts for the information he received on the assassination.[46] Perhaps this was a Zealot group that Paul was formerly affiliated with (6:12; 8:1–3) when he was "ravaging the church." His nephew could have had remote connections with them even if he was no longer involved. Although this cannot be proven, it can be assumed that a violent Zealot group existed in Jerusalem. Paul's words in Acts 22:3 describing himself as "a Zealot for God, *just as you all are today*" coupled with 21:31, "they were seeking to kill [Paul]," indicates that zealotry was a virulent expression of Jewish faith at that time and in that place.

As with Paul's early life, nothing is known about his sister. Was she older or younger than Paul? Did she precede Paul to Jerusalem, or did she come at a later date? What are the details regarding her migration to Jerusalem? Since single women did not usually move out of their nuclear families, one can assume that she was married when she moved to Jerusalem and that her husband probably initiated the move. Perhaps this was motivated by a desire to return to the Jewish homeland, or perhaps employment was the cause of the move. If she preceded Paul to Jerusalem, did Paul stay with her when he came to the city? We can surmise that she was emancipated at the same time as Paul. Both were probably quite young.

46. Jürgen Roloff, *Die Apostelgeschichte*, NTD 5 (Vandenhoeck & Ruprecht, 1988), 331.

| 5 |

Paul's Writings: The Letter to the Galatians

To be the slave of God is the highest boast of a man,
a treasure more precious than freedom, wealth and power.
Philo, *De cherubim*, 106 (Colson and Whitaker, LCL 227, 73)

UP TO THIS POINT, WE have presented indirect evidence that Paul was a slave. Some of this could be termed secondhand testimony (e.g., Jerome's comments), and other evidence could be construed as circumstantial evidence (e.g., statements from the Acts of the Apostles). But what about Paul's writings? Are there clues in his letters that suggest that he was a slave earlier in life? Indeed, there are. A disproportionate amount of slave terminology occurs in Paul's letters compared to the rest of the New Testament.[1] Most of this terminology is found in the apostle's letters to the Romans, Corinthians, Galatians, and Philemon. Noteworthy are the particularly revealing comments that were expressed in the letter to the Galatians. Furthermore, as one might expect, the preponderance of the cognates for "freedom" is even

1. The noun δοῦλος (slave) is used 124 times in the NT, 19 of which are in the undisputed Pauline writings (7 additional times in Ephesians and Colossians); the adjective δοῦλος is used twice in the NT (both Paul's); the noun δουλεία (slavery) is used 5 times in the NT, 5 of them in Paul; the verb δουλεύω is found 25 times in the NT, and of those 13 are in Paul's undisputed writings (2 more in Ephesians and Colossians); and the verb δουλόω occurs 8 times in the NT, with 5 of those in Paul.

more distinctively Pauline.[2] Like the slave terminology, the words associated with freedom are found primarily in Romans 6–7 and 1 Corinthians 7. While these statistics mean little by themselves, coupled with the evidence presented in this volume they lend corroborative support to the claims submitted here. If Paul was a slave, one might expect the experience to affect his thoughts, writings, and theology.[3]

Paul's Letter to the Galatians

The date and recipients of Paul's letter to the Galatians are issues on which scholars cannot agree. According to one theory, the letter was written to churches that Paul and Barnabas visited on the so-called first mission. This would include the churches at Pisidian Antioch, Iconium, Lystra, and Derbe. If these were the recipients of the letter, it would be Paul's earliest known letter, dated around AD 48 to 50. On the other hand, many scholars believe that Paul wrote this letter to churches established during his so-called second mission. This would include possible churches established at Pessinus, Gordion, Ankara, and possibly Tavium. Scholars who subscribe to this theory assign the letter's date to the mid-50s.

I am persuaded to follow the majority of scholars who support the South Galatia theory. This is due to several factors, although I will only mention a few. Christians and churches from the cities of North Galatia are never mentioned by name in the New Testament; thus, it is not clear that Paul ever traveled in that region. Also, the references to Barnabas in the letter (Gal 2:1, 9, 13) make better sense if the Galatians knew Barnabas, who traveled with Paul only on the first mission, not the second. I also believe that the fourteen years mentioned in Galatians 2:1 fit into a chronology that is better suited to the South Galatian theory.

Perhaps it was because of the proximity of Galatia to Paul's home in Tarsus, in nearby Cilicia, or perhaps because it was Paul's earliest letter, but this epistle to the Galatians was his most personal letter. In it, Paul revealed

---

2. The noun ἐλευθερία (freedom) occurs 11 times in the NT, with 7 of those in Paul; the adjective ἐλεύθερος (free) occurs 23 times in the NT, with 14 of those in Paul's undisputed letters (an additional 2 in Ephesians and Colossians); and the verb ἐλευθερόω occurs 7 times in the NT, with 5 of those in Paul's writings. The related ἀπελεύθερος occurs only in 1 Corinthians 7:22.

3. The discourses of Epictetus, a former slave and contemporary of Paul, likewise contain a disproportionate number of references to slavery and freedom. As in Paul's writings, Epictetus's references included both metaphorical uses of the terms as well as literal expressions.

more biographical information than in any of his other letters. Perhaps Paul was forced to do so because his opponents (the Judaizers) offered disparaging comments, denigrating his past. Paul wrote: "You have heard of my former manner of life in Judaism" (1:13). From whom did the Galatians

FIGURE 47. Kilistra (Gökyurt), an ancient Hellenistic and Roman town in Lycaonia. Numerous rock-cut dwellings can be seen at the site along with a Byzantine church.

FIGURE 48. Kilistra rock-cut dwellings. The location of biblical Lystra is disputed. Many believe the site was located at a mound (tel) west of Hatunsuray. However, a larger ancient settlement was located another ten miles west of this mound. This settlement today is known as Kilistra. Many modern Turkish city names preserve the ancient city names, albeit with small changes. Kilistra preserves the name "Lystra" and seems to be the more likely site of ancient Lystra.

hear this information: from Paul himself, from his opponents, or from both? What did these Judaizers have to say about Paul?

Paul's comment in 3:1 indicates that outsiders had deceived the Galatians: "You foolish Galatians, who has bewitched you?" This verse includes an unusual word: βασκαίνω. This is the only place the word is used in the New Testament. It usually means "to bewitch or to cast a spell," but it can also be understood as "to malign or to disparage."[4] Delling claims that the original meaning is "to do hurt to someone through unfavourable words."[5] The cognate noun βάσκανος refers to a sorcerer or slanderer, and the adjective is translated as "slanderous or malicious." One could plausibly argue that Paul used this word because his opponents were bewitching the Galatians, in part by maligning Paul. The Judaizers likely undermined Paul's authority by highlighting the ignoble aspects of his past. Paul wrote this letter to set the record straight.

Galatians 1:10

Not much can be determined from Paul's references to himself as the δοῦλος (slave) of Christ in the introductions of his letters to the Romans and Philippians.[6] Though some have noted that it was unusual for freeborn Greeks to use such terminology,[7] the expression had much more currency in the East, and Paul might simply have been following a Jewish precedent.[8] The case of Galatians 1:10, however, is different.

---

4. LSJ, 310.

5. Gerhard Delling, "βασκαίνω," *TDNT* 1:594.

6. I do not think an autobiographical reference to Paul's past can be demonstrated from the title "slave" alone. However, I am not convinced that Paul used it to claim the power and authority of Christ, as argued by Martin, *Slavery as Salvation*, 50–60. Martin asserts that far from expressing humility, Paul used this title to claim his leadership status. Martin claims that Paul was claiming to be Christ's slave agent, a slave who would manage the affairs of a rich and powerful master. The chief problem for this argument is that the normal terms for such a slave manager are οἰκονόμος and πραγματευτής. Paul introduces himself as such nowhere.

7. H. W. Pleket, "Religious History as the History of Mentality: The 'Believer' as Servant of the Deity in the Greek World," in *Faith, Hope and Worship: Aspects of Religious Mentality in the Ancient World*, ed. H. S. Versnel (Brill, 1981), 166–71, follows Franz Bömer, *Untersuchungen über die Religion der Sklaven in Griechenland und Rom*, 4 vols. (F. Steiner, 1958–63), 2:89, saying that in Greek territory it would be more probable for slaves or freedmen to use the term δοῦλος θεοῦ than for free persons to do so.

8. Most commentaries suggest that Paul borrowed the concept from the Old Testament use of the "servant of Yahweh." This is developed most extensively by John Byron, *Slavery*

In Galatians 1:1, Paul identified himself simply as an apostle. However, in the words that follow, he went out of his way to indicate that his apostleship is not in the service of other men but rather in the service of God. This is borne out by comparing Galatians 1:1 with 1:10–12:

> An apostle not sent from men, nor by a man but sent by Jesus Christ and God the Father. (1:1)
>
> For am I now placating [πείθω] men or God?[9] Or am I striving to please [ἀρέσκειν] men? If I was still [ἔτι] trying to please [ἤρεσκον] men, I would not be a slave of Christ. (1:10)
>
> The gospel which was preached by me is not according to man. (1:11)
>
> For I neither received it from man, nor was I taught it, but I received it through a revelation of Jesus Christ. (1:12)

Paul wanted to demonstrate that his apostolic ministry to the gentiles was distinct from the Jerusalem church's ministry to the Jews, yet no less divinely inspired (Gal 2:7–9).

In Galatians 1:10, Paul first posed a question about whether he was placating (πείθω) men or God. He followed with a second question that was similar to the first, except that the verb was changed to ἀρέσκειν. We can

---

Metaphors in Early Judaism and Pauline Christianity: A Traditio-Historical and Exegetical Examination, WUNT 2.162 (Mohr Siebeck, 2003). Cf. Ernst Käsemann, *Commentary on Romans*, trans. and ed. Geoffrey W. Bromiley (Eerdmans, 1980), 5; C. E. B. Cranfield, *A Critical and Exegetical Commentary on the Epistle to the Romans*, ICC (T&T Clark, 1975), 1:50–51; and Dunn, *Romans 1–8*, 7–9.

9. Betz, Bruce, and Martyn all translate πείθω as a reference to rhetoric ("to persuade") employed to manipulate people. Betz, *Galatians*, 54–55; F. F. Bruce, *The Epistle to the Galatians*, NIGTC (Eerdmans, 1982), 84–85; and J. Louis Martyn, *Galatians*, AB 33A (Doubleday, 1997), 138. This interpretation is problematic when applied to God. Betz tries to avoid this difficulty by asserting that "persuading God" is a reference to magic. Thus, as a rhetorical question Betz claims that Paul was denying that he used rhetoric to manipulate men and denying that he used magic to manipulate God. Martyn, on the other hand, believes that ἀνθρώπους πείθω ἤ τὸν θεόν is an alternative. He rightly recognizes many similar antinomies (1:10b, 11–12) in the context of this statement and concludes that 1:10a should be understood as an antinomy as well. Thus for Martyn, though the term πείθω had a rhetorical connotation as applied to men, it had a relational connotation as applied to God. This leads Martyn to the contorted translation "Am I now engaged in rhetorical arguments designed to sway the crowds; or am I intent on pleasing God?" (136), where the same verb simultaneously possessed two distinct meanings. Furthermore, by asserting that πείθω refers to rhetoric, interpreters are forced to conclude that Paul argued against the use of rhetoric while at the same time employing it, since Galatians is highly rhetorical. Consequently, it is better to understand πείθω relationally rather than rhetorically.

assume with the majority of scholars[10] that Paul was repeating questions his opponents were raising.[11] Beginning with Galatians 1:10b, Paul responded to these accusations with an autobiographical section (his largest) that ran from 1:10b to 2:14.[12]

What was the distinction between the two questions at the beginning of 1:10? They are virtually the same except for the verbs employed. Πείθω and ἀρέσκω may at times share the same semantic domain (to please, to placate, to seek the favor of), but their distinctions are important.[13] The first verb, πείθω, often translated as "persuade," means to please from a position of strength.[14] It often persuades or pleases by means of words, deeds, bribes, or even torture. The second verb, ἀρέσκω, however, usually has the connotations of pleasing or persuading superiors from a position of weak-

10. B. R. Gaventa parts company with the majority, saying: "Often this statement is taken to be a response to Paul's opponents, who charge that he proclaims a law-free gospel among Gentiles in order to please them. But this interpretation must ignore the adverb ἔτι ('still'). The time in which Paul was pleasing to human beings was prior to his call, when he pleased his peers and elders by observing and promoting the Law (vv. 13–14; cf. 5:11)." "Galatians 1 and 2: Autobiography as Paradigm," *NovT* 28 (1986): 314. Gaventa's objection disappears, however, when one recognizes that Paul's past was used by his opponents to malign him. Nevertheless, Gaventa is right that ἔτι refers back further in Paul's life. Brian J. Dodd, "Christ's Slave, People Pleasers and Galatians 1:10," *NTS* 42 (1996): 90–91, and Betz, *Galatians*, 56, are more neutral in asserting that there is no evidence to indicate that these questions came from Paul's opponents.

11. In the preceding verses (1:7–9) Paul excoriated those who were disturbing the Galatians and distorting the gospel. "If anyone should preach a gospel contrary to what you received, let him be accursed." These opponents are typically described as Judaizers who claimed that Paul's gospel was incomplete and that gentile converts needed to be circumcised and obey the Torah, two issues that Paul deals with at length in this letter.

12. To understand Paul's letter as apologetic does not preclude seeing this section as autobiographical. Gaventa, "Galatians 1 and 2," 322–26, is particularly helpful here. Also see George Lyons, *Pauline Autobiography: Toward a New Understanding* (Society of Biblical Literature, 1985); and Martyn, *Galatians*, 157.

13. "These verbs can have virtually the same force." Martyn, *Galatians*, 138; so also Betz, *Galatians*, 55.

14. Philo described the coercion used by Alexander the Great to force Calanus to travel with him: "And when he failed to persuade [ἔπειθεν] him declared that he would compel him to follow him" (*Prob.* 95 [Colson, LCL, 65]). Philo noted that Calanus refused to be "enslaved" by Alexander. Likewise, Philo described the construction of the Egyptian city named Πειθώ by Hebrew slaves (*Post.* 54–55). Philo defined the word πειθώ, meaning "persuasion" or "harassing mouth," as a description of the Egyptian overlords. The passive form of the verb meant "to be persuaded" or "to obey," and Philo used this frequently in reference to the commands of kings (*Legat.* 80), commanders (*Spec.* 2.230), masters (*Somn.* 2.108), and parents (*Ebr.* 33). See also Jeremiah 36:8 LXX (prophets and diviners persuading commoners); 2 Maccabees 7:26 and 4 Maccabees 16:24 (parents persuading children); 2 Maccabees 10:20 (persuasion by bribery); and 4 Maccabees 8:12; 9:18; 12:4–5 (persuasion by torture).

ness.[15] In this sense, ἀρέσκω is generally used in regard to the persuasion of subordinates and is often associated with slavery.[16]

The second question (using ἀρέσκω) seems likely to have originated with Paul's opponents as a way of denigrating his teachings. Paul's opponents were evidently aware that he was previously a slave, and they used this question to suggest in a disparaging manner that he was still a servant of others. Paul rebutted this assertion, using a contrary-to-fact condition that included ἔτι and the same verb (ἤρεσκον). Since Paul responded using ἔτι, likely his opponents claimed he was still (ἔτι) acting as the slave of others and not acting in God's interests. Paul's use of ἔτι is a concession that for him, such slave conditions once existed.[17] Also, the fact that Paul responded to this second question first indicates that it was a put-down that he hastily dismissed before responding to the first question's more serious charge.[18] This contrast between slavery to men and slavery to Christ was starkly illustrated when Paul juxtaposed the phrases "pleasing men"

---

15. Ἀρέσκω is used less frequently than πείθω, but Philo used the word to describe the requests of a servant (*Legat.* 3.194). In the Septuagint, the term was used to describe sacrifices pleasing to God (Mal 3:4), attempts by people to please or persuade rulers and commanders (Wis 14:19; 1 Macc 6:60), and instances when underlings were encouraged to persuade (Sir 20:27) and placate (Sir 20:28) powerful people.

16. The word is frequently used to express a slave's desire to please his master. For the close association of ἀρέσκω with slavery, see Peter Marshall, *Enmity in Corinth: Social Conventions in Paul's Relations with the Corinthians,* WUNT 2:23 (Mohr Siebeck, 1987), 73, 78, 316; and Martin, *Slavery as Salvation*, 51–52.

17. Scholars recognize that ἔτι ("still") implies that Paul described his pre-Christian life in servile terms. Yet, most have taken this as no more than a metaphor. So Martyn: "Referring to his earlier consumptive zeal to please his nomistic teachers (1:14), he implies that in that life he was, as Epictetus would have said, the slave of those he was trying to please." *Galatians*, 140. Similarly, Betz: "The word ἔτι (still) refers to Paul's pre-Christian existence. . . . It is incompatible with being a slave of Christ." *Galatians*, 56.

Two factors lead me to conclude that Paul was speaking of slavery during the early years of his life. First, the autobiographical data that follows this verse refers to Paul's adolescent and adult life and training in Judaism (1:13–14) without extending the slave metaphor. Second, I find Hester's analysis of the rhetorical structure of this section to be convincing. James D. Hester, "The Rhetorical Structure of Galatians 1:11–2:14," *JBL* 103 (1984): 223–33, sees 1:6–10 as the exordium, 1:11–14 as the stasis and transition, and 1:15–2:10 as the narratio.

18. Marshall describes how a Greek or Roman would respond to such an attack: "A free man could be ridiculed as a servile person, and often was. In return, he will assert his free status and vigorously attack his opponents in like manner. . . . He will never denigrate himself in servile terms." *Enmity in Corinth*, 305–6. Paul did not respond in this manner. Rather, he promoted his status by asserting his freedom from human control and his association with a higher authority, Christ. As Martin states, "In the patronal society of the Greco-Roman city, slaves of lower-class persons held little power or prestige, but the slave agent of an upper-class person was to be reckoned with." *Slavery as Salvation*, 56.

with "slave of Christ" (εἰ ἔτι ἀνθρώποις ἤρεσκον, Χριστοῦ δοῦλος οὐκ ἄν ἤμην).[19] The statement can thus be expressed: "If I was still enslaved to men, I would not be a slave of Christ" or perhaps "If I was still slavishly pleasing men, I would not be a slave of Christ." The combination of ἀνθρώποις with ἤρεσκον ("pleasing men") is used only in reference to slavery.[20] The words are combined as one—ἀνθρωπάρεσκος (man-pleaser)—in Eph 6:6 and Col 3:22. There, Paul instructs slaves to serve their masters, not as man-pleasers but as slaves of Christ. Paul's appropriation of the expression "slave of Christ" in Galatians 1:10 is different from the title he used for himself in the introductions of his letters. In this verse, the contrary-to-fact condition and the use of the temporal expression "still" strongly assert that the slave status he once possessed is no longer applicable and that he now has a new master.

Galatians 2:4

In Paul's recollection of the dispute in Jerusalem (Gal 2:1–10), he brought up the issue again. In his perception, the false brethren (v. 4) attacked his freedom (ἐλευθερίαν) and that of his followers in an attempt to enslave them (καταδουλώσουσιν). The issue of freedom (ἐλευθερία and its cognates) is a significant issue in this letter, occurring eleven times.[21] The word that Paul chose to express "enslave" (καταδουλώσουσιν) is used only twice in the New Testament. In the other instance (2 Cor 11:20), Paul used the term to rebuke the Corinthian church for allowing his opponents to abuse and enslave them.[22] The term is a compound word combining κατά with δουλόω, strengthening the concept and emphasizing the attempt to enslave Paul and his disciples.[23] The Judaizers who demanded Torah observance and circumcision imposed their beliefs on Paul and his followers. Paul interpreted their

19. Dodd, "Christ's Slave," 98–99, correctly observes that the phrase Χριστοῦ δοῦλος is emphatic, unique in Paul's writings (all other occurrences transpose the words), and polemical.

20. Hans Bietenhard, "Please - ἀρέσκω," *NIDNTT*, 2:817; Werner Foerster, "ἀρέσκω," *TDNT* 1:456.

21. "Freedom, in short, is a very large part of the message of the letter taken as a whole." Martyn, *Galatians*, 196.

22. Murray J. Harris states, "In the compounded form καταδουλόω the prefix κατα- may be 'perfective' in the sense that the servitude was total, 'reduce to abject slavery.'" *The Second Epistle to the Corinthians: A Commentary on the Greek Text*, NIGTC (Eerdmans, 2005), 784.

23. Rengstorf, citing the term's use in Hellenistic literature and the Septuagint, asserts that "καταδουλόω is to some extent a stronger form of δουλόω. The basic meaning is 'to make a slave,' or 'to enslave.'" Karl H. Rengstorf, "δουλόω," *TDNT* 2:279.

actions as an attempt to rob his disciples of their freedom and impose harsh slavery on them. Paul's Jewish or Jewish Christian opponents in Jerusalem knew that he had been a slave. They certainly knew he was a member of the Synagogue of the Freedmen and may have thrown pejorative insinuations in his face. Even if nothing of the sort was said, Paul's mind churned up thoughts of slavery that he expressed in terms that evoked his past.

Galatians 3:28–4:12a

Some commentators assert that verse 28 is awkwardly placed in the text. Paul's argument thus far was that the Mosaic law has been eclipsed, so both Jews and gentiles are now children of God (3:26). As Moo notes, "This well-known saying about the way traditional religious, social and gender barriers are transcended in Christ is not explicitly tied to its context: unusually for Greek, there is no particle or conjunction that introduced the verse."[24] Moreover, although the statement "There is neither Jew nor Greek" fits the context of the argument, the two following pairs ("neither slave nor free, neither male nor female") are not related to the issue. Martyn believes that Paul was quoting from an early Christian tradition: "It is in fact part of a baptismal liturgy. . . . In writing to the Galatians, however, he is interested only in the first pair."[25] Something similar to this expression is also repeated in 1 Corinthians 12:13 and Colossians 3:11. In both cases the third pair (neither male nor female) is missing. Early Christian tradition or not, Paul's insertion of these contrasting pairs provided him with a transition to what follows in chapter 4. The first pair (neither Jew nor Greek) summed up Paul's argument in chapter 3. The Mosaic law does not distinguish Jews from Greeks in God's plan of salvation. The second pair (neither slave nor free) introduces the following discussion in chapter 4: slavery as experienced by Paul, the Galatians, and the slave descendants of Hagar.

Throughout this section verbs can be found in the first person, second person, and third person. The third-person verbs describe the general principles of Paul's thought.[26] The second-person verbs apply these principles

24. Douglas J. Moo, *Galatians*, BECNT (Baker Academic, 2013), 252.

25. Martyn, *Galatians*, 378.

26. These are found in 3:28 and 4:1–2, 4–5, where Paul claimed there were no status distinctions with God. Jews, Greeks, slaves, free persons, men, and women were equally regarded as heirs. However, until the time set by the Father, heirs were no different from slaves as long as they were under guardians. But when the time was fulfilled, God sent his Son to redeem the heirs.

to the Galatian problems.[27] And the first-person verbs describe Paul's personal attachment to the discussion.[28] Paul utilized the first person in 4:3, 5, 11, and 12 to demonstrate with personal illustrations that real change can take place. In the first instance Paul identified himself with the readers of the letter, stating that "when we were children, we were made slaves under the principles of this world." Interpreters have generally understood this as referring metaphorically to slavery under the Law (Torah). According to this understanding, Paul was saying that Jews (Paul included) were enslaved to the Torah.[29] However, several observations work against this. First, most Jews would be disinclined to think of themselves as slaves.[30] Second, Jews would be loath to think of themselves as enslaved "to elemental principles of the world." Third, Paul uses the term νήπιος, which refers to a specific age of childhood (the preliterate age up to five years) rather than the more generic term τέκνον used in the second half of the chapter when he unquestionably refers to the Jews. Fourth, the term "we" is emphatic along with the pluperfect paraphrastic construction (ἤμεθα δεδουλωμένοι), which implies a past slavery that does not currently exist.[31] Paul's argument is that the Jewish

---

27. These include 3:28b–29 and 4:6–10. The Galatians probably included the Jews, Greeks, slaves, free persons, men, and women mentioned in 3:28. Though they may have been differentiated in the past, Paul claimed that they were all one in Christ, Abraham's offspring, and heirs of the promise. Following the statements in 4:1–5, Paul suggested that since the Galatians were already Abraham's offspring and heirs of the promise, the Law did nothing to enhance the promise but rather impeded it. Thus, the Law must be tossed aside. God sent his Spirit to the Galatians as evidence of this adoption. Finally, the Galatians were cautioned not to turn back to "the weak and worthless elemental things."

28. Paul's first-person verbs are usually plural and demonstrate that his experiences in his former life were analogous to the Galatians' life apart from Christ. So Martyn, *Galatians*, 334–36. Moo, on the other hand, claims "it is very difficult to find any consistent pattern in Paul's use of pronouns in Galatians." *Galatians*, 260.

29. Bruce, *Galatians*, 193. Likewise, Witherington, *Grace in Galatia*, 284. Betz believes that both Jews and gentiles are intended. *Galatians*, 204. So also Ronald Y. K. Fung, *The Epistle to the Galatians*, NICNT (Eerdmans, 1988), 181.

30. Though Jews were permitted to obtain slaves (Lev 25:44–46), even Jewish slaves (Exod 21:1–6), slavery was considered the fate of gentile people rather than Jewish people. Jewish slavery was thought to be an infrequent and temporary setback. Cf. Garnsey, *Ideas of Slavery*, 155–56. According to Philo, slavery was banned by the Essenes (*Prob.* 79) and Therapeutae (*Contempl.* 70). According to Josephus, the fourth philosophy of the Jews had an unconquerable passion for liberty, believed that God was their only master, and consigned vengeance for those who served another master (Romans). *Ant.* 18.4–10, 23–25.

31. Daniel B. Wallace lists the paraphrastic construction as an "intensive pluperfect" and notes that it was simultaneous with the phrase "when we were infants." "An implication to be drawn from the context (but not from the pluperfect alone) is that the enslavement was now past." *Greek Grammar Beyond the Basics: An Exegetical Syntax of the New Testament* (Zondervan, 1996), 585.

people are *still* bound and burdened by the Torah. And fifth, it is difficult to see how Paul, as a Jew, could say he was "enslaved" to sin when he says elsewhere that his prior life as a Jew was "blameless" (Phil 3:6), and earlier in Galatians he touted his religious achievements (1:14).[32]

More likely, Paul identifies himself with the Galatian Christians. The "we" in 4:3 is joined to the "you" and "our" in 4:6–7. As Moo notes, "In this case, Paul's application of the situation he describes to the Galatian Christians in 4:8 makes it likely that the ἡμεῖς refers to Christians generally."[33] While it is understandable that Paul would describe the Galatians as enslaved to "the elemental principles of the world," it is difficult to understand how Paul could be so described. Here, the context of 4:2 clarifies Paul's thought.

Paul claims that the young child (νήπιος) was under "guardians" (ἐπιτρόπους) and "stewards" (οἰκονόμους). These were technical Roman terms describing a child's overseers. Witherington declares that "one must consider both Roman and Hellenistic Law as viable options to explain the origin of this analogy."[34] Liddell, Scott, and Jones offer translations of "guardian" (ἐπίτρόπος) as "one to whom the charge of anything is entrusted, steward, trustee, administrator."[35] The guardian was generally a friend of a wealthy nobleman who exercised general oversight of the nobleman's affairs in his absence. The guardian offered his services freely. The "steward" (οἰκονόμος), on the other hand, was a skilled slave who was in charge of other slaves and entrusted with the management of his owner's property, business, and affairs. His services were by obligation. Wealthy noblemen generally had both guardians and stewards.

Moo notes a problem. If the "young child" is understood as the child of a free person, the "steward" would not have authority over the child. The steward, "οἰκονόμος, is apparently never used in this way elsewhere. The word refers to a steward or manager of property."[36] It is true that the steward had no authority over the master's children. However, the steward *did* have charge over other slaves. Thus it should be understood that Paul's statement, "when we were young children," refers to children who were slaves, which included Paul.

---

32. The statements in Romans 7 likely do not represent Paul's pre-Christian understanding of himself as a Jew, as reflected in the broad consensus of scholarship.

33. Moo, *Galatians*, 260.

34. Witherington, *Grace in Galatia*, 282.

35. LSJ, s.v. "ἐπίτρόπος."

36. Moo, *Galatians*, 259.

Considering Paul's earlier discussion (3:1–27), one might suspect that the phrase "under the elemental things of the world" (ὑπὸ τὰ στοιχεῖα τοῦ κόσμου) in 4:3 referred to slavery "under the Law." The following verses (4:4–5) seem to connect with similar terminology in 3:13 and describe how God sent his son "under the Law" in order to redeem those "under the Law." Both 3:13 and 4:5 use the uncommon word "redeem" (ἐξαγοράζω), used only here and in Ephesians 5:16 and Colossians 4:5. But if Paul was referring to bondage under the Law, why did he not simply say "enslaved under the Law?" The word *Law* held different meanings for the Jews and the Galatians. Paul's argument throughout the letter was that the Law (Torah) had run its course and expired. In the Mediterranean world, however, the word "law" pertained to Roman law, which was still in full effect. Paul's phrase "elemental principles of the world" encompassed both understandings of the word *law*. Paul expresses in 4:3 that as a child, he was enslaved under *both* the Torah and Roman law; that is, the elemental principles of the world. But, when God sent forth his Son, he was redeemed from those laws. The term ἐξαγοράζω had particular relevance for Paul. It referred to the purchase (redemption) of slaves from the slave market. Paul's redemption was freedom from the burden of slavery as well as freedom from the burden of the Torah.

Paul cautioned the Galatians not to be enslaved to "the weak and worthless elemental things" (4:9). That is, they should not allow the Judaizers to enslave them to the weak and depreciated covenant law of the past. The phrase "made slaves under the principles (στοιχεῖα) of this world" in 4:3 must be understood in relation to the similar phrase "weak and worthless principles" (τὰ ἀσθενῆ καὶ πτωχά στοιχεῖα) in 4:9. These expressions are some of the most vexing terms in Pauline studies.[37] The phrase in 4:8, "however at that time," connects the Galatians' pre-Christian life to Paul's early pre-Christian life: "when we were children" (4:3). In 4:8, Paul referred to the Galatians' experiences with idolatry and paganism.[38] Here Paul used "you,"

---

37. Eduard Schweizer, "Slaves of the Elements and Worshipers of Angels: Gal 4:3, 9 and Col 2:8, 18, 20," *JBL* 107 (1988): 455–68, surveys all the literature surrounding the first century and concludes that the phrase τὰ στοιχεῖα τοῦ κόσμου refers to the four cosmic elements: earth, water, air, and fire. As applied to the Galatians in 4:9, this could be understood broadly as a reference to heathen gods or demons that control nature's course. For Paul's personal reference in 4:3, however, this is more problematic.

38. Byron, *Slavery Metaphors in Early Judaism*, 190–92, believes this phrase refers to idolatry in 4:9 but follows James M. Scott, *Adoption as Sons of God: An Exegetical Investigation into the Background of Huiothesia in the Pauline Corpus*, WUNT 2.48 (Mohr Siebeck, 1992). Scott interprets στοιχεῖα in 4:3 as a reference to Egyptian officials under whom Israel

rather than the "we" he used in 4:3, and it is clear that Paul was talking about the Galatians' slavery to pagan practices.[39] However, in the next verse (4:9), Paul described the enlightened Galatians who "have come to know God." He challenged them not to allow others to encumber them with another kind of slavery—slavery to the Torah. As Paul earlier stated, the Torah had faithfully discharged its duties as a tutor (that is, a slave whose task was to convey the children to Christ, the instructor; 3:24–25) but was no longer master over them.

Paul wrote "the elemental principles of the world" (τὰ στοιχεῖα τοῦ κόσμου) as a broad and encompassing expression.[40] The στοιχεῖα (principles) represent the "system," that is, the institutional machinations of the world, the system of laws and customs that are foisted on all people. Paul was twice freed from these (slavery and the Torah), and he was calling the Galatians to follow his lead. "I beg of you, brethren, become as I am, because I also was as you are" (4:12). The "we" expression in 4:3 was inclusive and applied not only to his childhood slavery and his slavery to the Torah but also to the Galatians' bondage to sin (under the umbrella of Hagar's descendants, taken up in the latter part of Gal 4). These slave burdens were lifted, as Paul explained in 4:5: "That he might redeem [ἐξαγοράσῃ—a word loaded with slave connotations][41] those under the law, that *we* might receive adoption." Thus, the apostle described his personal history as a parallel to the Galatians' struggle.

---

was enslaved during the exodus. The lack of references to Moses, Egypt, and the exodus makes this latter interpretation implausible.

39. Sam K. Williams, "*Promise* in Galatians: A Reading of Paul's Reading of Scripture," *JBL* 107 (1988): 714–15, distinguishes between the "we" and "you" in these verses, and he determines that the "we" in verse 3 is an exclusive we (meaning Paul and fellow Jews) rather than an inclusive we (meaning Paul and the Galatians). The problem with seeing this as an exclusive we is that Paul was uniting himself with the Galatians in 3:28 ("there is neither Jew nor Greek"), and he joins the Galatians in 4:6 ("God has sent forth the Spirit of His Son into *our* hearts"). This sense is carried on in 4:1–3 and 4:8. The τότε (then) in 4:8 seems to refer clearly to the ὅτε (when) in 4:3. Moreover, the use of στοιχεῖα in both 4:3 and 4:9 is compelling evidence that the "we" in 4:3 is inclusive.

40. Generally speaking, the word στοιχεῖα referred to fundamental principles. When applied to logic, the word referred to the principles of reasoning. When applied to physics, the word referred to the elements or basic components of structure. LSJ, "στοιχεῖον," 1647.

41. Bömer, *Religion der Sklaven*, 2:138–39, remarks that sacral manumission among the Greeks was expressed by the word πρίαμαι and not by ἀγοράζω. Since Paul uses only ἀγοράζω and ἐξαγοράζω, it seems he was not taking his cues from Greco-Roman sacral manumission. Nevertheless, ἐξαγοράζω "refers to the action of one person redeeming another by delivering him from slavery." Martyn, *Galatians*, 317.

The analogy of childhood heirs, who are equated with slaves in 4:1–2, is directly tied to Paul and the Galatian Christians with the words "so also we, while we were children" (4:3). Both Paul and the Galatians were destined to receive the inheritance as they were redeemed and adopted as sons (4:5). Though Paul and the Galatians were future heirs, as children they were nonetheless slaves under guardians, tutors, and stewards.[42] Consequently, rather than interpreting this as a simple metaphor, one can see in this statement an autobiographical reflection of Paul's past history in slavery that had come to an end, as the pluperfect participle (ἤμεθα δεδουλωμένοι, 4:3) indicates. This was the rags-to-riches story that Paul and the Galatians shared. Just as Paul had been redeemed from slavery to become an heir of God, so also the Galatians had made the transition from slavery (as Hagar's children) to receive adoption as God's heirs.[43]

In the concluding verses of this section (4:11–12a),[44] Paul lamented that he may have labored in vain and that the Galatians may not escape from their slavery.[45] He exhorted the Galatians to "become as I am, because I

---

42. The terms ἐπίτροπος and οἰκονόμος commonly designated household positions, the latter commonly occupied by a trusted slave. Betz notes, "Probably, Paul's association of the two terms came about because of the mention of slavery (4:3; also 4:1), since οἰκονόμος ('administrator') can designate the supervisor of slaves." *Galatians*, 204.

43. J. C. O'Neill noted the incompatibility of verses 1–3 with verses 4–7. According to O'Neill, verses 1–3 deal with a true son who is a minor under a guardian, and verses 4–7 deal with an actual slave. O'Neill concluded that the text has been glossed by two different people. See *The Recovery of Paul's Letter to the Galatians* (SPCK, 1972), 56–59. Seeing this as a gloss, however, is a cop-out. Paul created this incongruity because he needed to describe himself and the Galatians in 4:1–3 as heirs of the promise (Abraham's offspring in 3:29; Paul, a genealogical heir, and the Galatians, adopted heirs), and he also wanted to describe himself in 4:4–7 as a slave in terms similar to the Galatians. The Galatians were slaves as Hagar's children; Paul was a slave literally.

44. Surprisingly Bruce, *Galatians*, 208, Betz, *Galatians*, 220, and Martyn, *Galatians*, 418, see 4:12a as the introduction to the following section (4:12–20) rather than the conclusion to the preceding section (4:1–12a), although they provide no rationale for doing so. There is no logical connection between 4:12a and the section that follows. Conversely, throughout the preceding section Paul emphasized his kinship with the Galatians. Nevertheless, Martyn suggests a connection to the first part of chapter 4 when he links the personal pronouns of 4:12 to the plural pronouns in 4:3 and 4:5–6. "In those instances, Paul has underlined the absolute solidarity of himself with the Galatians. Moreover, this solidarity can be seen *ante Christum* as well as *post Christum*." Martyn, *Galatians*, 420.

45. The Galatians' slavery can be understood in two ways: enslavement to the Torah (as imposed on them by the Judaizers), and enslavement as descendants of Hagar (whereby the Galatians were thought not to receive the full inheritance of salvation). Paul's hope was that they would escape from the encumbrance of the Torah and be adopted (fully integrated) into the house of God.

also was as you were" (γίνεσθε ὡς ἐγώ, ὅτι κἀγὼ ὡς ὑμεῖς, 4:12a).[46] Paul was exhorting the Galatians to overcome their bondage as he had overcome his. Just as slaves are subject to the lifestyle imposed on them by their masters, so also children are enslaved to the culture of their parents (Hagar, in the case of the Galatians). Paul was paralleling his life with that of the Galatians. Separating the "we" sections (referring to Paul) from the "you" sections (referring to the Galatians) makes this more evident (implied statements are in brackets):

1. As children we [Paul included] [did not know Christ] and had been enslaved (ἤμεθα δεδουλωμένοι) under the elementary principles of this world. (v. 3)

2. When the fullness of time came, God sent His Son to redeem (ἐξαγοράσῃ) those under the Law. (vv. 4–5)

3. That we might receive adoption as sons (υἱοθεσίαν). (v. 5)

4. As children you [Galatians] did not know God and were enslaved (ἐδουλεύσατε) to things which by nature are not gods. (v. 8)

5. Now that you have come to know God, [you have been redeemed] and you are no longer a slave (οὐκέτι εἶ δοῦλος). (vv. 6–7)

6. Now you have become a son and an heir (εἰ δὲ υἱός καὶ κληρονόμος). (vv. 6–7)

7. Do not be enslaved again by these weak and worthless principles. (v. 9)

Galatians 4:22–5:1

In Galatians 4:22–5:1, Paul expanded the thoughts presented in 3:28–4:12a. The connection between these passages is supported not only by their proximity but also by the common elements found in each. Both passages deal with the children of Abraham (3:29; 4:22), both promote the heirs of the promise rather than slaves (3:29–4:1; 4:23–28), both address redemption and

46. Distinct from εἶναι (to be), γίνεσθε required a change in being. Paul was asking the Galatians to alter their past, just as he had altered his. A similar expression occurs in Pseudo-Justin, *Or. Graec.* 5.7 (probably a quotation of Paul): γίνεσθε ὡς ἐγώ, ὅτι κἀγὼ ἤμην ὡς ὑμεῖς.

the covenants inaugurated through sons born of a woman (4:4, 22–23), both exclaim that the Galatians are not slaves but free sons (4:7, 25–28, 30–31), and both exhort the Galatians not to turn back to a life of slavery (4:9; 5:1).[47] Most scholars recognize that Paul was responding in this section to Judaizers who were twisting biblical texts from Genesis to state their case.

As difficult as it is to reconstruct the arguments of Paul's opponents in this letter, there is ample evidence that the Judaizers used scriptural texts to assert that gentile believers were illegitimate heirs of the promise. It seems that gentile believers were caricatured as descendants of the slave Hagar who needed to comply with the Torah and be circumcised.[48] Thus, the Galatians were considered slaves born of the slave woman Hagar. The pejorative approach taken by the Judaizers cast aspersions not only on the Galatians but also on Paul. As in Galatians 1:10, Paul's opponents evidently knew of his past slavery and used this to malign his ministry. Paul's response engaged in contemporary Jewish exegesis and incorporated his own personal experiences in order to refute the Judaizers' contentions.

---

47. Most scholars follow Charles Kingsley Barrett, *Freedom and Obligation: A Study of the Epistle to the Galatians* (Westminster John Knox, 1985), 22–29, who claims that the Hagar and Sarah allegory is a continuation of Paul's reply to the Judaizers' exegesis of the Genesis texts. Consequently, one must see a continuation of the thought and logic of Paul's response from 3:6 to 5:1. Hence, the slavery slurs of the Judaizers in 3:28–4:12a were further processed by Paul in 4:21–5:1. Peder Borgen, "Some Hebrew and Pagan Features in Philo's and Paul's Interpretation of Hagar and Ishmael," in *The New Testament and Hellenistic Judaism*, ed. Peder Borgen and Søren Giverson (Aarhus University Press, 1995), 163, argues that Philo represents a Hellenistic Jewish tradition that interpreted Hagar similarly to the Judaizers. In Philo, Hagar was understood as an Egyptian by birth but a Hebrew by choice, a slave bodily but free mentally (*Abr.* 251). Hagar became the prototype proselyte. The Judaizers may have utilized such texts to insist that the Galatians pursue circumcision and Torah observance leading to proselytism.

Paul interpreted Hagar differently. For him, Hagar was always a slave. She could represent the matriarch of pagan gentiles (as in Jewish exegesis), but she could also represent people enslaved to the Torah. Paul did not align the Galatians with Hagar but with the free woman. They were adopted (4:5) as Abraham's descendants and thus were free. Philo also mentioned that Hagar's children were adopted (θέσις, *Abr.* 250) as proselytes, but Paul refused to follow this exegesis, since it implied circumcision and Torah observance for the Galatians.

48. Barrett argues that Paul was involved in an exegetical argument with Judaizers who appealed to the Abraham texts in Genesis. The key text was Genesis 21:10, "Cast out the slave woman and her son, for the son of the slave woman shall not be an heir with the son of the free woman." *Freedom and Obligation*, 22–25. Likewise, Byron comments, "Paul is engaged in an exegetical polemic against his opponents and is seeking to deflect the accusation that Gentile believers are the 'illegitimate sons of slaves.'" *Slavery Metaphors in Early Judaism*, 182.

The Abraham texts are central to the material throughout Galatians 3:6–5:1. Our interest, however, is in two sections—3:28–4:12a and 4:21–5:1—where Paul interprets the Genesis texts in order to challenge the slavery slurs leveled by the Judaizers. The transitional statement, "there is neither Jew nor Greek, neither slave nor free man, neither male nor female, for we are all one in Christ Jesus" (3:28), implies that the Judaizers used the inferior status of gentiles, slaves, and women to further their case.[49] In the sections that followed, Paul argued first that the gentiles (descendants of Hagar and slaves, according to the Judaizers' exegesis of the texts) became the free adoptive sons of Abraham, and second that the Jews (freeborn sons of Abraham) became slaves.[50]

In 4:1–12a and again in 4:21–31, Paul laid out his interpretation of the texts. Both of these sections included eschatological reversals and personal references to his past experiences in order to illustrate his argument. Likewise, in both sections, Paul employed a diachronic correlation ("as in the past . . . so now") to connect those past experiences with the present problem. Briefly, Paul's discussion can be outlined as follows:

Galatians 4:1–12a

Eschatological Reversal: Sons and Slaves

Gentiles (Galatians) were children (νήπιοι) who were slaves (δοῦλοι). (vv. 1–3)

Gentiles (Galatians) were adopted as [Abraham's] sons (υἱοθεσίαν). (v. 5)

Gentiles (Galatians) are no longer slaves (δοῦλος), but sons (υἱός, 3x). (vv. 6–7)

Biographical Link

Paul includes himself in the eschatological reversal:

> So also *we* (emphatic construction), when *we* were children, *we* were enslaved . . . *we* might receive adoption. . . . God sent the Spirit of his Son into *our* hearts. (vv. 3–6)

---

49. Martyn asks, "Did the Teachers' demand of circumcision and their scriptural equation of circumcision with the covenant function to imply that they were bringing the female members of Paul's churches into God's covenantal people on an inferior level?" *Galatians*, 380n260.

50. Such eschatological reversals are common in the Jesus tradition: "If anyone wants to be first, they shall be last of all, and a servant of all" (Mark 9:35); "Whoever wants to be great among you shall be your servant, and whoever wants to be first among you shall be slave of all" (Mark 10:43–44).

Diachronic Correlation

At that time you were slaves, . . . but now you are sons [τότε μὲν . . . νῦν δὲ]. (vv. 8–9)

Biographical Link with a Diachronic Correlation

Become as I am, for I was as you were. (v. 12)

Galatians 4:21–31

Eschatological Reversal: Sons and Slaves

Abraham had two sons (υἱοὺς): one slave and one free (v. 22)

The slave = according to the flesh (v. 23)

The free = through the promise (v. 23)

Judaizers = sons of Torah = sons of flesh = Hagar's sons = slaves = present Jerusalem (vv. 24–25)

Gentiles = sons of the promise = sons of the Spirit = free sons = Jerusalem above (vv. 26–29)

Biographical Link with a Diachronic Correlation

As at that time, the one who was born in the flesh persecuted the one in Spirit, so also now [ὥσπερ τότε . . . οὕτως καὶ νῦν]. (v. 29)

Cast out the slave woman. *We* are not children of the slave, but of the free. (vv. 30–31)

Paul was arguing that he was once zealously Torah observant (like the Judaizers) and could be described as a son of the flesh. As such, Paul was enslaved. He narrated this biographically in the first eschatological reversal (4:1–12), which referred to his early life in slavery (νήπιοι, "early childhood," vv. 1, 3). Paul was "redeemed" from this slavery when God "adopted" him as a son (v. 5). This concept was expanded in the second eschatological reversal (4:21–31), which referred to his pre-Christian, Torah-centered existence as slavery to the Law. In this state, Paul formerly persecuted the church, just as the Judaizers were persecuting the Galatian gentiles (v. 29). Paul and the Galatians, however, were freed from the Torah and became children of the promise and of the Jerusalem above (τέκνον, descendants, in vv. 28, 31).

Paul's personal reflections highlighted the primary issue: The Judaizers' assertion that uncircumcised gentiles had only a slave's stake in the inheritance of salvation, which Paul argued to the contrary. He could relate to these assertions at two levels (as an actual slave and as a Jew who was enslaved to the Law). Thus, in responding to these charges, Paul added his personal experiences to his exegesis of the Genesis texts pertaining to the Galatian gentiles.

The Judaizers' argument was about heredity. The Galatians were gentiles and, like Hagar, were without the Torah and thus outside the covenant. Paul's argument in response was theological: Ethnic, status, and gender distinctions were irrelevant, and the Torah had been abrogated. The Judaizers (and formerly Paul himself) were enslaved to the flesh (Torah), while the Galatians had received the promise, had been adopted as sons of the Spirit, and were free.

Throughout Paul's exegesis, he never identified the Galatians as the descendants of Hagar the slave woman. However, this assertion was made by Paul's opponents, who connected them to the Genesis texts. Instead, in Paul's mind, the Galatians were identified with the free woman, although she was never explicitly identified as Sarah (4:23, 31). They were adopted (v. 5), "children of the promise" (vv. 23, 28), born of the Spirit (v. 29), and free (5:1). In a surprising twist, Paul characterized the Jews and Judaizers as descendants of the slave woman Hagar (vv. 24–25). They were born of the flesh (vv. 23, 29) and slaves (vv. 24–25). Paul describes this as an allegory (ἀλληγορούμενα).

Martyn argues that Paul's unusual allegory incorporated an autobiographical reference to Paul's own mission.[51] The Septuagint's account of Genesis 16–21 uses the verb τίκτω, typically used to refer to women giving birth. Paul, however, changed this to the verb γεννάω, typically used to refer to a man fathering a child.[52] Consequently, Martyn believes that the phrase "the one born according to the flesh" (4:23, 29) referred to Torah-compliant churches founded by the Jerusalem church and that the expressions "the one born through the promise" and "the one born according to the Spirit" in Galatians 4:23 and 29 referred to Torah-free churches that Paul himself founded.[53]

It seems Paul was suggesting that those "born according to the flesh" were Jews and Jewish Christians who were myopically attached to the Torah

51. J. Louis Martyn, *Theological Issues in the Letters of Paul* (Abingdon, 1997), 197–98; so also Witherington, *Grace in Galatia*, 331.

52. The word τίκτω was most often used as a reference to women giving birth and expressed the physical reality of labor. Conversely, γεννάω was used almost exclusively to refer to men fathering and raising children. Cf. LSJ, "γεννάω," 344, and "τίκτω," 1792; also Gerhard Bauer, "Birth - τίκτω," *NIDNTT*, 1:186–87. When Paul uses the participle of γεννάω in verse 24, he uses the feminine form because of the preponderance of feminine pronouns in verses 24–26.

53. Martyn, *Galatians*, 433–45.

(including Paul in his early years), while those "born according to the Spirit" were Christians (both the Galatians and Paul) who had experienced the Spirit and salvation apart from the Torah (cf. Gal 3:2–3).[54] In Paul's mind, the distinction here was not racial but rather between two modes of following God: through Spirit or flesh.[55] Paul could identify with both of these groups. The first-person plural pronouns and first-person verbs (as in 3:28–4:12a) indicate Paul's personal attachment. Paul associated with those "born according to the Spirit." He considered himself the son of another mother: "The Jerusalem above is free, she is *our* mother" (v. 26), and "*we* are not children of the slave woman, but of the free woman" (v. 31). But Paul also suggested that he was once associated with those "born according to the flesh." His words in 5:1 make this clear: "It was for freedom that Christ set us free; therefore, keep standing firm and do not be subject again to a yoke of slavery." The words "freedom,"[56] "set free," "us," "again,"[57] "yoke of slavery," and "do not be subject to"[58] all link him to a former experience of slavery.

Paul's depiction of Hagar as the "present Jerusalem" (the mother of those enslaved to the Torah) and his portrayal of the free woman as the "higher Jerusalem" (the mother of the free gentiles) were preposterous ways

---

54. The contrasts between faith and Torah, as well as Spirit and flesh, are themes in the introduction to the Abraham texts that follow Galatians 3:1–5. In these verses the Galatians were driven by the Spirit, and the advocates of the Torah were directed by "the flesh."

55. Martyn, *Theological Issues*, 201n16, observes that the phrases ὁ κατὰ σάρκα and τὸν κατὰ πνεῦμα should be understood adverbially rather than adjectivally. The traditional adjectival interpretation suggests that Jews as a race were born according to the flesh and outside of God's covenant, while Christians were born according to the spirit and thereby the new covenant people. However, recognizing these phrases as adverbial indicates that Paul referred to the manner in which one follows God.

56. Betz, *Galatians*, 255–56, asserts that freedom "is the basic concept underlying Paul's argument throughout the letter. . . . In Galatians Paul uses various concepts to describe mankind's situation outside of the Christ-event as one of slavery by the evil elements dominating the world." Though Betz falls short of reading this back into Paul's biography, he states that Paul's "freedom is not merely a theory but an experience of that freedom. . . . It is characteristic of Paul's theology that theory and experience cannot be separated; every item of doctrine is at the same time reflection of experience, and every experience is accompanied by reflection and theory" (256).

57. Most scholars follow Ernest DeWitt Burton and abbreviate the meaning of this word: "πάλιν recalls the fact that as Gentiles they had been in slavery, and classes the burden of Jewish legalism with that of heathenism." *Critical and Exegetical Commentary on the Epistle to the Galatians*, ICC (T&T Clark, 1921), 271. But this is not enough. One has to recognize that when Paul said, "Christ set us free," the force of πάλιν must refer to him as well.

58. The term ἐνέχεσθε evokes "the imagery of cruel subjection of the slaves under their masters, and the heavy burden of suppression which the enslaved have to bear." Betz, *Galatians*, 258.

of describing Abraham's descendants and the gentiles.[59] How could descendants of Abraham be enslaved to other masters?[60] Anticipating that question, Paul inserted his personal experiences into the allegory.[61]

Perhaps this becomes most clear in 4:29, where Paul made the puzzling statement that "the one born according to the flesh persecuted the one according to the Spirit." The Genesis account made no mention of Ishmael persecuting Isaac,[62] so it is not likely that Paul's comments were a reference to the patriarchal narratives.[63] Instead, Paul described *his* past persecution of the church. Paul framed this statement with another diachronic correlation, ὥσπερ τότε . . . οὕτως καὶ νῦν ("just as it was in the past . . . so also it is now"). With this connection, Paul was able to expand the meaning of the Genesis text. But what was his point? This statement was only vaguely connected to Ishmael and Isaac. While Paul formerly persecuted the church, even more germane to the context is the Judaizers' current persecution of the Galatian church. Thus:

Ishmael's (one fleshly born) persecution of Isaac (one spiritually born)?

---

59. In 4:25, Paul said that Hagar was Mount Sinai and that this "corresponds" (συστοιχεῖ) to the present Jerusalem. This is the only occurrence of συστοιχέω in the NT, and it is interesting that the cognate word στοιχεῖα appears in 4:3, 9. Was Paul using this term as an intentional link to his earlier discussion, thus suggesting that Mount Sinai (the Law) had become the enslaving principle for the present Jerusalem?

60. The slavery of gentiles to Jews was permissible, as was the temporary slavery of one Jew to another. However, the concept of being "chosen" did not allow Jews to accept the idea of being enslaved to gentiles. Thus, the manumission of fellow Jews by whatever means was obligatory. As Garnsey notes: "Slavery was the fate of others, not of Jews. Jews could be subjected only to temporary slavery, unless they chose to stay with their masters." *Ideas of Slavery*, 155.

61. In Fairchild, "Paul's Pre-Christian Zealot Associations," 514–32, I suggest that Paul's family (and Paul himself) had connections to fanatical Torah-observant "Zealots" in Galilee. Torah-inspired resistance to Roman rule eventually led to the conquest of his home village, Gischala, and the sale of its Jewish inhabitants as slaves (e.g., Josephus, *J.W.* 1.222; *Ant.* 14.275).

62. Some interpreters claim Paul was asserting that Ishmael persecuted Isaac. So Dieter Lührmann, *Galatians: A Continental Commentary* (Fortress, 1992), 92; Bruce, *Galatians*, 223–24; and Betz, *Galatians*, 249–250. These scholars have appealed to rabbinic traditions as Paul's source for this information. For instance, Bruce cites rabbinic traditions suggesting that Ishmael may have taunted Isaac, been involved in idolatry, or endangered the child's life. However, none of these activities would be an apt description of persecution (ἐδίωκεν). Furthermore, as Bruce acknowledges: "These observations are all later than Paul's day; whether there were earlier forms of any [such traditions] . . . we cannot say." *Galatians*, 224.

63. Instead, Martyn sees "the one born according to the flesh" as the Jerusalem church and "the one born according to the Spirit" as Paul's Torah-free churches. Thus, he comes to the implausible conclusion that the Jerusalem church was persecuting the Torah-free gentile churches. *Galatians*, 444–45.

> As in the past Paul (one fleshly born) persecuted the church (one spiritually born), so also now the Judaizers (fleshly born) persecute the church (spiritually born).

In the following verses (4:30–31), Paul exhorted his readers (the Galatians) to cast out the slave (fleshly born) and to be free (spiritually born).

Paul used the Ishmael and Isaac narratives primarily because these Genesis texts were being utilized by the Judaizers to undermine the status of Galatian gentile believers. In response, Paul turned the tables, allegorizing these narratives and employing eschatological reversals to indicate that the Torah-free gentiles were the adopted spirit-born descendants of Abraham, while the Torah-enslaved Jews and Judaizers were the fleshly born descendants of Abraham. Paul's argument was all the more forceful because he was deeply involved on both sides of the issue. He was fleshly born, enslaved, Torah fixated, and had persecuted the church. Yet, following his rebirth, Paul was spiritually born, freed, Torah free, and was being persecuted by those who remained ardently attached to the Torah. When Paul employed a first-person verb in 4:31 ("We are not children of a bondwoman, but of the free woman") and a first-person pronoun in 5:1 ("It was for freedom that Christ set us free"), he used them in the same autobiographical way that the first-person verb was used in 4:12. That is, though he was formerly enslaved, his slavery was past. His two concluding statements are parallel:

> Become as I am [free], because I also was as you were [enslaved]. (4:12)

> It was for freedom that Christ set us free; therefore keep standing firm and do not be subject again to a yoke of slavery. (5:1)

Galatians 6:17

The next-to-last verse in Galatians contains a cryptic statement that scholars have interpreted in various ways. In 6:17 Paul made an appeal: "Do not let anyone trouble me anymore, for I bear the brand-marks (στίγματα) of Jesus on my body." This stigmata (στίγματα) can scarcely be a reference to the stigmata of Christ—wounds on the hands, side, and forehead that correspond to Christ's wounds on the cross. Later Christian mystics claimed to bear these marks while suffering with Christ.[64] Most interpreters see this verse as a reference to the wounds or scars he accumulated over many years

64. Nor is it plausible that this would be a decorative Christian tattoo, such as a cross or a chi. This was first suggested by Erich Dinkler, "Jesu Wort vom Kreuztragen," in *Neutes-*

of ministry.[65] This understanding of the word, however, is highly unlikely. It is never used elsewhere in the New Testament to refer to wounds or scars, and it is rarely used in other literature in this manner.[66] Paul talked about his whippings and beatings (2 Cor 6:5; 11:23–25), sufferings and afflictions (1 Thess 3:4, 7), and the puzzling thorn in the flesh (2 Cor 12:7), but he never referred to any of these as στίγματα.[67] Additionally, if these στίγματα were wounds or scars of the apostle, the verse would be understood as an appeal for pity.[68] The sense would be: "Leave me alone. Can't you see that I have suffered enough?" Such an interpretation is quite out of character for Paul, who took suffering as his destiny (1 Thess 3:3).

Instead, the reference to the stigmata must be understood as a reference to a tattoo or brand that Paul received as a slave.[69] These marks (usually a tattoo) were quite common among slaves of the time.[70] The marks were

---

tamentliche Studien für R. Bultmann: Zu seinem siebzigsten Geburtstag am 20. August 1954, BZNW 21 (Töpelmann, 1954), 110–29, and is thought possible by Betz, *Galatians*, 324.

65. This is the most popular understanding, supported by Betz, *Galatians*, 324–25; Bruce, *Galatians*, 275–76; Martyn, *Galatians*, 568–69; and Ralph P. Martin "Mark, Brand - στίγμα," *NIDNTT* 2:573.

66. C. P. Jones, "*Stigma*: Tattooing and Branding in Graeco-Roman Antiquity," *JRS* 77 (1987): 140–41, argues persuasively that στίγματα almost always designates tattoos, though the term can, rarely, refer to brand marks. There are several other words suitable to describe wounds or scars. So also F. H. Thompson, *The Archaeology of Greek and Roman Slavery* (Bloomsbury, 2003), 241–42. Thompson notes that the tattoo may have been as small as a single letter, and these were commonly applied to slaves, criminals, and prisoners of war.

67. Elsewhere in the NT, wounds are referred to as τραῦμα (Luke 10:34), τραυματίζω (Luke 20:12, Acts 19:16), or μώλωψ (1 Pet 2:24) Josephus relates that Antipater disrobed in order to reveal his scars (τραύματα), which demonstrated his loyalty to Caesar (*J.W.* 1.197).

68. Betz discounts this but claims that Paul was making an emotional appeal characteristic of the philosophers. *Galatians*, 324. See also Hans Dieter Betz, *Der Apostel Paulus und die sokratische Tradition: Eine exegetische Untersuchung zu seiner "Apologie" 2 Korinther 10–13*, BHTh 45 (Mohr, 1972), 15–17.

69. Branding was usually designated with the word χαρακτήρ or καυτήριον. Though the branding of humans was practiced by the Babylonians, Egyptians, and Persians, there is no evidence of it among the Greeks, and evidence of its practice among the Romans is sparse. Jones, "*Stigma*: Tattooing and Branding," 155. Martin adds: "Certain points argue that the reference here would be understood as the tattoo—or, somewhat less likely, a brand—sometimes placed on slaves. For one thing, 'tattooed' or 'branded' was a common way of referring to slaves." *Slavery as Salvation*, 59.

70. According to Jones, "*Stigma*: Tattooing and Branding," 140–41, tattoos in antiquity could be (1) decorative (only among the barbarians), (2) religious (among the Eastern nations, such as the Egyptians and Syrians), and (3) punitive (among the Persians, Greeks, and Romans). Jones further notes that penal tattooing was inflicted on slaves, criminals, and prisoners of war, many of whom were sold as slaves (146). A text cited by Jones may suggest that even good slaves were tattooed by their owners (148).

well known and easily recognized, so much so that in Martial's satires of Roman life, he often referred to slave brands or tattoos without any further clarification. On one occasion, Martial (writing in Latin) even inserted the Greek term στίγματα to refer to such marks.[71] Juvenal, another satirist and contemporary of Martial, lived in the last half of the first century. His *Satires* also described the brands of slaves.[72] At the beginning of the first century, Gaius Petronius Arbiter, yet another satirist, wrote *Satyricon*, a bawdy fiction about Trimalchio, a freed slave who became wealthy and lived a licentious life. The work has numerous references to the brands of slaves.[73] Philo, in his treatise *Every Good Man Is Free*, also wrote of generations of slaves who have been subject to "the branding iron, the fetter, and immemorial thralldom."[74] Since Paul had gained his freedom, he now described the mark as a symbol of slave ownership to Christ. The sense of the statement is: "Do not let anyone malign the gospel I preach; I am accountable only to my master, Christ."

Excursus: Slave of God Inscriptions in Galatia

Christian funerary inscriptions are common throughout the Mediterranean world. Over the first three centuries, at times and in places where Christians were persecuted, the grave markers generally did not identify the deceased as Christians. Thus, in many instances, it is difficult or impossible to determine if the deceased were Christians. In other cases, discreet symbols or embedded clues suggest that the inscription marked the burial of Christians.[75] A small "+" representing the cross might be placed on a loaf as an inconspicuous clue for the bread of the Eucharist. In other instances, a word beginning with the Greek chi might be turned upright in the shape of a cross (+ rather than χ). In central Anatolia, the Eumeneian formula condemning the vandalization of the tomb ("he will be subject to

71. Martial, *Epigrams* 2.29, describes a well-clad, bejeweled nobleman who was hiding the brands of slavery under patches on his forehead. In 3.21, Martial mentions a branded slave who saved the life of his master. In *Epigrams* 8.75, he refers to four branded slaves carrying a corpse, and in 10.56, he utilizes the term *stigmata* in reference to the brands of slaves.

72. Juvenal, *The Satires*, trans. Niall Rudd, Oxford World's Classics (Oxford University Press, 1991), 10.180–85, 14.20–25.

73. Petronius, *Satyricon*, 45, 69, 103, 105, 107 (Walsh).

74. Philo, *Every Good Man Is Free*, trans. by Colson, *Prob.* LCL, 10.

75. I note several examples in Mark R. Fairchild, *The Underwater Basilica of Nicaea: Archaeology in the Birthplace of Christian Theology* (IVP Academic, 2024), 28–31.

God") was fairly common. In Phrygia, the explicit expression "Christians for Christians" on several Christian tombstones was a bold proclamation of their faith.[76] This phrase was unique to the region of Phrygia.

In the adjoining Roman province of Galatia, Christians adopted a title that Paul himself used. This was a distinctive feature of Christian funerary inscriptions in Galatia; there are numerous tombstones with the epithet "Slave of God." It is hard to escape the conclusion that these epithets not only echoed Paul's appropriation of the title but also reflected his use of the concept throughout his letter to the Galatians. At the outset of the letter, Paul described himself as "a slave of Christ" (1:10). The apostle exclaimed, "you are no longer a slave, but a son; and if a son, then an heir through God" (4:7). In the context of slavery, Paul exhorted the Galatians to "become as I am, for I was as you are" (4:12). Reading between the lines, it appears that many of the Galatian Christians did exactly that and went so far as to include the expression on their tombstones.

In my examination of Christian inscriptions from Anatolia,[77] I have noticed an inordinately large number of inscriptions that cite the names of Paul and Thecla, particularly in Lycaonia. I am not the first to note this. Breytenbach and Zimmermann claim, "From the 3rd to the 5th centuries AD, the name Παῦλος became by far the most used male name in funerary inscriptions from the region."[78] This and other factors have led Breytenbach and Zimmermann to weigh in on the disputed question of whether Paul's letter to the Galatians was addressed to churches established in north Galatia (Pessinus, Ankara, and Tavium) or south Galatia (Iconium, Lystra, and Derbe). They conclude that the recipients of Paul's letter to the Galatians were the Lycaonian Galatian churches in the south. "Taking all these facts together, there is cumulative evidence that the addressees of the Letter to the Galatians should best be placed in Lycaonia."[79] They state:

> It is obvious that the places where the name Paulus is attested are the locations where the apostles Barnabas and Paul founded the first congregations in the south of the province of Galatia (Iconium and Lystra) and the Phrygian-Galatian borderland, which Paul and his co-workers had visited on

76. Elsa Gibson, *The "Christians for Christians" Inscriptions of Phrygia: Greek Texts, Translations and Commentary*, HTS 32 (Scholars Press, 1978).

77. Inscriptiones Christianae Graecae, https://icg.uni-kiel.de/.

78. Cilliers Breytenbach and Christiane Zimmermann, *Early Christianity in Lycaonia and Adjacent Areas: From Paul to Amphilochius of Iconium*, Early Christianity in Asia Minor 101 (Brill, 2017), 61.

79. Breytenbach and Zimmermann, 91.

> the second (Acts 16:1–6) and third missionary journeys (Acts 18:23). Although people were not directly named after Paul the apostle, the name Paulus clearly became popular where the apostle Paul had exerted influence in the first century. Did the impact of Paul go beyond his name? Did his letters leave their mark on Christian tombstones?[80]

I would suggest that the impact of Paul's letter *did* in fact go beyond his name. The inscriptional evidence indicates that his repeated references to himself as a slave of God, along with his plea to the Galatians to become slaves of God, resulted not only in the proliferation of the name Paul but also in the epitaph "slave of God" or "slave of Christ" and the personal name Theodoulos (Theodoule).

Statistically, 67 percent (157 of 233) of the slave of God inscriptions come from north Galatia. If we include the twenty-eight inscriptions from Lycaonia (south Galatia), the percentage jumps up to 79 percent (185 of 233). If we include the neighboring Roman province of Phrygia, 98 percent (228 of 233) of the slave of God inscriptions come from this area of Anatolia.

Slave of God Inscriptions

Location	Total	"Slave of God"	"Slave of Christ"	"Your Slave"	"Theodoulos" or "Theodoule"
Cappadocia					
Caria	3				
Cilicia					
Galatia	157	143	4	7	3
Lydia					
Lycaonia	28	5	8	10	5
Phrygia	43	14	3	23	3
Pisidia	2	1		1	
Pontus					
Totals	**233**	**163**	**15**	**44**	**11**

These inscriptions are primarily funerary inscriptions and votive inscriptions. The votive inscriptions often directly address the Lord (κύριος) and describe the slave in the second person "your slave" (τοῦ δούλου σου).

80. Breytenbach and Zimmermann, 90.

These could probably be numbered with the slave of Christ inscriptions. The votive inscriptions often follow the formula κυριὲ βοήθι τοῦ δούλου σου, requesting help or mercy: "O Lord, help your slave." Eleven inscriptions offer the names of individuals, male (θεόδουλος) or female (θεοδούλη), meaning "God's slave."

The fact that these inscriptions are largely isolated to Galatia and the nearby provinces suggests that Paul's letter to the churches in Galatia resonated with the people in this area. Many named their children and grandchildren after him, and many took the title "slave of God" to designate their submission to Christ. The persistence of this title up through the fourth and fifth centuries is remarkable.

Conclusions from Galatians

The frequent use of slave terminology—coupled with autobiographical data throughout Paul's letter to the Galatians—leads to the conclusion that Paul was not using the concept of slavery exclusively as a metaphor. Rather, Paul was sharing his past personal struggle with a life in slavery. "Paul's metaphorical usage of slave language throughout Galatians dominates the letter and signifies a major contributor to Paul's thought processes as he attempts to influence the Galatian church in his favor."[81] When writing to the Galatians, Paul was contending with a Judaizing distortion of his gospel. These Judaizers described uncircumcised gentiles as the slave children of the bondwoman Hagar. Their objective was to burden (or in Paul's mind "enslave") the Galatians with the Jewish Law and circumcision. The struggle to keep the Galatians free from the constraints of the Torah caused Paul to frame his arguments using similar experiences from his life that had left a permanent impression on him.

Paul's opponents used their knowledge of his slavery to denigrate his teaching. To counter that, in his opening statements Paul emphasized that he was no longer a slave of people but rather a slave of Christ (Gal 1:10). Elsewhere in the letter, he stated that as a child he was made a slave according to the custom of this world (4:3). Nevertheless, he exhorted the Galatians to become free, just as he had done (4:12). Later, he allegorized the story of Hagar in such a way as to incorporate personal references to his slavery. He capped this with concluding statements: "We are not

81. Barrier, "Paul and His Master," 36.

children of a bondwoman, but of the free woman" (4:31), and "It was for freedom that Christ set us free" (5:1). Finally, when Paul referred to the "stigmata" on his body (6:17), he was almost certainly referring to a slave's tattoo.

When the data from Galatians is combined with the traditions cited at the beginning of this essay, the conclusion carries even more weight. There is every reason to believe that the tradition from Jerome is reliable and suggests that Paul's Roman citizenship originated from slavery and

Top left to right, FIGURE 49. Funerary inscription with cross: "Here lies the slave of God." Byzantine period. Tavium. FIGURE 50. Funerary inscription with cross: "Here lies the slave of God, Epiphania." Byzantine period. Tavium. FIGURE 51. Funerary inscription with crosses: "Here lies the slave of God, Theodote." Byzantine period. Tavium.

Bottom left to right, FIGURE 52. Funerary inscription with cross: "Here lies the slave of God, Epiphania daughter of . . ." Byzantine period. Tavium. FIGURE 53. Funerary inscription with crosses: "[Here lies the] slave of God, Heasper." Byzantine period. Boğazkale. FIGURE 54. Funerary inscription with cross: "Here lies the slave of God, who . . ." Byzantine period. Boğazkale.

manumission. This was probably also true for many other Jews who held Roman citizenship. Similarly, there is circumstantial evidence indicating that Paul was a member of the Synagogue of the Freedmen mentioned in Acts 6:9. Taken together, it is safe to conclude that Paul was a former slave and that this experience continued to influence his thought throughout his life.

Top left to right, FIGURE 55. Damaged funerary inscription: "Slave of God, having passed through the sea, is entombed here." Byzantine period. Boğazkale. FIGURE 56. Funerary inscription with rosette and crosses: "Here lies the slave of God, Theodouros Paramon Arius." Byzantine period. Ankara. FIGURE 57. Funerary inscription with cross: "Here lies the slave of God, Platon Neophytis." Byzantine period. Ankara.

Bottom left to right, FIGURE 58. Funerary inscription with large cross: "Here lies the slave of God, Platon." Byzantine period. Ankara. FIGURE 59. Funerary inscription embedded in a modern building: "Here lies the slave of God, Georgios, son of Stabos Larios." Tavium. FIGURE 60. Funerary inscription with cross embedded in a modern building: "Here lies the slave of God." Tavium.

| 6 |
Paul's Writings: The Letters to the Corinthians

In this country live a considerable part of the very populous nation of the Jews . . . called Essenes. . . . Not a single slave is to be found among them, but all are free, exchanging services with each other, and they denounce the owners of slaves, not merely for their injustice in outraging the law of equality, but also for their impiety in annulling the statute of Nature.

Philo, *Every Good Man is Free* 75, 79 (Colson, LCL 363, 55, 57)

Paul's Letters to the Corinthians

PAUL FIRST VISITED CORINTH AROUND AD 50 and settled there for eighteen months (Acts 18:11) while he established a church. By the time of Paul, the city had eclipsed Athens in population and was the provincial capital of Achaia. As an important seaport, it was socially diverse, consisting of people from assorted ethnicities, religious perspectives, wealth, and status.[1] This diversity in the city and in the church contributed significantly to the problems that Paul faced as he nurtured the Christian faith in Corinth. We know from 1 Corinthians 5:9 and from 2 Corinthians 2:3–4, 7:8, and 7:12 that Paul wrote at least four letters to the Corinthians to address these issues. Only two of those letters were canonized. Paul wrote the letter known as 1 Corin-

1. Cf. Gerd Theissen, *The Social Setting of Pauline Christianity: Essays on Corinth*, trans. John H. Schütz (Fortress, 1982); Daniel N. Schowalter and Steven J. Friesen, eds. *Urban Religion in Roman Corinth*, HTS 53 (Harvard University Press, 2005).

FIGURE 61. The Corinthian Forum. Paul, Aquila, and Priscilla worked here as tentmakers while ministering to the people of Corinth.

thians between AD 53 and 55 while residing in Ephesus. Roughly a third of the population of Corinth were slaves, and another third were freed slaves.[2]

Even if those figures are overstated, the city of Corinth was teeming with people who had personally experienced life in servitude. Thus, it is not surprising that Paul offered his thoughts on the institution. He did so tactfully, recognizing that the practice was too deeply established, socially and economically anchored, and politically charged to be undone. He encourages slaves to become free, if possible, but he falls short of calling for the upheaval that would ensue if he condemned the practice. The Mediterranean world, and Romans in particular, were well aware of the trauma of the earlier slave revolts.

1 Corinthians 6:20

In the context of the well-known immoral behavior rampant in Corinth, Paul exhorted the Corinthians to flee immorality and stated that their bodies were temples of the Holy Spirit. Paul stated, "You are not your own" (6:19) and "You have been bought with a price" (6:20). The English word *agora* comes from the Greek ἀγοράζω ("bought") and describes a transaction in the market or, in this case, the slave market. In the past, scholars followed Adolf Deissmann's research based on the sacral manumissions written on

2. Murphy-O'Connor, *1 Corinthians*, xi. Most scholars concur with Murphy-O'Connor's conclusions.

the walls of the Delphic Oracle.[3] This practice freed slaves through a payment to Apollo, either a monetary payment or a sacrifice to the god. The reference to "temple" in the previous verse seemed to support Deissmann's conclusions. However, despite the similarities, this is not what Paul was describing.[4]

The word that Paul used, "bought" (ἠγοράσθητε), differed from the term commonly used in the Delphic inscriptions (πριᾶμαι). Rather than a payment for freedom, Paul was describing the sale of a slave from one party to another. In verse 19, Paul claimed, "You are not your own." Christ's purchase was not meant to free the Corinthians to act freely and independently. Instead, they had been purchased with the blood of Christ (not an animal sacrifice) and had now become slaves of Christ. The illustration relates not only to the Corinthians but to Paul as well. Following his conversion, he realized that his manumission was not a release to self-determination but instead a sale from one human master to God himself. As Ciampa and Rosner state: "Here in 1 Corinthians 6:20 Paul has in view a change of ownership, not a manumission resulting in unqualified freedom."[5] "When Christ buys a person, the salvific element of the metaphor is not in the movement from slavery to freedom but in the movement from a lower level of slavery (as the slave of just anybody or the slave of sin) to a higher level of slavery (as the slave of Christ)."[6] For the Corinthians (whether slave or free), Paul's message was that they were purchased by a new owner, Christ, and that they were not free to engage in sexual behavior contrary to the will of their owner. Their bodies were a temple for the Holy Spirit. They were not a brothel.

This is the understanding of the apostle when he introduces himself as "Paul, the slave of Christ" (Rom 1:1; Phil 1:1). He, like many of the Corinthian Christians, had been bought by a new master. In earthly terms, he was a freedman. But in reality, Paul's manumission was a mirage. He was still enslaved to a cruel master, sin (Rom 6–7). Now he had been purchased by a master of higher rank, a master of righteousness. Paul, however, did not leave it at that. He went on to claim that he had a stewardship (οἰκονομίαν)

3. Adolf Deissmann, *Light from the Ancient East: The New Testament Illustrated by Recently Discovered Texts of the Graeco-Roman World*, trans. Lionel R. M. Strachan (Harper & Brothers, 1922), 319–30.

4. Martin, *Slavery as Salvation*, 63.

5. Roy E. Ciampa and Brian S. Rosner, *The First Letter to the Corinthians*, PNTC (Eerdmans, 2010), 265.

6. Martin, *Slavery as Salvation*, 63.

entrusted to him (1 Cor 9:17). Stewards were trusted slaves who carried the status and authority of their master. Thus, Paul's role as a slave of Christ not only connoted the humble status of a slave but also the steward's authority of his master, Christ himself.

1 Corinthians 7:21–24

The same words "you were bought with a price" (ἠγοράσθητε . . . τιμῆς) from 1 Corinthians 6:20 are repeated a few verses later in 7:23. However, the context is different. Whereas the former passage dealt with sexual impurity and the necessity of maintaining purity for one's new master, this passage focuses more on the matter of slavery itself and the prospect of manumission. "In order to understand Paul's rhetoric in 1 Corinthians 7:22–23, which depends on the status-improvement meaning of slavery to Christ, one must recognize that salvation is here depicted as upward mobility within slavery."[7] Verse 23 is the conclusion of Paul's teaching in verses 21–22. Given that it was a touchy issue in Roman society, Paul is purposely succinct in his instruction: "Do not become slaves of men" (7:23).

FIGURE 62. Funerary relief of a family of freedmen, depicted with their slaves. 50 BC. Thessaloniki Archaeological Museum. See gallery for color version.

7. Martin, 63.

Just as the issue is politically charged today, the issue was perhaps even more thorny 2,000 years ago. Slavery was an institution deeply embedded in Mediterranean culture. In fact, slavery was established in civilizations as far back as we can discern in recorded history. Almost no one in the first century questioned the legitimacy of slavery or attempted to tear down the practice. Aristotle defended it as a matter of creation. He believed some people were incapable of functioning properly while free and needed the constraints of slavery.

Slavery was ubiquitous. Jews had slaves, and some slaves even had their own slaves. Just as the economy of the American South was heavily reliant on slavery two hundred years ago, the Roman economy was dependent on slavery. Eliminating slavery would have led to the collapse of the economy and the demise of the Roman way of life. The brutality and injustice of the institution culminated with the slave wars in the century prior to the Christian era (see chapter 2). The destruction, death, turmoil, and carnage of those wars struck a chord of fear in the Roman psyche that would never be forgotten. The wars also led to changes in the treatment of slaves and to laws addressing some of the abuses. Nevertheless, the overturning of slavery was not possible in the first century.

In this context, Paul was circumspect when he addressed the issue with the Corinthians. As mentioned previously, an inordinate proportion of the Corinthian population was, or had been, enslaved. Paul was not plotting to create a social movement through civil unrest and institutional upheaval, knowing that the outcome would give rise to violence, death, and destruction. Instead, he offered words of hope in whatever circumstances his readers found themselves. In these three verses, the apostle dropped the seeds of hope that, in time, germinated and sprouted an abolitionist movement in America and elsewhere.[8]

Paul's words were few and temperate, within the bounds of Roman law. Paul did not malign the practice of slavery, yet he did not condone it.

> Were you called while a slave? Do not let it be a concern. But if you are able also to become free, rather make use of it. For he who was called in the Lord

8. On a personal note, my ancestors were neighbors of the abolitionist John Brown when he lived in Richmond Township in northwest Pennsylvania. Our family's relationship with John Brown is largely unknown since the workings of the Underground Railroad were secretive. Yet, it seems that my ancestor Samuel Stufflebeam worked at Brown's tannery, the ruins of which still stand at New Richmond, and he assisted in the Underground Railroad that functioned at the site. Stufflebeam's son was named after the abolitionist, John Brown Stufflebeam.

> while a slave, is the Lord's freedman; likewise, he who was called while free, is Christ's slave. You were bought with a price; do not become slaves of men. (1 Cor 7:21–23)

One might wish that Paul would have offered words "off the record." I am sure the apostle would have been much more candid about the institution, having experienced slavery from within. Yet, Paul was cautious in his speech. Christianity was already being persecuted throughout the first century, and Paul knew that taking on the maelstrom of slavery was too cumbersome for the time. Christianity's aspirations were more ethereal and less concerned with the mundane. The matters of life were (and are) important, but the attainment of the kingdom was paramount.

With this in mind, Paul assured his readers that their status in Christ was secure. Paul's words to the slaves, "Do not let it be a concern" (v. 21), would have been received in various ways. For slaves subjected to hard labor and grim living conditions, some might respond: Who is he to say don't worry about it? Yet, Paul spoke as an insider with experience. Paul could not change their condition, but he also knew that there was hope: "You have been bought with a price."

The latter part of verse 21 is debated. Some interpret the phrase "but if you are able to become free, rather make use of it" as instruction to remain in a state of slavery rather than seizing the opportunity to become free. The sense of the verse would be to encourage slaves to remain as slaves and make the most of it.[9] This, however, seems an unlikely interpretation since the word "but" (ἀλλά) is a strong adversative statement to being a slave. Paul was suggesting that slaves who have an opportunity for freedom should avail themselves of the chance to become freed persons.[10]

Freedom certainly has its benefits. In Paul's words to Philemon, the apostle appealed to him to manumit Onesimus "no longer as a slave, but more than a slave" (Phlm 16). Paul admits, "I wished to keep him with me" (v. 13). He evidently recognized that Onesimus had ministerial gifts and, as a freed slave, he was "useful" (v. 11).[11] Freed, Onesimus could engage in ministry for the gospel. As a slave, his movement and availability would

---

9. Thiselton, *First Epistle to the Corinthians*, 558–59.

10. Most scholars agree. Cf. Ciampa and Rosner, *First Letter to the Corinthians*, 320; Fee, *First Epistle to the Corinthians*, 350–51; Joseph A. Fitzmyer, *First Corinthians*, AB 32 (Yale University Press, 2008), 309–10; David E. Garland, *1 Corinthians*, BECNT (Baker Academic, 2003), 309.

11. The name Onesimus was a common slave name and means "useful." Paul was using a play on words in this verse.

have been limited. Once again, Paul worded this letter tactfully and sensitively. He was careful not to command Philemon to release Onesimus. "Although I have enough confidence in Christ to order you to do that which is proper, yet for love's sake I rather appeal to you . . . but without your consent I did not want to do anything, that your goodness should not be as it were by compulsion, but of your own free will" (vv. 8–9). Paul wrote this letter from a Roman prison, aware of the fact that it might be read by officials. As with 1 Corinthians 7:21–24, Paul wrote circumspectly, not attacking the institution of slavery and instead confining his request within the parameters of Roman law. Thus, Paul encouraged slaves who had the opportunity to take advantage of the moment.

Regardless of whether such an opportunity should arise, Paul offered the Corinthian slaves and freedmen encouraging words. For those who embraced Christ while a slave, the good news was that they were the Lord's freedmen (7:22a). This involved a massive increase in status. Freed slaves generally retained a relationship with their former masters and often served them in their free life. A patron-client relationship involved mutual support and trust. In many cases, the freed slave was adopted into the household of their master, received their master's praenomen, and assumed a higher status. The status of the freed slave was derived from that of their master. The status of a senator's freed slave was near the pinnacle of one's expectations. Here, however, Paul was describing a status much higher. Paul was claiming that the Christian slave was given the highest status of a freedman—a freedman of Christ himself. Paul frequently described the Christian's adoption into the household of God. "For you have not received a spirit of slavery leading to fear again, but you have received a spirit of adoption as sons by which we cry out, 'Abba! Father!'" (Rom 8:15). For the Christian slaves at Corinth, this was a rags-to-riches elevation in status.

Those who were called while free, Paul asserts, are slaves of Christ (1 Cor 7:22b). This section has as much to do with status as it does freedom. Just as Christian slaves are elevated to freedmen, so also free people are conceived as slaves of Christ. This, too, is an elevation of the free person's status. Martin comments, Paul "turns around and establishes a difference between metaphorical slaves of Christ and metaphorical freed persons of Christ in order to stress the lower status (relatively speaking, that is) of the slaves of Christ (higher-status Christians)."[12] In the balance, the Christian slave

12. Martin, *Slavery as Salvation*, 65.

(deemed a freed person of Christ) actually possessed a slightly higher status than the free Christian (described as a slave of Christ). The distinction is slight, but nonetheless, those who were free believers in the Corinthian church had a lower status than the slave believers. By this, the "boasting" of the rich and powerful free Christians that Paul addresses at the church (1 Cor 5:2, 6) is dampened by the realization that the slaves are regarded as having higher status due to their association with Christ.

Whether slave or free, Paul reminds his readers that *all* were bought with a price (7:23). Christ has purchased all believers from the slave market or other masters. His command is "do not become slaves of men." Why would anyone stoop to serve a master of lower status?

1 Corinthians 9:1, 17, 19

Paul begins this new section with four rhetorical questions that can all be answered in the affirmative: "Am I not free? Am I not an apostle? Have I not seen Jesus our Lord? Are you not my work in the Lord?" (1 Cor 9:1). Most Corinthians likely knew the correct response to each of these questions. Yet, some Corinthians doubted that Paul was an apostle (1 Cor 9:2, 15:9; 2 Cor 11:5; 12:11), some doubted that he had seen the Lord (1 Cor 15:8), and some did not receive Paul as the patriarch who engendered their salvation (1 Cor 1:12–16; 3:4–6; 2 Cor 3:13).[13] The next two verses confirm this: "If to others I am not an apostle, at least I am to you" (9:2), and "My defense to those who examine me is this" (9:3). Earlier in 4:3, he addressed his critics: "It is a very small thing that I should be examined by you." Again, later in 10:29, Paul queried his antagonists: "Why is my freedom [ἐλευθερία] judged by another's conscience?" Were there some in Corinth who also questioned whether Paul was truly free? With so many in Corinth who were slaves and freed slaves, was Paul no better than them? As Paul already stated in 7:21–23, earthly status does not matter. However, the Corinthians thought differently. Paul "uses status-specific language and concentrates on status

13. Fee believes this is Paul's response to a letter he received from Corinth: "After an opening salvo in which Paul reasserts his apostleship (vv. 1–2), he sets out to defend himself against those who are calling him into question (v. 3)." *First Epistle to the Corinthians*, 433–39. Charles Kingsley Barrett adds, "Paul would hardly have spent so long on the question of apostolic rights if his own apostolic status had not been questioned in Corinth." *The First Epistle to the Corinthians*, HNTC (Harper & Row, 1968), 200. So also Fitzmyer, *First Corinthians*, 353. Thiselton rejects this, believing that Paul was defending his right to receive wages, which he rejected anyway. *First Epistle to the Corinthians*, 666.

images in chapter 9 precisely because his goal is to change the behavior of a particular group in Corinth, those who are themselves taking their own high positions too seriously."[14]

Some may have doubted that Paul, even as a freedman, was acting as a servant of God. Was Paul still obligated to a former human master as were most freed slaves? Where was Paul's true fealty and what were his motives when he came to Corinth? The answers to these questions were what Paul hoped to resolve in the verses that followed.

"If I do this voluntarily, I have a reward; but if against my will, I have a stewardship entrusted to me" (9:17). Stewards (οἰκονόμος) were, almost without exception, slaves who managed their master's affairs. Indeed, Paul was obliged to his master. Paul claimed that he was acting as a steward of Christ.[15] As such, he was obliged to preach the gospel without charge, rather than for personal enrichment or the benefit of a human master. Paul called himself a steward earlier in 1 Corinthians 4:1–3: "Let a man regard us in this manner, as servants of Christ and stewards of the mysteries of God. In this case, moreover, it is required of stewards that one be found trustworthy. But for me it is a very small thing that I should be examined by you, or by any human court; in fact, I do not even examine myself." Paul further clarified his status in 9:19: "For though I am free [ἐλεύθερος, echoing 9:1] from all things, I have made myself a slave [ἐδούλωσα] to all, so that I may win more." "Because he is a slave of Christ Paul does not accept financial support; he must therefore find some other way to support himself. Faced with this necessity, Paul becomes a manual laborer. Doing so does involve a step down in status, which is exactly what he wants, as will become clear in his enslavement, not to Christ, but to all in 9:19–23."[16]

Paul's critics assumed that if he was a true apostle, he would receive the wages of a philosopher or sophist. But Paul did not. His manual labor pointed to a much lower status. Martin asserts: "Paul refused support in order to maintain his independence and freedom from the control of the Corinthian church. Unfortunately for Paul, so the theory goes, he could only

---

14. Martin, *Slavery as Salvation*, 79.

15. Almost all stewards were slaves. "The primary meaning of the word has to do with the management of a household and, by extension, the management of businesses, cities, states and governments. Nevertheless, in the early Roman imperial period the word *oikonomos* almost always points to someone of servile status." Martin, 74. For further discussion of οἰκονόμος, see chapter 2 of this work.

16. Martin, 85.

maintain that freedom paradoxically by practicing what was considered a slavish trade."[17]

So, what does Paul's trade have to do with the matter? Based on Paul's intellect, superior writing skills, and high standing within Judaism (Phil 3:4–6), most scholars conclude that he came from a well-to-do Pharisaic family. However, Acts 18:3 tells us that Paul collaborated with Aquila and Priscilla in tentmaking at Corinth. The phrase "because he was of the same trade" assumes that Paul's tentmaking skills came from his father. In most cases, children followed the occupation of their fathers. Meeks reports that tentmaking was a lowly occupation.[18] The question is how a wealthy Pharisaic family became involved in an ignoble occupation commonly assumed by slaves. Was this a trade picked up by his father during the family's slavery in Tarsus?

Hock approached the issue from a different perspective.[19] "What, therefore, do we do with Paul's tentmaking when considering his social class? . . . By entering the workshop he had brought about a considerable loss of status, since as Cicero put it, a workshop can in no way be an appropriate place for a free man."[20] Hock's analysis of Paul's words in 1 Corinthians reflects an acknowledgment that such work was that of a slave (1 Cor 9:19; 2 Cor 11:7). Hock concludes, "By working at a slavish and demeaning trade Paul sensed a considerable loss of status, a loss that makes sense only if he were from a relatively high social class."[21] The question boils down to how a respected, well-to-do Pharisaic family could be reduced to working in a slavish trade dealing with the remains of dead animals. This, of course, takes us back to Tarsus. It is not likely that Paul's father would have migrated to Tarsus to take up a trade in tentmaking. Details such as this affirm the tradition that Jerome received.

Paul's connection with Aquila and Priscilla is also interesting. Acts 18:2 states that they were natives of Pontus. How did they arrive in Rome? Most of the Jews living in Rome were slaves and emancipated slaves. Did the families of Aquila and Priscilla suffer the same fate as Paul's? Both Aquila and Priscilla are Roman names. Were they emancipated and adopted into

---

17. Martin, 70.

18. Wayne A. Meeks, *The First Urban Christians: The Social World of the Apostle Paul* (Yale University Press, 1983), 59.

19. Hock, "Paul's Tentmaking," 555–64.

20. Hock, 558–60.

21. Hock, 564. Hock does not elaborate on how Paul learned the trade.

their master's household? Acts 18:2 tells us that an edict from Claudius forced all Jews, including Jewish Christians, out of Rome.[22] Aquila and Priscilla withdrew to Corinth, where they could join thousands of other Jewish slaves and freed slaves. Was there a "synagogue of freedmen" in Corinth, as in Jerusalem (Acts 6:9)? Of the 150,000 people in Corinth, a third of them freedmen, perhaps Paul met them there. It seems that Paul sought out others of the same status.

1 Corinthians 12:13

One of the issues confronting the Corinthian church was the diversity of its members. This was evident with members who represented the gamut of the social order: the wealthy and powerful, the nobility, as well as the peasants and slaves. Distinctions in race, gender, education, and various tiers of status were represented in the church. Because it was an important seaport, people from across the Mediterranean settled in Corinth, resulting in a diverse, cosmopolitan city. Sometime after it was rebuilt as a Roman colony in 44 BC, Corinth was named the capital of the province of Achaea. Differences in language, culture, status, and wealth contributed to the chief problem that Paul addressed in 1 Corinthians: divisions. The problem is broached immediately after the introduction of the letter: "I exhort you, brethren by the name of our Lord Jesus Christ, that you all agree, and there be no divisions among you, but you be made complete in the same mind and in the same judgment. For I have been informed concerning you, my brethren, by Chloe's people, that there are quarrels among you" (1:10–11). The problem manifested itself in several of the problems that Paul addressed throughout the letter: differences between the wise and the foolish (chs. 1–3), competing Christian philosophies (1:12, 3–4), immoral sexual behavior (ch. 5), lawsuits between Christians (ch. 6), liberty and the eating of meat sacrificed to idols (chs. 9–10), neglect of others at the Lord's Supper (ch. 11), and disputes about gifts of the Spirit (chs. 12–14) and the resurrection (ch. 15).

In his letter, Paul responded to several questions posed by the Corinthians. In 12:1, the apostle addressed the issue of spiritual gifts and the status of those who possessed them. Some Corinthians held the unspoken assumption that certain spiritual gifts were more important than others and that church leaders should be appointed from among those who shared the

22. This was also mentioned in Suetonius, *Claud.* 25.

more important gifts. "Paul is reacting against some Corinthian Christians who are vaunting one gift over another (especially speaking in tongues as the main gift of the Spirit)."[23]

Paul resorted to using the body as a metaphor for the church. All parts of a body are necessary for it to function optimally. Eyes, ears, hands, and feet function in coordination with one another. Although the church is diverse, the "less honorable members" (vv. 22–23) are no less honorable than the most honorable (vv. 23–24). Many commentators have found parallels in Greco-Roman literature. The first-century BC historian Dionysius of Halicarnassus described a speech by the fifth-century statesman Menenius Agrippa in which he attempted to put down an uprising by the plebeians against the patricians.

> A commonwealth resembles in some measure a human body. For each of them is composite and consists of many parts; and no one of their parts either has the same function or performs the same service, as the others. . . . The feet should say that the whole body rests on them; the hands, that they ply the crafts, secure provisions, fight with enemies, and contribute many other advantages toward the common good; the shoulder, that they bear all the burdens; the mouth, that it speaks; the head that sees and hears and, comprehending the other senses, possesses all those by which the thing is preserved. . . . Now consider the same condition existing in a commonwealth. For this also is composed of many classes of people not at all resembling one another, every one of which contributes some particular service to the common good, just as its members do to the body.[24]

Fitzmyer believes that Paul borrowed this metaphor: "Paul would then have taken over this Greek philosophical notion and given it his own distinctive Christian nuance, the church as 'the body of Christ.'"[25] If Paul borrowed this from the secular domain, one difference is striking. The purpose of Menenius's speech was to quell the plebeian revolt and to keep the patricians in power, thus preserving the status and economic distinctions between the plebeians and patricians. Paul, on the other hand, used the metaphor to level the status of those who were considered most honorable and least honorable. All members of the body of Christ had important roles in the body and should have equal honor. "God has so composed

23. Fitzmyer, *First Corinthians*, 454.

24. Dionysius of Halicarnassus, *Ant. rom.* 6.86.1–4 (Cary, LCL). This is cited in a similar fashion by Livy, *Ab urbe cond.* 2.32.9–12.

25. Fitzmyer, *First Corinthians*, 476.

the body, giving more abundant honor to that member which lacked, that there should be no division in the body, but that the members should have the same care for one another" (12:24–25). Thus, Paul could say: "Though they are many, they are one body, so also is Christ. For by one Spirit, we were all baptized into one body, whether Jews or Greeks, whether slaves or free" (12:12–13).

The passage reveals little about Paul's past but reflects his enlightened understanding of the place of slaves in society. Similar statements are found in Galatians 3:28 and Colossians 3:11. In Colossians 3:11, the Colossians are encouraged to be renewed in the image of Christ. In this renewal, "there is no distinction between Greek and Jew, circumcised and uncircumcised, barbarian, Scythian, slave and freeman." Galatians 3:28 states, "There is neither Jew nor Greek, there is neither slave nor free man, there is neither male nor female; for you are all one in Christ Jesus." These thoughts culminated in Paul's letter to Philemon, where he pleads for the slave Onesimus's manumission: "I have sent him back to you in person, that is, sending my very heart" (v. 12).

2 Corinthians 4:1–5

In this "second letter" to the Corinthians,[26] Paul was forced to explain and defend his ministry to some in the Corinthian church who had cast aspersions on his credibility and authority. Earlier in 1 Corinthians 1:12, it is clear that some followers had turned away from Paul and were following the teachings of Apollos, others were following Peter, and still others were following Christ alone. As in nearby Athens, the Corinthians believed that Paul, Apollos, and Peter were competing with each other with their Christian philosophies. However, in 3:4–9, Paul underscored the understanding that these Christian leaders were all on the same team, serving the same master, Jesus Christ. "I [Paul] planted and Apollos watered, but God caused the growth" (1 Cor 3:6).

By the time Paul wrote 2 Corinthians, the situation had become worse. In chapters 10–13, Paul recognized his weaknesses but adamantly maintained his position as an apostle. Paul's opponents highlighted the fact that he was not personally dynamic and that he was a poor speaker. "For they say, 'His letters are weighty and strong, but his personal presence is unim-

26. This was actually Paul's fourth letter to the Corinthian church. Prior to 1 Corinthians, Paul wrote an earlier letter mentioned in 1 Corinthians 5:9. Likewise, prior to 2 Corinthians, Paul wrote a so-called painful letter mentioned in 2 Corinthians 2:1–4 and 7:8–9.

pressive, and his speech contemptible'" (2 Cor 10:10). In 11:6, Paul affirmed this assessment of his speech: "But even if I am unskilled in speech, yet I am not so in knowledge." This was a concessive statement, acknowledging that these statements were true.[27] In Athens, Paul was criticized and described as an "idle babbler" (Acts 17:18), and he was promptly dismissed after his speech on the Areopagus. Paul lacked the oratorical skills of the skilled philosophers in Athens. The comparison with Apollos (1 Cor 1:12; 3:4), who was described as "eloquent" (Acts 18:24), suggests that Paul's presence and speech did not measure up to that of Apollos.[28]

In 2 Corinthians 4, Paul addressed his ministry to the Corinthians. Since he had received "this ministry," he had "renounced the things hidden because of shame" (v. 2), (ἀπειπάμεθα τὰ κρυπτὰ τῆς αἰσχύνης). This verse is wholly ambiguous, and perhaps the apostle intended it that way. Most commentators believe it has something to do with the deceptive practices of Paul's opponents.[29] But Paul tackled the issue of his opponents only in chapters 10–13. From these chapters, it is clear that the boastful arrogance of Paul's opponents was neither hidden nor shameful. They tried to humiliate Paul, accusing him of lacking the attributes in which they took great pride.

In contrast, I consider 2 Corinthians 4:2 to be a reference to Paul's humble and shameful past. The word ἀπειπάμεθα (we have renounced) came from the archaic ἀπολέγω, which, depending upon the context, could mean "to pick out, reject, to decline, refuse or to speak of fully."[30] Κρυπτὰ referred to things hidden or concealed.[31] Αἰσχύνης translates as shame or disgrace. Bultmann commented: "It is the disgrace one brings on oneself by one's own action. This is perhaps the meaning in 2 C. 4:2 also . . . either hidden things which bring shame . . . or hidden shameful things."[32]

---

27. Harris, *Second Epistle to the Corinthians*, 748; and Victor Paul Furnish, *II Corinthians*, AB 32A (Doubleday, 1984), 490.

28. Rhetoric was a cardinal element of a Greco-Roman education. Those who excelled became politicians, statesmen, leaders of philosophical schools, and private teachers. Paul lacked such skills. Perhaps the "thorn in the flesh" (12:7) that Paul experienced was a speech impediment that inhibited the apostle's oral abilities. God's response was, "My power is perfected in weakness" (12:7). That is, God's Spirit is powerful even through a weak vessel such as Paul.

29. Harris, *Second Epistle to the Corinthians*, 324–25; Furnish, *II Corinthians*, 246; and Margaret E. Thrall, *A Critical and Exegetical Commentary on the Second Epistle to the Corinthians*, ICC (T&T Clark, 1994), 1:297.

30. LSJ, 206.

31. Rudolf Meyer, "κρύπτω, κρυπτός," *TDNT* 3:957–87.

32. Rudolf Bultmann, "αἰσχύνη," *TDNT* 1:190; and Rudolf Bultmann, *The Second Letter to the Corinthians* (Augsburg Fortress, 1985), 100.

I propose that we translate 2 Corinthians 4:2 as: "But we speak fully of the hidden things of shame,[33] not walking in deceit or distorting the word of God but in the manifestation of the truth we commend ourselves to everyone's conscience before God." The question is: What were the hidden things of shame? Writing to Corinthians, two-thirds of whom were slaves or freed slaves, Paul could speak more openly of his past. Although Paul was discreet, he did not hide his past experiences of slavery from certain Corinthians who had endured slavery. Earlier, in 1 Corinthians, Paul wrote, "To the Jews I became as a Jew, that I might win Jews. . . . To those who are without law, as without law . . . that I might win those who are without law. To the weak I became weak that I might win the weak" (1 Cor 9:20–22). Perhaps he could have added, "To the slaves, I became a slave in order to win slaves." Could Paul be talking about his "hidden things of shame?" To others, this shame was hidden. But to other slaves, Paul spoke openly so that he might win those people to Christ. Possibly, this disclosure was turned against Paul by his opponents to shame him. Nonetheless, Paul continued: "We do not preach ourselves but Christ Jesus as Lord, and ourselves as your slaves (δούλους) because of Jesus" (2 Cor 4:5).[34] Strangely, this is the only place where Paul describes himself as a slave of someone other than Christ. There is no shame in serving other slaves.

In first-century Greco-Roman culture, slaves could be loaned to other masters. In such cases, the owner might receive a rental fee or the slave would return his wages to his primary master.[35] Paul recognized that his master, Jesus, had given him to the Corinthians as their slave. "Acknowledgment of the lordship of Jesus leads naturally and inevitably to lowly service to one's fellow believers. To confess that 'Jesus is Lord' is to say to other Christians 'I am your slave'; slavery to Christ is exhibited in slavery to Christians."[36]

If, as mentioned in an earlier chapter, the stigmata that Paul bore (Gal 6:17; most likely a tattoo identifying him as a slave) could not be hidden, he may be defending himself against any thought that his status as a former slave would have diminished the truth of the gospel. Martial described a

33. "Expressed negatively it means not hiding shameful things." Furnish, *II Corinthians*, 246.

34. Harris astutely observes, "In the history of the English Bible there has been a curious but inappropriate reluctance to translate δοῦλος by 'slave,' except where the context demands it." *Second Epistle to the Corinthians*, 333.

35. Barth and Blanke, *Philemon*, 11.

36. Harris, *Second Epistle to the Corinthians*, 333.

wealthy man sitting in the front rows of Marcellus's theater, "whose starred brow is plastered by many a patch. Don't you know what he is? Remove the patches: you will read."[37] He was hiding the brands of slavery under the patches. Petronius's fictional *Satyricon* portrays Eumolpus shaving the heads of his slaves, saying, "I didn't want those letters branded on their faces to be overshadowed by their hair and so hidden from people's discerning eyes."[38] Paul, for obvious reasons, was not eager to reveal his status as a former slave. However, if his tattoo or brand was conspicuous, questions regarding his past would have been something that he needed to address. For some congregations, this might not be a big deal, but his opponents at Corinth picked up on anything they could use to disparage Paul's apostolic authority.

37. Martial, *Epigrams*, 2.29 (Bailey, LCL).
38. Petronius, *Satyricon*, 105 (Walsh).

| 7 |
Paul's Writings: The Letter to the Romans

For many slaves their name is a thing of shame,
but their mind is freer than those who are not slaves.

Euripides, Fragments, 832 (Collard and Cropp, LCL 504, 455)

AROUND AD 58, WHILE IN Corinth, Paul wrote a letter to the churches in Rome as he was finishing his so-called third mission. In this letter, Paul expressed his hope that he would finally come to Rome and share his understanding of the gospel (1:13; 15:22–24). Although this letter was not a comprehensive theology, it was the most detailed explanation of Paul's teachings. Here Paul viewed sin and salvation through the lens of slavery. From his perspective, slavery served as a fitting analogy for the coercive power of sin over human behavior. The first-person personal pronouns he used in chapter 7 reflected his struggle and frustration to be free.

Romans 6

Outside of Paul's letter to the Galatians, the bulk of Paul's slave and freedom terminology occurs in his epistles to the Romans and the Corinthians. One could say that this is logical, because Romans and 1 Corinthians are Paul's two longest letters. However, these two cities also had larger slave populations per capita than any other cities in the Mediterranean. In chapter 2, we noted estimates that the percentage of slaves in Rome ranged from 25 to 40 percent, while in Corinth around a third were slaves and another third were freed slaves. Slavery became a useful metaphor for these congregations. But was Paul's discussion of slavery just a metaphor, or was his discourse more personal? Earlier, when discussing slavery in his letter to the Galatians, we noted his use of the first-person pronouns. The same pattern is evident in his letter to the Romans. Are these signs that Paul was referring to his own personal experiences in his teaching?

In Romans 6, Paul described the human attachment to sin by means of a slavery metaphor. Paul began the chapter by explaining that those who have been baptized have been united with Christ in his death and resurrection (vv. 3–5). The Jewish practice of baptism (immersion into a mikvah) was a purification rite, representing the washing away of sins. Priests regularly engaged in such immersions, and worshipers entering the Jerusalem temple were required to immerse in a mikvah. Paul expanded on this meaning for the sacrament. The immersion correlates the lowering of the individual into the water with the death and burial of Christ (v. 4). The believer has been united with Christ in his death. "'Burial with Christ' is a description of the participation of the believer in Christ's own burial, a participation that is mediated by baptism."[1] With this, we may hear echoes of the oral traditions circulating regarding Jesus's words: "If anyone wishes to come after me, he must deny himself, and take up his cross and follow me" (Mark 8:34). Paul's point is the definitive break with the past (death) and the beginning of a new life. Perhaps he was aware of Jesus's words to Nicodemus: "You must be born again" (John 3:7) and "unless one is born of water and the Spirit, he cannot enter the kingdom of God" (3:5).[2] As the Christian is raised up out of the water, the initiate participates in Christ's resurrection and is resurrected to a new life (Rom 6:5). Baptism quickly became the primary ritual for (1) purification, (2) unification with Christ through his death and new birth, and (3) the chief entry rite for admission into the covenant community of God (the church).

Expanding on union with Christ and new birth, Paul related baptismal practice to slavery. "Knowing this, that our old self was crucified with him, in order that our body of sin might be done away with, so that we would no longer be slaves [τοῦ μηκέτι δουλεύειν ἡμᾶς] to sin" (v. 6). "Our old self," or "our body of sin," was nailed to the cross and buried, and a new person

---

1. Douglas J. Moo, *The Epistle to the Romans*, NICNT (Eerdmans, 1996), 363. Moo further notes, "Baptism, then, is not the place, or time, at which we are buried with Christ, but the instrument (*dia*) through which we are buried with him" (364).

2. There is a great deal of dispute regarding this phrase. Does it refer to baptism or natural birth followed by a rebirth through the Spirit?

emerged from the grave (waters), resurrected and liberated from slavery to our old master. With this metaphor, Paul personified sin as a slave master.

Why did Paul abruptly abandon the baptism metaphor and turn to the metaphor of slavery?[3] Slavery was an imperfect metaphor to describe the transformation of the believer, a point that Paul conceded in verse 19. Death certainly ends one's burden of servitude to an earthly master, but rebirth in slavery to another master, such as righteousness (vv. 18–19), was not an appealing prospect for his readers. There were other metaphors more appropriate: perhaps an agricultural metaphor of a plant's death at the end of the year and its rebirth in the spring; the darkness at the end of the day and the dawn of a new day; or the conquest of an odious evil ruler and replacement with a benevolent new king. So, why did Paul quickly jettison the baptism metaphor and pick up the slave metaphor? It goes back to Paul's worldview that was established early in his life. Paul viewed the world through the eyes of his most traumatic experience: slavery.

The personification of sin as a nefarious taskmaster driving his minions toward deeds of unrighteousness continues in verses 13–20:

> And do not go on presenting the members of your body to sin as instruments of unrighteousness; but present yourselves to God as those alive from the dead, and your members as instruments of righteousness to God. For sin shall not be master over you, for you are not under law but under grace. What then? Shall we sin because we are not under law but under grace? May it never be! Do you not know that when you present yourselves to someone as slaves for obedience, you are slaves of the one whom you obey, either of sin resulting in death, or of obedience resulting in righteousness? But thanks be to God that though you were slaves of sin, you became obedient from the heart to that form of teaching to which you were committed, and having been freed from sin, you became slaves of righteousness. I am speaking in human terms because of the weakness of your flesh. For just as you presented your members as slaves to impurity and to lawlessness, resulting in further lawlessness, so now present your members as slaves to righteousness, resulting in sanctification. For when you were slaves of sin, you were free in regard to righteousness.

Paul wrote this letter while in Corinth and sent it to the church in Rome. Dunn recognizes how this section would resonate with those in Corinth and in Rome:

3. "After mentioning baptism in vv. 3–4, Paul drops the subject, never to resume it in this chapter." Moo, *Romans*, 364.

> In first-century Corinth, from where Paul was writing, at least one-third of the population would have been slaves, and almost as many again may have been freedmen, freed slaves. . . . And the Christian community in Rome was probably made up of a majority of slaves and freed persons, as both the history of the Jewish community in Rome and the evidence of chap. 16 strongly suggest.[4]

One can imagine that these words would evoke a visceral response from his readers and probably conjured up similar memories of Paul's past.

In this section Paul used the word *present* (παρίστημι) five times as a voluntary act of the individual (vv. 13 [2x], 16, and 19 [2x]). The term has varied meanings depending on the context, but here it is best understood as "dispose," "surrender," or "submit."[5] Twice in verse 13, the apostle used the term ὅπλα, translated "instruments" in the NASB, NIV, ESV, and NRSV. Käsemann, however, argues that Paul was utilizing military imagery here. The word ὅπλα is translated "weapons" in the only other New Testament examples: John 18:3; Romans 13:12; 2 Corinthians 6:7; 10:4.[6] The Greek word in these instances is the same word used for the Hoplite soldiers, untrained volunteers for war who sometimes functioned as mercenaries. The Corinthians and Romans were well aware of the Hoplites. Although the Hoplites originated in

FIGURE 63. Arch of Titus in the Roman Forum. Jewish slaves paraded through Rome carrying the menorah and table of showbread from the Jerusalem temple.

FIGURE 64. Roman Colosseum, where slaves were routinely executed in the spectacle.

4. Dunn, *Romans 1–8*, 341.

5. LSJ, 1340. Dunn translates it as "put at the disposal of" and comments that it is "acknowledgment of a superior power and authority to whom the only proper response is submission and obedience." *Romans 1–8*, 337.

6. Käsemann, *Commentary on Romans*, 177. Schreiner and Thielman both follow this interpretation. Thomas R. Schreiner, *Romans*, BECNT (Baker Academic, 1998), 324. Frank Thielman, *Romans*, ZECNT (Zondervan, 2018), 311.

Greece, the Romans as well as the Greeks employed Hoplite-style warfare. Paul's reference here continues his thought of slavery. The imagery evokes the voluntary act of a person selling himself into slavery in a war of unrighteousness. Paul beckons the Romans to enlist ("present yourselves") in the war of righteousness. Here, Paul may have been describing the transition from the wretched state of slavery in a war of unrighteousness to a superior form of slavery fighting for righteousness.

As noted in earlier chapters, slavery can increase the standing for some slaves. Not only can the welfare of a slave increase under a beneficent master, but in some cases the financial and social standing of a slave could increase. Martin emphasizes the upward mobility of this passage:

> Once we have placed slavery in its full Greco-Roman context, we can see its possibilities for use as a salvific image. An obvious way it symbolizes salvation is by recalling the benefits a slave might expect from a good master as opposed to a bad one. In Rom. 6:20–23, Paul can speak of slavery to God as the positive counterpart to slavery to sin by contrasting the returns or benefits of slavery to one master, sin, with those of slavery to a better master, God.[7]

Paul was one of those who personally benefited from the transition.

In the apostle's mind, he thought the metaphor was a suitable description of the Christian's fight with sin. As an alternative to "presenting yourselves" to sin, Paul proposed that they "present" themselves to God and fight for righteousness. This amounts to enslavement to a righteous master. Nevertheless, the metaphor is awkward at best. In verse 19a, Paul acknowledged as much by inserting the word ἀνθρώπινον.[8] The phrase could be rendered: "I am speaking in a foolish way because of the weakness of your flesh." Commenting on this verse, Cranfield opines:

> Paul is clearly aware of the fact that the figure of slavery is inadequate, unworthy and misleading as a way of speaking about the believer's relation to δικαιοσύνη [righteousness] . . . that is why he apologizes for the all too human nature of his language. . . . In almost every respect the image is inappropriate for Paul's purpose. Of course, the Christian's relation to righteousness, to obe-

7. Martin, *Slavery as Salvation*, 62. Schreiner misses this point, saying, "The illustration from slavery is inadequate because the relationship believers have with God is shorn of all the negative elements present in slavery." *Romans*, 333.

8. Among the varied possible translations, LSJ suggests "human folly" or "fallible human understanding" (141).

> dience (v. 16), to God (v. 22), is not at all the unjust, humiliating, degrading, grievous thing that slavery has always been.[9]

Yet, this analogy resonated in Paul's thoughts and reverberated with echoes of his past. This section is replete with structural contrasts that illustrate the transition to a new master:

> Consider yourselves to be dead to sin but alive to God in Jesus Christ. (v. 11)
>
> Do not present your body to sin as weapons for unrighteousness but present yourself to God as weapons for righteousness. (v. 13)
>
> Sin shall not be master over you; you are not under the law but under grace. (v. 14)
>
> You are slaves of the one whom you obey, either of sin resulting in death or obedience resulting in righteousness. (v. 16)
>
> Having been freed from sin, you became slaves of righteousness. (v. 18)
>
> You presented your members as slaves to impurity; now present your members as slaves to righteousness. (v. 19)
>
> When you were slaves of sin, you were free in regard to righteousness. (v. 20)
>
> Now having been freed from sin and enslaved to God. (v. 22)
>
> The wages of sin is death; the free gift of God is eternal life. (v. 23)

As is common in Paul's ethical exhortations, his indicative statements form the foundation of his imperative commands.[10] That is, based on what God has done through Jesus Christ in freeing us from sin (the indicative mood verbs), we are charged with becoming slaves of God and righteousness (the imperative mood verbs).

This section introduces another important concept associated with slavery: freedom (ἐλεύθερος). Freedom is mentioned three times in this section (vv. 18, 20, 22). In addition to Paul's frequent use of slave terminology, he also frequently described the Christian life as an emancipation from slavery. The contrast between slavery and freedom is laid out in parallel expressions:

---

9. Cranfield, *Romans*, 1:325.

10. "Romans 6 is the classic biblical text on the importance of relating the 'indicative' of what God has done for us with the 'imperative' of what we are to do." Moo, *Romans*, 390.

> Having been freed (ἐλευθερωθέντες) from sin, you became slaves of righteousness. (v. 18)
>
> For when you were slaves of sin, you were free (ἐλεύθεροι) in regard to righteousness. (v. 20)
>
> Having been freed (ἐλευθερωθέντες) from sin and enslaved to God. (v. 22)

Paul's understanding of freedom from sin does not imply that people are autonomous and able to make their own standards of right and wrong. Instead, they are free (or obliged) to choose God's standards of righteousness. This is expressed well by Moo:

> In a world in which "freedom" has taken on all kinds of historical and social baggage, we must remember that Paul's concept of freedom is not that of autonomous self-direction but of deliverance from those enslaving powers that would prevent the human being from becoming what God intended.[11]

Romans 7

These concepts of war and slavery continue in chapter 7. Paul reiterates the contrasts of "consider yourselves dead to sin, but alive to God" (6:11) and "freed from sin and enslaved to God" (6:22) a few verses later in 7:6: "We have been released from the Law, having died to that by which we were bound, so that we are enslaved [δουλεύειν] in the newness of the Spirit."

However, Paul's account takes a dark turn two verses later. The second-person verbs and pronouns from chapter 6 have been replaced with first-person verbs and pronouns in chapter 7. Was Paul reflecting on his past? Romans 7:7–25 is one of the most debated passages in all of Scripture. Was Paul describing his past life in Judaism? Was he describing his life and struggles as a Christian? Or was he using first-person terminology to describe the struggles and temptations of anyone who wishes to please God?

As in 6:13–20, Paul again used military terminology in 7:8–11 to recount how the Law overcame him, leading to his spiritual death:

> But sin, seizing an opportunity [ἀφορμήν] through the commandment, produced in me coveting of every kind; for apart from the Law sin is dead. I was once alive apart from the Law; but when the commandment came, sin became alive and I died; and this commandment, which was to result in life, proved to result in death for me; for sin, seizing an opportunity [ἀφορμήν] through the commandment, deceived me and through it killed me.

11. Moo, *Romans*, 402.

Liddell, Scott, and Jones translate "opportunity" (ἀφορμήν in vv. 8, 11) as a "starting point, especially in war, a base of operations."[12] Dunn claims that the metaphor is military: "This is one of the most vigorous of the personifications of sin as a power, underscoring the human experience of sin as an oppressive force acting upon the individual."[13] More of this violent imagery of war is relayed in verse 14: "The Law is spiritual, but I am flesh, sold into bondage to sin." Again, Dunn asserts that with πεπραμένος ("being sold into slavery") "the metaphor of slavery so prominent in 6:16–23 is recalled; though since defeated captives in war were usually sold as slaves, the imagery of successful surprise attack (vv. 8, 11) also naturally leads into that of slavery."[14] Paul can be understood to describe the anthropomorphized "sin" as an enemy that has attacked and subjugated our body and sold it as a slave to unrighteousness. By looking through the lens of his family's experience in Galilee, Paul recalled a trope that was deeply embedded in his thought world. Whether consciously or unconsciously, past traumatic events have a way of conditioning our thoughts and speech.

If it is acknowledged that Paul's family spent his early years in Tarsus in slavery, then his words have a deeper meaning. Certain aspects of Paul's life were beyond his control. From 7:15–24, Paul made it clear that he was incapable of escape from this slavery.

> What I am doing, I do not understand; for I do not do what I want, but I do what I hate. (v. 15)
>
> If I do what I do not want to do. (v. 16)
>
> But now I am no longer the one doing it, but sin which dwells in me. (v. 17)
>
> I know that nothing good dwells in me. (v. 18)
>
> For I do not do the good that I want. (v. 19)
>
> If I am doing what I do not want, I am no longer the one doing it, but sin dwelling in me. (v. 20)

In these six verses, Paul stated six times that he was unable to do as he wished or wanted: θέλω (vv. 15, 16, 18, 19 [2x], 20). Although the section most directly refers to a failure to do good, the verses parallel the experience of a slave whose will was restricted by the wishes of his master. Even for a pious Jew who wished to follow Torah, the demands of the master could

12. LSJ, 292.
13. Dunn, *Romans 1–8*, 380.
14. Dunn, 388.

suppress and frustrate the will of the slave. As a slave, Paul could not live as he wished. The exact same expression is found in verses 17 and 20: "I am no longer the one doing it, but sin dwelling in me" (ἐγὼ κατεργάζομαι αὐτὸ ἀλλὰ ἡ οἰκοῦσα ἐν ἐμοὶ ἁμαρτία). This reveals that the apostle's life was out of his control. The phrase "sin dwelling in me" was a tactful way of describing slavery. Paul was reluctant to insert the word "slavery" into this section. To explicitly describe slavery as sin would be a direct challenge to an institution that was fundamental to Roman law and life. Nevertheless, the association with slavery and the connotations of slavery through war are more clearly established later in verses 23–25.

More war terminology appears in the following verses, mingled with the enslavement of captives taken in war and sold in slave markets.

> I see a different law in the members of my body waging war [ἀντιστρατευόμενον] against the law of my mind and making me a prisoner [αἰχμαλωτίζοντα] of the law of sin which is in my members. Wretched man that I am! Who will set me free [ῥύσεται] from the body of this death? Thanks be to God through Jesus Christ our Lord so then, on the one hand I myself am serving [δουλεύω] the law of God in my mind, but the law of sin in my flesh. (7:23–25)

Thielman comments:

> The metaphors of warfare and captivity were very much alive for Paul's readership, many of whom were Greek-speaking immigrants, slaves, and former slaves living among the narrow streets and crowded conditions across the Tiber and below the Janiculum Hill. Their parents and grandparents, in many cases, would have probably immigrated to Rome as wartime captives. The vividness of Paul's language would have added to the dark picture Paul painted.[15]

Dunn maintains that Paul's protracted engagement with the war metaphor goes back to chapter 6 and continues to chapter 8. There is a "sharp existential edge to this sustained usage."[16] Moreover, "the metaphor is expressed in its most extreme form here since it speaks not only of warfare but of defeat. This is consistent with the other most prominent metaphor in preceding sections, slavery, since defeat in battle usually resulted in the prisoners of war being sold as slaves."[17]

The uncommon word ῥύομαι (set me free) in verse 24 has a different meaning than the more common σώζω (to save or to rescue), although there

---

15. Thielman, *Romans*, 363.
16. Dunn, *Romans 1–8*, 395.
17. Dunn, 395.

is a slight overlap in semantic domains. The rescue from danger or harm (to deliver) is prevalent in most instances of ῥύομαι, while that meaning is "comparatively rare" for σώζω.[18] Unlike σώζω, ῥύομαι is used twelve times in the Septuagint with the sense of releasing or buying back.[19] In Exodus 6:6, the word is used to describe Israel's bondage in Egypt: "I will deliver you from the slavery. I will also redeem you." In the context of Romans 7 (the struggle with sin in the context of war and slavery), we must understand ῥύσεται (set me free) to refer to rescue from slavery as a prisoner of war. Through his family's history, Paul was keenly aware of slavery due to war. In the broader context of slavery, Paul used the word to suggest the practice of manumission through the purchase of the slave's freedom.

When Paul described the addictive power of sin over human behavior and God's rescue from sin, he chose the metaphor of slavery, the imagery of war, the sale of slaves in markets, the freedom from harsh masters, and the enslavement to God and righteousness. Other metaphors could have easily been co-opted to illustrate the web of sin's entanglements, but Paul chose this one. Furthermore, Paul's illustrative additions to the slavery metaphor, his first-person personal pronouns in Romans 7 (as well as in his letter to the Galatians), along with the strong emotions expressed in the text, suggest that the issue penetrates deeper into Paul's past, a past marked by his family's capture, sale, and servile life in Tarsus.

We cannot escape from our past. It is our shadow that follows us wherever we go. Our current thoughts and actions are an extension of our past, which sets us on a trajectory to our future. Traumatic events are a recurrent nightmare that haunts us even at a subconscious level. Our thoughts echo the traumas of our past, particularly those from our childhood and adolescence. Paul's early childhood and perhaps some of his adolescent years were spent in slavery before he was manumitted. Once freed, Paul moved to Jerusalem, perhaps with his sister, and began rabbinic school with the famed Gamaliel. Yet, he never forgot his roots.

Romans 8

The arduous, slavish struggle with the law and sin that Paul described in Romans 6–7 was overcome through faith in Christ. At the end of chapter 7,

---

18. Johannes Schneider and Colin Brown, "Rescue, Deliver, Preserve, Save—ῥύομαι," *NIDNTT*, 3:202–3, 211.

19. Wilhelm Kasch, "ῥύομαι," *TDNT* 6:999. So also, J. Schneider and C. Brown, *NIDNTT*, 3:201.

Paul's frustration boiled over: "Wretched man that I am! Who will set me free [ῥύσεται] from the body of this death?" (v. 24). The answer followed in chapter 8: "The law of the Spirit of life in Christ Jesus has set you free [ἠλευθέρωσεν] from the law of sin and of death" (v. 2).

Commentaries generally miss the contrasting parallelism of Paul's words:

> Who will set me free [ῥύσεται] from the body of this death? (7:24)
>
> The Spirit of life . . . has set you free [ἠλευθέρωσεν] from the law of sin and of death. (8:2)

From this, it is clear that Paul is substituting a different verb in 8:2. As we noted above, ῥύομαι has the meaning of rescue from war and the slavery that results from it. In 7:24, the question is: Who will redeem me from being a war slave? The answer in 8:2 makes this clear. The Holy Spirit (Spirit of life) has become Paul's redeemer, the one who rescued him from the slave market. The meaning of ἠλευθέρωσεν is restricted to freedom as it relates to slavery. The word is never used in the New Testament to refer to political freedom.[20] Paul's question in 7:24 is a plea for rescue from the slavery of sin that he was incapable of remedying on his own. He was reaching out to someone who could buy him and release him from his quandary. The response in 8:2 reveals the deliverer. The deliverer is not another slave master who would entangle him in other matters but rather "the Spirit of life in Christ Jesus," a master of much higher caliber who had better plans for him. The transition between Romans 7 and 8 represents the transformation of Paul's status from a slave of sin and human masters to a slave of Christ. Service in Christ is a liberation from sin and earthly entanglements. Slavery to God is freedom from human masters.

This new freedom, however, presents us with the reality of our choices for how we live our lives. We still live in a physical realm subjugated by Satan and his evil agents. Do we consciously choose to live by the Spirit? How does living by the Spirit impact the choices we make in the flesh? Paul asserts that followers of Christ "do not walk according to the flesh but according to the Spirit. For those who are according to the flesh set their minds on the things of the flesh, but those who are according to the Spirit set their minds on the things of the Spirit" (8:4–5).

Such words speak to the mental state of believers. But what about the physical necessities of life in this world? People experience bodily needs that

---

20. Jürgen Blunck, "Freedom - ἐλευθερία," *NIDNTT*, 1:715–21.

must be addressed for life to continue. Those bodily needs lead us down the path of the flesh. Do those needs lead us back to the dilemma that Paul expressed in 7:14–24? "The mind set on the flesh is death . . . the mind set on the flesh is hostile toward God; for it does not subject itself to the law of God, for it is not even able to do so and those who are in the flesh cannot please God" (8:6–8).

The philosopher Epictetus, himself a freed slave, approached the issue of addictive behaviors in a similar fashion to what Paul expressed in Romans 7–8.

> Every habit and faculty is confirmed and strengthened by the corresponding actions. . . . In general, therefore, if you want to do something, make a habit of it; if you want not to do something, refrain from doing it. . . . The same principle holds true in the affairs of the mind; when you are angry, you may be sure, not merely that this evil has befallen you, but also that you have strengthened the habit, and have, as it were, added fuel to the flame. . . . In this way, without doubt, the infirmities of our mind and character spring up. . . . Certain imprints and weals are left behind on the mind, and unless a man erases them perfectly, the next time he is scourged upon the old scars, he has weals no longer but wounds. If, therefore, you wish not to be hot-tempered, do not feed your habit, set before it nothing on which it can grow. . . . How, then, may this be done? Make it your wish finally to satisfy your own self, make it your wish to appear beautiful in the sight of God. Set your desire upon becoming pure in the presence of your pure self and of God.[21]

Interestingly, Epictetus twice used the singular for God (θεός), rather than the plural that one would expect from a polytheist. Could Epictetus have been influenced by Paul's writings?

Paul's answer goes beyond the good advice of Epictetus: "However, you are not in the flesh but in the Spirit, if indeed the Spirit of God dwells in you. But if anyone does not have the Spirit of Christ, he does not belong to him. If Christ is in you, though the body is dead because of sin, yet the spirit is alive because of righteousness" (8:9–10). It is not just a matter of trying harder to please God. The key is the indwelling Spirit of God, who empowers us to make godly choices. "If by the Spirit you are putting to death the deeds of the body, you will live. For all who are being led by the Spirit of God, these are sons of God" (vv. 13b–14). Without the Spirit of God, the human mind is set on the flesh, is hostile to God, cannot please God, and leads to death

21. Epictetus, *Diatr.* 2.18.

(vv. 6, 7, 13). Such a condition leads us back to the entrapment of slavery to sin (v. 15). For many of Paul's readers, there was no escape from slavery. But the Spirit of life could liberate them from the snares of sin.

The indwelling Spirit of God has ramifications for our present life in this world. "The Spirit himself testifies with our spirit that we are children of God, and if children, heirs also, heirs of God and fellow heirs with Christ, if we truly suffer with him, we may also be glorified with him" (vv. 16–17). Three of these words are connected with the Greek prefix συν (together with). Since we are children of God, we are heirs together with (συγκληρονόμοι) Christ. If this is true, we suffer together with him (συνπάσχομεν), and we may be glorified together with him (συνδοξασθῶμεν). The concepts are connected. We are unified in Christ's sonship, his suffering, and his glorification. In his letter to the Colossians, Paul wrote, "I rejoice in my sufferings for your sake, and in my flesh, I do my share on behalf of his body (which is the church) in filling up that which is lacking in Christ's afflictions" (1:24). This was played out with the austere life of ascetic monks in the early church, but the practicalities of life make that impossible for most people. In the midst of our modern comforts, it seems we have lost a sense of how to suffer as Christ suffered. We commonly think that suffering only comes when nonbelievers harass or mock us for our Christian faith. Somehow, I think it involves more than that. Perhaps suffering in today's world may involve standing firm in the Christian faith in the face of evil or injustice. There may be daily acts of participating in the suffering of others through fasting and self-deprivation.

In 8:15, Paul expands on the notion of an emancipated slave. "For you have not received a spirit of slavery leading to fear again, but you have received a spirit of adoption as sons by which we cry out, 'Abba! Father!'" (8:15). The utter contrast of this verse is remarkable. There is some debate regarding the spirit (πνεῦμα) in this verse. Some claim that it refers to the human spirit or the spirit of the age,[22] but in light of a parallel expression in Galatians 4:5–6 ("God sent forth the Spirit of His Son"), it is likely the Holy Spirit that Paul has in mind here. This becomes a *description* of the spirit that Paul mentioned earlier in 8:2 ("the Spirit of life"), 8:4 ("walk according to the Spirit), 8:5–6 ("the mind set on the Spirit"), 8:9 ("the Spirit of God that dwells in you"), and 8:11. This Spirit does *not* lead back into slavery and fear (8:15a) but rather leads to an enhanced position with God as adoptive sons.[23]

---

22. Dunn, *Romans 1–8*, 451–52.

23. Joseph A. Fitzmyer, *Romans*, AB 33. (Doubleday, 1993), 499–500. Cranfield seems to follow this interpretation, *Romans*, 1:396, as does Moo, *Romans*, 500.

As mentioned in previous chapters, some freed slaves were adopted into their master's family.[24] As Gardner notes, "A patron lacking direct heirs might prefer to adopt a known and trusted freedman rather than a free outsider."[25] Lyall pointed out that Paul gained his understanding of adoption from Roman law rather than Jewish law or practice. "No Jewish legal writing contains any provisions which can be construed as adoption."[26] According to Roman law, "The adoptee is taken out of his previous state and is placed in a new relationship with his new *paterfamilias*. All his old debts are canceled, and in effect he starts a new life. From that time the *paterfamilias* owns all the property and acquisitions of the adoptee, controls his personal relationships, and has rights of discipline."[27] There are only five places in the New Testament where the term adoption (υἱοθεσία) is used. All are in Paul's writings (Rom 8:15, 23; 9:4; Gal 4:5; Eph 1:5), and the Septuagint never uses the word. Seeing that Paul did not receive his understanding of adoption from his Jewish heritage, how did he come to know the process from slave to freedman to adoptee? In Roman law, adoptees were *usually* given the *nomen* or *cognomen* of their adopted parents. Lindsay claims that in formal adoptions there was a stronger compulsion to take the name of the adopter. This was probably the manner in which Paul received his Roman name, Paul.[28] The entire scenario presupposes a familiarity with slavery and adoption that reflects his personal history.

Returning to the parallel expression in Paul's letter to the Galatians, we see similarities and verbal agreements with Romans 8. "God sent forth his Son . . . that he might redeem those who were under the law, that we might receive the adoption as sons. And because you are sons, God has sent forth the Spirit of his Son into our hearts, crying 'Abba Father!'" (Gal 4:4–6). What are we to make of these parallel elements?

> Romans 8:2, 15: "set free" (ἐλευθερόω), "adoption" (υἱοθεσία), "Spirit" (πνεῦμα), "crying" (κράζω), "Abba Father" (αββα ὁ πατήρ)
>
> Galatians 4:5–6: "redeem" (ἐξαγοράζω), "adoption" (υἱοθεσία), "Spirit" (πνεῦμα), "crying" (κράζω), "Abba Father" (αββα ὁ πατήρ)

---

24. Gardner, "Adoption of Roman Freedmen," 236–57. "Roman freedmen could be, and were, adopted by Roman citizens" (236).

25. Gardner, 243.

26. Francis Lyall, "Roman Law in the Writings of Paul: Adoption," *JBL* 88 (1969): 459. So also Dunn, *Romans 1–8*, 452.

27. Lyall, 466.

28. Lindsay, *Adoption in the Roman World*, 87–96.

The time span between the writing of these letters makes it unlikely that Paul was copying an expression from his letter to the Galatians. Rather, I would suggest that Paul often repeated these words and concepts to explain his transition from being a slave to becoming a freedman, to faith in Christ, and ultimately to adoption as a son of God.

In Romans 8:19–23, Paul broadened this concept of slavery in order to include all of creation as captive to bondage. Paul, no doubt, had Genesis 3 in mind as he wrote this. Creation was thrown into bondage to sin due to humanity's fall. Paul states that creation was cowed to "futility" (ματαιότητι). He used the verbal form of this word earlier in Romans 1:21, describing the downward spiral of humanity after the fall. This futility designates the inability of creation and human beings to fulfill their created purpose as God intended.[29] Creation was unwillingly (οὐχ ἑκοῦσα) forced to submit (ὑπετάγη) to the bondage of sin because of the one who forcibly subjugated (ὑποτάξαντα) it (v. 20). Here, Paul acknowledged Satan's dominion over the material realm, including people.[30] The concept here follows Paul's earlier discussion in 7:15–24 about his struggle with sin, culminating in his cry: "Wretched man that I am! Who will set me free from the body of this death?"

The final words in 8:20, "on the basis of hope," constitute the grounds for the future declaration: "that the creation itself also will be set free (ἐλευθερωθησεται) from its slavery (δουλείας) to corruption into the freedom (ἐλευθερίαν) of the glory of the children of God" (v. 21). Not only has the Spirit of life in Christ Jesus set us free (ἠλευθέρωσεν, 8:2), but now we see that creation itself will be freed from the burden of sin. The terms used in 8:21 evoke the same imagery of slavery and freedom that Paul had discussed earlier in Romans 6–7.

The expression "groan" with its cognates occurs three times in verses 22, 23, and 26. In the first instance, creation collectively groans (συστενάζει). The preposition σύν attached to the verb στενάζω indicates the act of a group. Paul did not clarify who or what is collectively groaning. He could have been referring to all creation, both the inanimate (anthropomorphized) and the animate, metaphorically groaning at the burden of sin and decay. Or perhaps he was anticipating the next verse, where the verb is used without

29. Cranfield, *Romans*, 413–14.

30. Many interpreters understand the phrase to refer to God. See Moo, *Romans*, 515–16. However, I see this as a reference to Satan, the person to whom God ceded power and control over fallen creation. The force of the adjective διά with the accusative case indicates cause. God is not the cause of this fallen realm.

the preposition. Thus all creation—the rocks, vegetation, and animals (v. 22) together with humans (v. 23)—suffer and groan as we wait for redemption. But this is not all. In verse 26, Paul used the noun στεναγμοῖς to say that the Holy Spirit also is involved with "groanings" as he intercedes on our behalf.

Returning to verse 23, Paul completed the thought with the terminal eschatological condition of the believers: "our adoption as sons and the redemption of our bodies." The anticipated "Spirit of adoption" from verse 15 finds its future fulfillment as the adoptive sons of God who have experienced deliverance (redemption). Paul's understanding of adoption came from Roman law, according to which *all former debts* were canceled. The metaphor of adoption was a perfect analogy to describe the believer's experience of forgiveness from the bondage and debts of sin. Paul's choice of terms here was not coincidental but rather stemmed from his experience.[31]

31. "Paul further defines 'adoption as sons' with the phrase 'the deliverance of our bodies.' The term 'deliverance' (ἀπολύτρωσις) sometimes referred to the rescue of someone from slavery (e.g., Philo, *Good Person* 114), and in this context where Paul has just spoken of the slavery of creation to decay (Rom 8:21), it clearly carries these connotations." Thielman, *Romans*, 406.

| 8 |

Paul's Writings: The Letter to Philemon

A slave of Aristogenes, son of Chrysippus, of Alabanda, ambassador, has escaped in Alexandria, by name Hermon also called Nilus, by birth a Syrian from Bambyce, about eighteen years old, of medium stature, beardless, with good legs, a dimple on the chin, a mole by the left side of the nose, a scar above the left corner of the mouth, tattooed on the right wrist with two barbaric letters. He has taken with him three octadrachmas of coined gold, ten pearls, an iron ring on which an oil-flask and strigils are represented. and is wearing a cloak and a loincloth. Whoever brings back this slave shall receive two talents of copper.

Papyrus Parisiensis 10[1]

PAUL'S SHORTEST CANONICAL LETTER WAS a personal letter to Philemon, a resident of Colossae in Phrygia. Philemon was a wealthy businessman and slave owner. One of his slaves, Onesimus, escaped from Philemon and, in the process, evidently stole money from his master. Onesimus fled to Rome, somehow became a Christian, and met the imprisoned Paul in the city. Paul convinced him to act in accordance with Roman law and return to Philemon. This letter was sent with Tychicus, who was accompanied by Onesimus as they returned to Colossae and Philemon.

Tychicus also carried other letters that he delivered while traveling to Colossae: one to the church in Ephesus (Eph 6:21), another to the church

1. A second-century BC announcement of reward for the return of an escaped slave originally posted in Alexandria, Egypt. A. S. Hunt and C. C. Edgar, trans., *Select Papri*, vol. 2, *Public Documents*, LCL 282 (Harvard University Press, 1934), 234.

at Colossae (Col 4:7), perhaps a third to the church at Laodicea (Col 4:16), and conceivably a fourth to the church at Hierapolis (Col 4:13). A ship from Rome would have docked at Ephesus, and the journey inland would have taken travelers through the cities of Hierapolis and Laodicea before arriving at Colossae. The journey from the coast would have involved around 120 miles.

Background to the Letter

It is important that we recreate the context of the letter and the historical setting of Colossae. By examining ancient literary texts and adding recently discovered archaeological research, we can better understand the developments that led to Paul's letter to Philemon.

Colossae was part of a cluster of four cities in the Lycus Valley of Phrygia. These four nearby cities—Colossae, Laodicea, Hierapolis, and Tripolis—were centrally located on important roads that led to the largest Anatolian ports at Smyrna to the north, Miletus to the south, and Ephesus in the middle. The area was blessed with access to three river valleys leading to the coast. The Meles River flowed west and northwest, emptying into the Aegean Sea at Smyrna, one of the metropolis cities on the coast. The Cayster River flowed west, leading to Ephesus, the largest city in Asia and the largest port. To the south, the Meander River meandered west and southwest to another large port at Miletus.

Dio Chrysostom, the first century orator and historian, commented on this area, stating that the largest and most serviceable rivers of the land have their headwaters in the area of Celaenae (Apamea), Phrygia. Here were the markets where goods from Cappadocia, Pamphylia, and Pisidia poured in. Here also people gathered for various businesses, including judicial proceedings, artisan work, slave auctions, prostitution, and trade.[2] These businesses contributed to the region's prosperity, allowing Dio to state that the area had "money in greatest abundance with the result that the place thrives."[3]

Due to their geography, the quad cities unsurprisingly became important trade and banking centers.[4] Goods from the interior of Anatolia were brought to this area, where the sellers met with merchants who negotiated

2. Dio Chrysostom, *Cel. Phryg.* 13–16.

3. Dio Chrysostom, *Cel. Phryg.* 16.

4. Cicero, *Fam.* 3.5.4.

prices and shipped the merchandise to the ports on the Aegean Sea. These cities were not particularly large during the first century, but together, they became a formidable economic power on the borders of the Roman province of Asia. In addition to the financial boon of trade, local agriculture and textile production added to the local economy. Cadwallader cites several inscriptions found at Hierapolis, Laodicea, and Colossae that reference associations of dyers, fullers, and leather workers. Funerary steles from the Denizli Museum depict women from the region with weaving implements.[5] Even today, fields of cotton surround the ancient sites, and textile production is a chief contributor to the economy of Denizli. Many of the production centers for European clothiers are located in the area.

Recent archaeological work at these sites confirms what we read from the ancient literary texts. Furthest to the northwest was the city of Tripolis. The ancient city was located one mile east of the village of Yenicekent and eleven miles northwest of Hierapolis. The Directorate for Museums in Denizli and Pamukkale University began excavations at Tripolis in 2012. Significant for our purposes, three agoras have been unearthed at Tripolis. Most cities of larger size only had one agora. The presence of three agoras in Tripolis underscores the importance of trade in the city.

Southeast of Tripolis, the city of Hierapolis was established at hot springs. Today, the springs, rich in calcium, have produced beautiful travertine formations, much larger than those at Yellowstone in Wyoming. The site is listed as a World Heritage Site. The hot springs were thought to be therapeutic, and ancient people came to Hierapolis for the healing springs as well as for commercial activities. Many of those who sought healing did not survive. The necropolis at Hierapolis surrounds the city on all sides and is the largest in all of Anatolia. The wealth of the city is evident from the numerous and magnificent temple tombs, mausolea, tumuli, and sarcophagi. The legacy of trade is inscribed on one of the monumental tombs. The mausoleum of Titus Flavius Zeuxis, dated to the first century AD, claims that Zeuxis, a merchant, sailed to Italy seventy-two times with products

5. Alan H. Cadwallader, *Fragments of Colossae: Sifting Through the Traces* (ATF Press, 2015), 120–30. "The evidence from texts and images suggests that a high proportion of females were involved in wool processes such as carding, spinning and weaving but there is a distinct lack of inscriptional evidence of associations for or including these women. . . . The suggestion is that women were engaged in these activities at home operating a cottage industry, even if the industry contributed to public markets and trade" (122–23).

from the area.[6] The agora at Hierapolis is one of the largest in Anatolia, measuring 560 feet by 920 feet.

Five miles south of Hierapolis was the city of Laodicea. Strabo notes that Laodicea was formerly a small town but quickly became one of the largest cities in Phrygia due to its fertile land and the prosperity of its people. The countryside around Laodicea was known for its sheep, whose black wool was soft and surpassed the quality of other wool.[7] Excavations at Laodicea began in 2003 by Pamukkale University under the direction of Celal Şimşek. Three agoras have been excavated to date, and the extraordinary wealth of the city is evident from the remains. While many cities had their main streets (*cardo maximus* and *decumanus maximus*) colonnaded, Laodicea had the financial resources to colonnade several secondary streets in addition to its cardo and decumanus. Additionally, the city had the money for two theaters and six decorative fountains (*nymphaea*). Revelation testifies to Laodicea's pride, quoting the city slogan: "I am rich, I have prospered, and I have need of nothing" (3:17). When the city was destroyed by an earthquake in AD 60, the proud city refused Nero's imperial benefactions, preferring to rebuild with its own resources.[8]

Colossae, the easternmost city of the quad cities, was nine miles east of Laodicea and a little over a mile north of the modern village of Honaz. Although the ancient site has been identified, it has never been excavated.[9] A tributary of the Lycus River flows alongside the ruins, and the site is dominated by the ancient city mound. Some five centuries earlier than Paul, Xenophon wrote that Cyrus and the Persians stayed at Colossae for seven days, saying that the city was "large and prosperous."[10] It would appear that the population declined by the first century. Strabo described it as a small town.[11] Walking the site today, it is clear that the city was smaller than Tripolis, Hierapolis, and Laodicea. We can nevertheless assume that the city enjoyed a similar prosperity to its neighbors and was likewise involved in trade and commerce. A first- or second-century AD inscription found

6. Francesco D'Andria, *Hierapolis of Phrygia (Pamukkale): An Archaeological Guide* (Ege Yayınları, 2003), 66–68.

7. Strabo, *Geogr.* 12.8.16.

8. Tacitus, *Ann.* 14.27.

9. The Turkish Ministry of Culture and Tourism recently issued a permit for excavations at Colossae to Dr. Bariş Yener of the University of Pamukkale. Work at the site was expected to begin in the summer of 2025.

10. Xenophon, *Anab.* 1.2.6.

11. Strabo, *Geogr.* 12.8.13.

at Colossae mentions an interpreter, Markos son of Markos. The presence of this inscription suggests that merchants from the surrounding regions who spoke ancient Carian, Lycian, Pisidian, and Lycaonian languages plied their wares in Colossae.[12] Another inscription from Colossae, dated to the second century, is dedicated to a civic official who served as the overseer of the agora, the municipal clerk, and the warden responsible for regulating trade in the surrounding area. As Cadwallader notes: "These offices indicate that Colossae was an important city for the administration of trade."[13]

Unsurprisingly, the vocabulary Paul used in his letters to Philemon and the Colossians is loaded with commercial terminology. Barth and Blanke assert: "In no other Pauline letter are *legal and commercial* vocabulary and formulations found as densely as in PHM [Philemon]. Nearest to this letter stands Colossians with its references to a deposit made at a safe place and an IOU deleted in favor of the saints [Col 1:5; 2:14]."[14]

What Do We Know About Philemon?

Philemon was a resident of Colossae. The name of the town is not mentioned in the letter that bears his name, but Paul's letter to the Colossians makes this clear. Lohse has noted, "Almost all the names that appear in the last section of Col are also mentioned in Phlm."[15] The two letters were sent together from Paul's prison in Rome, and most commentators deal with the two letters together.

In the first verse, Philemon is described as "our beloved brother and fellow worker" (ἀδελφὸς . . . τῷ ἀγαπητῷ καὶ συνεργῷ ἡμῶν). The term "fellow worker" is used to refer to Timothy (1 Thess 3:2), Titus (2 Cor 8:23), and Aquila and Priscilla (Rom 16:3), so it can be assumed that Philemon ministered in a similar fashion. Paul mentioned "the church in your house" (v. 2). Thus, Philemon may have been the pastor of a congregation in Colossae. The parishioners of the earliest Christian churches worshiped in homes rather than in dedicated structures as today. Apphia, mentioned in

12. Cadwallader, *Fragments of Colossae*, 119. "As chief interpreter, Markos was the head of a team of interpreters in the civic administration. Located at Colossae it is possible that Markos and his team provided services to the Lycus Valley, especially those coming from the East, thereby adding to the contribution Colossae made to the region's trade" (119).

13. Cadwallader, 129–30.

14. Barth and Blanke, *Philemon*, 110 (emphasis original).

15. Eduard Lohse, *Colossians and Philemon*, Hermeneia (Fortress, 1971), 175.

verse 2 as "our sister," was Philemon's wife and was also a Christian. As the woman of the house, she would have been involved in important decisions.

Archippus, described as "our fellow soldier" (v. 2), was likely Philemon's son. He is also mentioned in the letter to the church at Colossae, where he is charged with attending to "the ministry that he received from the Lord" (Col 4:17). The two statements regarding Archippus as "fellow soldier" (συστρατιώτῃ) and the "ministry" (διακονίαν) that he received imply that he was actively engaged in ministry, probably as a pastor. The two preceding verses, Colossians 4:15–16, refer to the nearby church in Laodicea, and in 4:13 the nearby city of Hierapolis is mentioned. This has led some commentators to suggest that Archippus was ministering in the nearby church at Laodicea[16] and perhaps the church at Hierapolis as well. The historical-geographical setting of Colossae in the first century helps us understand the situation that Paul addressed in his letter to Philemon.

Philemon's slave, Onesimus (Phlm 10–16), is mentioned in Colossians 4:7–9 as accompanying Tychicus as they returned to Colossae. Onesimus is described as "one of your residents." Since Philemon owned the slave Onesimus, he was probably a wealthy resident of Colossae. He probably owned other slaves as well. It is not hard to imagine that he was involved in one or more of the numerous commercial activities known in the quad cities. Philemon's wealth is demonstrated by the fact that a church met in his home (Phlm 2). The small homes of peasants would not accommodate many believers, but the spacious homes or villas of affluent Christians served well for church gatherings. In nearby Laodicea, the home of a wealthy Christian has been identified by excavators as a house church. This is described as one of the earliest house churches known anywhere in the world.[17]

As the apostle claimed, Philemon owed his salvation to Paul's ministry (Phlm 19). How this happened is not clear. Most scholars assume Philemon met Paul during his ministry in Ephesus and converted to the faith. One of Paul's disciples, Epaphras, first shared the gospel with those in Colossae (Col 1:7). Epaphras was a resident of Colossae; he was responsible for sharing the gospel in Laodicea and Hierapolis as well as in Colossae (4:12–13). How

16. J. B. Lightfoot, *Saint Paul's Epistles to the Colossians and to Philemon* (Zondervan, 1959), 309. This was also the opinion of Theodore of Mopsuestia and is supported by the Apostolic Constitutions 7.46.

17. The director of excavations at Laodicea, Celal Şimşek, claims to have found a 20-room peristyle home encompassing an area of 2,000 square meters. The rooms surround an atrium encircled with eighteen columns. The house was used as early as the first century and at some point functioned as a house church, https://archaeology.org/news/.

Epaphras became a Christian is another mystery. In the course of Paul's third mission, the apostle spent three years in Ephesus (Acts 20:31). During that time, Paul established the school (or lecture hall) of Tyrannus, where he taught disciples for a period of two years (Acts 19:9–10). As a consequence, according to Luke, the author of Acts, "all of Asia heard the word of the Lord." Paul sent his trained disciples into the countryside to share the faith. It can be understood that Epaphras, the Colossian, was one of those disciples who met Paul in Ephesus, embraced the Christian faith, was trained in the school of Tyrannus, returned home, and shared the gospel in the quad cities of Colossae, Laodicea, Hierapolis, and perhaps Tripolis.

Epaphras may have been in Ephesus for commercial endeavors, as many traders, merchants, and their agents traveled to the coastal cities. Wealthy merchants generally did not accompany their goods to the ports since robbers and thieves posed significant dangers along the way. Instead, they would usually send a trained agent with the commodities. Most of these agents were slaves, known as an οἰκονόμος (steward, manager, or agent). It is probable that Epaphras was such an agent, although it is unlikely that he was a slave since he was free to continue his associations with Paul and traveled with him. It is possible to speculate that Epaphras may have been Philemon's agent and met Paul's disciples or Paul himself while taking products to the harbor at Ephesus.

What Do We Know About Onesimus?

All we know about Onesimus is (1) that he was a slave of Philemon,[18] (2) that he escaped or fled from his master,[19] (3) that he became a Christian, (4) that

18. Allen Dwight Callahan, "Paul's Epistle to Philemon: Toward an Alternative *Argumentum*," *HTR* 86 (1993): 357–76, argues that Onesimus was not a slave, but rather a brother who had a falling out with Philemon, which Paul attempted to patch up. This understanding of the letter fails to account for the name Onesimus, a common slave name, and inadequately addresses verses 15–16, which describe Onesimus as a slave.

19. Joseph A. Fitzmyer, *The Letter to Philemon*, AB 34C (Doubleday, 2000), 18, formerly believed that Onesimus was an escaped slave but has now adopted the view that Onesimus had some trouble with his master, Philemon, and fled to Paul in Rome in order that Paul might plead his case to Philemon. Thus, Onesimus was not a fugitive slave but temporarily fled to seek Paul's help. I find this explanation implausible, since Onesimus could have found someone in the Colossian community to mediate the issue rather than traveling thousands of miles to Rome to find Paul. Moreover, the reference to Onesimus's wrongdoing, what he owes Philemon, and Paul's willingness to repay it (vv. 18–19) best fits with a narrative of a slave who stole money and escaped to launch a new life in Rome.

he somehow met Paul (probably in Rome), and (5) that he returned home to Colossae and his master Philemon with this letter from Paul requesting that Onesimus be released from slavery. Those details are certainly helpful, but there are many gaps in the story, and much more can be plausibly pieced together. The name Onesimus was a common slave name, and it occurs frequently in inscriptions of slaves. The name Ὀνήσιμος means "useful." Since this was his birth name, it is probable that his parents were also slaves, perhaps also owned by Philemon.

In verse 11, Paul employed a play on words with Onesimus's name: Onesimus "who formerly was useless to you but now is useful both to you and to me." Although his name means "useful," Paul asserted that in his current condition as an escaped slave, Onesimus was "useless" to Philemon. However, as a Christian and a slave who had returned to Philemon, Onesimus was truly "useful." It is curious that when Paul wrote this verse, he did not use the actual word ὀνήσιμος, but rather ἄχρηστος (*achrēstos*) and εὔχρηστος (*euchrēstos*), which are an antonym and synonym with similar meanings—"useless" and "useful." Why? Was this intentional? The base word *chrēstos* is similar to the name of Christ, *Christos*. In fact, many early Christian funerary reliefs and the Roman historian Suetonius misspelled the word "Chrestos." Pronounced, the words would sound the same. Paul added prefixes to the terms: "a" (not) and "eu" (good). Could Paul be insinuating that the "unchristian" Onesimus was useless but the "good Christian" Onesimus was useful to both Paul and Philemon?

From what we know of Colossae, Onesimus, and Philemon, I suggest the following reconstruction. Onesimus was a slave entrusted with many of Philemon's financial matters as a steward or manager (οἰκονόμος).

The primary industry in the area was agriculture, but the area was better known as a robust commercial trade and banking center. Merchants in Tripolis, Hierapolis, Laodicea, and Colossae actively bought and sold various goods. Philemon was likely engaged in these activities either as a wealthy landowner selling agricultural products or as a merchant buying goods from the Anatolian interior and shipping them down to the ports for transport elsewhere.

Verses 18 and 19 in the letter indicate that Onesimus stole money from Philemon at the time of his escape. The most plausible scenario is that Onesimus was tasked with hauling Philemon's commercial goods to the Aegean coast and receiving payment for them at the harbor. Rather than return to Philemon with the money, Onesimus took the money and fled. At the harbor, there were ships sailing to a number of destinations, but many were bound for Rome, the largest city in the Mediterranean realm. Onesimus chose a ship heading for Rome, a city where approximately a quarter or more of the population were slaves. There, it would have been easy for Onesimus to disappear.

Clockwise, from top left, FIGURE 65. "Onesime [a woman] erected this monument in memory of her daughter Tryphaine and her husband Epaphrodeitos." Bursa. 3rd c. AD. Istanbul Archaeological Museum.

FIGURE 66. Sarcophagus with bilingual inscription for Otacilius Crispus and his wife Otaciliae Onesimus. Istanbul Archaeological Museum.

FIGURE 67. "Dionysios, son of Onesimos, honored his wife Tyche." AD 189–90. Uşak Archaeological Museum.

FIGURE 68. Funerary relief of "Onesimus, the steward [OIKONOMOΣ] of Aelius Menogenes, his daughter Onessime, and his wife Neike." AD 150–80. Thessaloniki Archaeological Museum.

After Paul returned to Jerusalem at the conclusion of his third mission, he was seized and imprisoned in Caesarea for two years. He subsequently appealed to have his case heard in Rome; he was transferred there and spent at least another two years awaiting trial (Acts 28). In prison, Paul wrote letters to the Philippians, Ephesians, Colossians, and to Philemon. These are collectively known as the Prison Epistles. There is some debate about where these were written. Some scholars believe they were written from Paul's Caesarean imprisonment, but most scholars believe they were written from his Roman imprisonment. Without getting into the details, I believe that Paul more likely wrote these from Rome, and it is far more likely that Onesimus would have fled to Rome rather than Caesarea.

At some point, Onesimus became a Christian. It is possible that Onesimus became a Christian while still in Philemon's household. He would not have been the first or last Christian to be tempted by money and freedom. However, based on Paul's words in verse 10, "Onesimus, whom I fathered in my imprisonment," it is more likely that Onesimus became one of Paul's converts in Rome. Onesimus may have met Christians in Rome who shared their faith and brought him to Paul, who was under house arrest, to hear more of the gospel. Or Onesimus may have heard from others that Paul was imprisoned in the city and could have come on his own initiative. In either case, the connection with Paul was providential.

At some point the Christian Onesimus came to the conviction that he must confront what he had done. First, he had stolen money from his master. But more importantly, his escape from bondage to Philemon was, according to Roman law, a more serious matter. Escaped slaves who were recaptured were typically severely beaten or killed.[20]

Did Paul know Onesimus before their meeting in Rome? As Philemon's steward, Onesimus probably came to Ephesus on several occasions doing business for his master. Epaphras, a fellow Colossian who was with Paul when he wrote this letter (v. 23), almost certainly knew Onesimus. Over time, Onesimus spent enough time with Paul that Paul established a close connection with the slave and recognized the ministerial gifts that he possessed (v. 13).

---

20. Lightfoot says: "Slaves were constantly crucified for far lighter offences than his." *Epistles to the Colossians and to Philemon*, 314. Barth and Blanke state: "The slave might be whipped or beaten until he was a cripple; he might be branded on his head or arms; the skin under his feet might be burned off by glowing iron plates; a metallic collar with his name and address might be fixed around his throat; he might even be killed as a warning to fellow slaves." *Philemon*, 30.

What Does This Letter Reveal About Paul?

Paul's relationship with Philemon was complex. On the one hand, Paul claimed to have never visited Colossae, Philemon's home (Col 2:1).[21] Yet, on the other hand, Philemon owed Paul a debt of gratitude for his salvation (Phlm 17, 19). The letter to the Colossians and the letter to Philemon were sent at the same time, probably from a Roman prison (around AD 60–62). So, the problem cannot be resolved by positing that Paul visited Philemon in Colossae sometime after he wrote his letter to the Colossians. Instead, most scholars suggest that Philemon met Paul in Ephesus during the apostle's three years in that city.

> What Paul means by saying that Philemon owes him his "very self" (*seauton*) is that Philemon is in debt to Paul for his eternal life. Paul was used by God in Philemon's conversion. Paul may have been involved indirectly: Philemon may have been converted through the ministry of one of Paul's fellow workers (Epaphras) during the apostle's three years in Ephesus or sometime thereafter. But it is more likely that Paul's involvement was direct, Paul having brought Philemon to faith during a visit of the latter to Ephesus while Paul was resident there.[22]

If this suggestion is true, it supports the belief that Philemon was a wealthy merchant engaged in business with the coastal cities. During one of his visits, he ran into Paul and converted to the faith. This, in turn, supports the contention that Onesimus was Philemon's steward. Wealthy merchants seldom traveled with goods in transit to the ports for fear of thieves along the way. Instead, that task was delegated to a steward who would complete the transaction and receive the payment. Wealthy merchants probably visited the coastal cities separately to network with business partners.

Even though Paul lacked the financial status of Philemon, deSilva suggests that Paul was acting as Philemon's patron.

> Although Paul lacks both property and a place in a community, he nevertheless claims to be able to exercise authority over Philemon on the basis of having brought Philemon the message of salvation. . . . We find a mixture of grounds on which Paul bases his request: on the one hand, Paul claims authority to command Philemon's obedience as Paul's client (Philem. 8, 14, 20); on the

21. The church was founded by Epaphras, Paul's disciple whom he discipled while in Ephesus (Col 1:7).

22. Douglas J. Moo, *The Letters to the Colossians and to Philemon*, PNTC (Eerdmans, 2008), 431. So also Lightfoot, *Epistles to the Colossians and to Philemon*, 305.

> other, he voices his preference to address Philemon as friend, coworker and partner (Philem. 1), and only actually makes his request on that basis (Philem. 9, 14, 17, 20).[23]

This is interesting because patron-client relationships were generally based on wealth, power, and status. Paul, a prisoner when he penned this letter, lacked the financial resources of Philemon. Yet, he offered to repay the stolen money (or debt) as if he actually had the funds necessary to repay what was owed. Likewise, Paul lacked the power and social status of Philemon. How was Paul able to assert himself in this manner to Philemon? Notwithstanding his humble state, his appeal stemmed from the spiritual authority that he wielded. After spending more than two years teaching disciples at the school of Tyrannus and sending out evangelists and teachers throughout all of Asia (Acts 19:9–10), Paul's spiritual status and reputation were extensive. In the broader social domain, Paul was nothing. But in the eyes of the early Christian communities established throughout Asia, Paul was the father of the faith. Among his many spiritual sons and daughters, Paul was the *pater familias* and exercised absolute authority over the household.

The apostle wrote that he was sending Onesimus back as if he were sending his own "heart" (v. 12). The word used here is not the customary Greek word καρδία. Instead, Paul used the word σπλάγχνα, denoting one's innermost feelings. Fitzmyer comments, "Paul sees Christian Onesimus as part of himself." The use of σπλάγχνα in this letter "shows how personally Paul was involved in the matter."[24] Why was he so personally involved? The depth of his emotions is remarkable. Similarly, Lohse asserts: "Paul, though, is sending Onesimus to Philemon with the express assurance that this slave means as much to him as his own heart. When Onesimus returns to his master, it is as if the Apostle himself had come to him."[25] Barth and Blanke go even further:

> Actually, Paul says still more. Not only is he Onesimus's loving father, mother, and subtly pleading advocate, but he plainly *identifies* himself with the slave and the slave with himself. Onesimus "is made one with me so that henceforth also to you [Philemon] he is quasi the *alter ego*" (W. Estius). According to E. Lohmeyer, in Philem 12 "I and thou [Paul and Onesimus] have been made

23. DeSilva, *Honor, Patronage, Kinship and Purity*, 124.

24. Fitzmyer, *Letter to Philemon*, 109. "Actually the apostle's unique and special love for Onesimus even goes beyond his cordial care for other Christians whom he calls his 'dear children,'" 361.

25. Lohse, *Colossians and Philemon*, 201.

> one person"; the formula used by Paul is "completely unique"; "the I of Paul is the thou of the slave"—so totally the apostle "empties himself."[26]

How can we explain Paul's over-the-top identification with Onesimus? Onesimus was not one of Paul's close traveling companions. Paul's exposure to Onesimus was probably limited to brief visits during Paul's house arrest. Yet, Paul connected with Onesimus more deeply than with his beloved Timothy or any other coworker in his ministry. Even the bonded relationships of those in the mystery religions or philosophies could not compare with Paul's feelings for Onesimus. "Paul's total self-identification with the slave goes far beyond the Stoics' and other humanitarians' sympathy with slaves. While the Stoics recognized that slaves, too, *have* a soul, Paul in fact confesses that Onesimus *is* his soul."[27] The answer is that Paul connected with Onesimus at a visceral level. Paul knew from personal experience what life was like as a slave.

Paul may have been alluding to Philemon's status as a merchant in verse 17: "If you regard me as your partner." The word for partner (κοινωνός) "normally denotes 'one who takes part in something with someone' (BAGD). Indeed, it may even have the nuance of one who is a partner in a common business pursuit or commercial endeavor. . . . The common interests would involve not merely 'faith and love' . . . but something more concrete, adding a 'commercial dimension to the whole affair,' as Dunn suggests."[28] As a partner, Paul implored Philemon to "welcome Onesimus as you would me."

The words "if he has wronged you," "owes you," and "charge that to my account" are all "examples of technical, commercial language that Paul introduces."[29] These terms reinforce the understanding of Philemon as a merchant and the conclusion that Onesimus ran off with Philemon's commercial funds. In concert with Paul's identification with Onesimus, the apostle asked Philemon to charge the stolen money to his account. Philemon knew that Paul was in no position to pay this charge, but the apostle was determined to make it right. His statement "I will repay it" (v. 19) is an emphatic construction.

The urgent stress that Paul placed in verses 10–20 regarding Onesimus and his entreaty to release him can best be explained by what is argued in

---

26. Barth and Blanke, *Philemon*, 360 (emphasis original).

27. Barth and Blanke, *Philemon*, 360 (emphasis original).

28. Fitzmyer, *Letter to Philemon*, 116. Cf. James D. G. Dunn, *The Epistles to the Colossians and Philemon* (Eerdmans, 1996), 336.

29. Fitzmyer, 117.

this volume. Paul passionately identified with Onesimus because he could see in him what he and his family endured in bondage. Writing from a Roman prison, Paul could not directly attack the unjust institution of slavery entrenched in Roman society. Paul, like every other Roman, knew that the upheaval of slavery would have ramifications for the economy of the Mediterranean world and would bring violence like what happened during the Roman Servile Wars a hundred years earlier. Paul's letter struck a blow against the institution, which began a slow and violent spiral toward its death. Today, 2,000 years after the emergence of the faith Paul promoted, the cadaver of slavery continues to convulse in its death throes.

| 9 |
Paul's Apocalypse: Understanding His Theology

Before Paul's Damascus Conversion

PAUL CLAIMED TO HAVE BEEN a Zealot and Pharisee (Gal 1:13; Phil 3:5–6). As such, we can get a sense of his thoughts and beliefs prior to his encounter with the risen Christ. In an earlier chapter, we detailed some of the fundamental beliefs of the Zealots. The term "Zealot" was used loosely and included rebels who chiefly rose up in opposition to Roman rule in Palestine. These groups had no central organization, unified theology, or universally accepted code of conduct. Like Paul, members of the Jewish sects could harbor Zealot sentiments in addition to their other beliefs.[1] One of Jesus's apostles, Simon, evidently was a Zealot (Matt 10:4; Mark 3:18; Luke 6:15 [ζηλωτὴν]; Acts 1:13 [ζηλωτὴς]). The rebels could target Romans, gentiles, or even fellow Jews who appeared to contravene the Jewish sacred traditions encapsulated in the Torah. The stimulus for Zealot violence was ostensibly offensive behavior deemed to be a violation of Jewish sacred traditions, but additional economic or political factors often contributed to the emergence of Zealot outbreaks.

Josephus described four groups: Sadducees, Pharisees, Essenes, and Zealots.[2] He was not particularly nuanced in his descriptions of their essential beliefs. However, he is our most valuable primary source. Among

1. Josephus mentioned a Pharisee named Saddok who rose up against the Pharisees around AD 6. *Ant.* 18.1.1; *J.W.* 2.8.1.

2. Josephus, *Ant.* 13.171–73, 18:11–23; *J.W.* 2.119–66.

the beliefs of the Pharisees, Josephus states: "Now for the Pharisees, they say that some actions, but not all, are the work of fate, and some of them are in our own power, and that they are liable to fate, but are not caused by fate."[3] Lacking clarity from Josephus, scholars have mined the New Testament, Dead Sea Scrolls, intertestamental Jewish literature, and rabbinic sources to understand more of what the Pharisees believed. Owing in large part to E. P. Sanders[4] and scholars who have refined his research, we understand a central tenet of Palestinian Judaism to be what is referred to today as covenantal nomism.

Covenantal nomism encompassed the following beliefs: (1) God graciously chose Israel (Abraham's descendants) as his people. (2) God entered into a covenant relationship with Israel. (3) The terms of the covenant were incorporated in the Torah (law of Moses). (4) The Torah was God's special gift to Israel. (5) The Torah was the means (or instrument) by which people could atone for their sins, achieve righteousness, and remain in God's favor.[5] (6) The Jewish people were saved by God's grace, not by their actions, although obedience was necessary to remain in the covenant. (7) Covenantal nomism involved a quantitative understanding of righteousness and salvation. If one's righteous deeds outweighed the deeds of unrighteousness, one was saved. (8) Without the Torah, no one could achieve righteousness. (9) Torah (not Roman law or civil law) became the standard of practice for the Jewish people. (10) All people within the covenant community abiding by the Torah and accruing righteousness were predestined for salvation.[6] (11) Gentiles living without the Torah, and thus unable to achieve righteousness, were predestined for condemnation. What developed was a corporate mentality that all Jews would be saved, and all gentiles would be condemned.

In any culture, there are people who are devout, others who are less devout and nominally engaged with their faith, and still others who are not religious at all. All people have varying levels of commitment to the God of their faith. Second Temple Judaism was diverse and included religious extremists, staunchly observant Jews, a passively observant majority

---

3. Josephus, *Ant.* 13.172.

4. E. P. Sanders, *Paul and Palestinian Judaism: A Comparison of Patterns of Religion* (Fortress, 1977).

5. "God has provided the Torah as a means of identifying Israel as a special people and of maintaining the covenant relationship." Donaldson, *Paul and the Gentiles*, 295.

6. "Jews who are so identified and who avail themselves of the Torah-prescribed means of maintaining their membership in the covenant community (who are 'righteous') are assured of divine blessing, especially that of salvation in the age to come." Donaldson, 295.

of peasants, and a small minority of rather silent people who were tangentially connected to the faith of their neighbors. However, living within the confines of a Jewish culture that was defined by the Torah, even marginal Jews obeyed the Torah more than they disobeyed it. Bearing in mind this corporate mentality, it was thought that all Jews would receive salvation. Only Jews who intentionally rejected the Jewish faith would be condemned. On the other hand, there were gentiles who were devout. Some, such as the God-fearers and devotees of Theos Hypsistos,[7] forsook the traditional polytheistic gods and became monotheists. However, most Jews thought that, without the Torah, it was impossible for gentiles to achieve righteousness. Thus, in first-century Judaism there arose a corporate mentality of predestination. All Jews would be saved, while all gentiles would be condemned.

A minority position emerged within first-century Judaism whereby it was thought that some righteous gentiles could be saved. The so-called Noahide laws harkened back to the covenant God made with Noah. These laws, generally seven in number, were a baseline for gentiles to achieve righteousness and salvation before the Torah was given. As it was a minority belief, it is hard to determine how widespread the belief in the Noahide laws was in first-century Judaism.[8] Some circles within Pharisaism, certainly few in

7. Worshipers of the "highest God"—these were gentiles who became henotheists or monotheists. Numerous inscriptions throughout the Mediterranean world indicate that this cult was widespread. Stephen Mitchell documents 376 of these inscriptions, most of them in the eastern Mediterranean. "The Cult of Theos Hypsistos Between Pagans, Jews, and Christians," in *Pagan Monotheism in Late Antiquity*, ed. Polymnia Athanassadi and Michael Frede (Oxford University Press, 1999), 81–148; also Stephen Mitchell, "Further Thoughts on the Cult of Theos Hypsistos," in *One God: Pagan Monotheism in the Roman Empire*, ed. Stephen Mitchell and Peter Van Nuffelen (Cambridge University Press, 2010), 167–208.

8. J. Duncan Derrett refers to the Noahide courts, applying Noahide laws, as "a jurisdiction which certainly existed in first-century Palestine, and which has been unaccountably overlooked by historians of comparative law." "'Bechuqey Hagoyim': Damascus Document IX, Again," *RevQ* 11 (1983): 411. Likewise, Louis Finkelstein, "Some Examples of the Maccabean Halaka," *JBL* 49 (1930), 20–42, who opts for a formative date during the Hasmonean period; Samuel Sandmel, *Judaism and Christian Beginnings* (Oxford University Press, 1978), 180–81; Alan F. Segal, *Paul the Convert: The Apostolate and Apostasy of Saul the Pharisee* (Yale University Press, 1990), 194–201, who avers a time during the Hellenistic period; E.P. Sanders, *Judaism: Practice and Belief* (Trinity Press International, 1992), 269; and Donaldson, *Paul and the Gentiles*, 65–69. Contra David Novak, "The Origin of the Noahide Laws," in *Perspectives on Jews and Judaism: Essays in Honor of Wolfe Kelman*, ed. Arthur A. Chiel (Rabbinical Assembly, 1978), who asserts that "there is no convincing evidence that this doctrine is earlier than the tannaitic period, specifically after the destruction of the Second Temple and the Christian schism" (309). Also, Novak, *The Image of the Non-Jew in Judaism: An Historical*

number, probably espoused the belief at least theoretically, if not practically. But the widespread and commonly known ban on fellowship with gentiles during the first century tells us that the common people did not entertain the thought that gentiles could be saved. The pre-Christian Paul did not.

Paul's encounter with the risen Jesus on the Damascus Road had a profound impact on him. During the apostle's seven to nine years in Cilicia following his conversion (Acts 9:30; Gal 1:21), before Barnabas called him to minister in Antioch (Acts 11:25–26), Paul went through a period of introspection and theological reconsideration when the Spirit of God revealed to him the fullness of the gospel. This is probably what Paul described as an "apocalypse" when he wrote to the Galatians (1:12). Paul was adamant that his gospel was not received from others. "For I would have you know, brethren, that the gospel which was preached by me is not according to man. I neither received it from man, nor was I taught it, but I received it through a revelation of Jesus Christ" (1:11–12). Here, Paul was designating a clean break with his former traditions. Later in his letter to the Corinthians, Paul described an apocalyptic experience "fourteen years ago" (2 Cor 12:2). This may have been the same "apocalypse" that Paul described in his letter to the Galatians. The "fourteen years" places this experience back during the seven- to nine-year Cilician period following his conversion (around AD 41). While Paul was going through this theological transformation, he continued to preach the gospel in the regions of Cilicia. There, he realized that God was doing a work among the gentile people, and he could see the work of the Spirit regenerating the lives of the people in the towns and villages of Cilicia. This was a profound breach with the Pharisaic teaching that he had acquired previously. Jewish beliefs, echoed among the Palestinian Jews and supported by the rabbis, held that uncircumcised gentiles could not be saved. What Paul witnessed in Cilicia taught him otherwise. It was at this point that he reassessed what is known today as "covenantal nomism."

It is impossible to know what kind of theological consternation this caused in the mind of the apostle, nor how long it took him to make this break with the long-established and deeply entrenched Jewish belief.

---

and Constructive Study of the Noahide Laws (Edwin Mellen, 1983). Markus Bockmuehl, "The Noachide Commandments and New Testament Ethics with Special Reference to Acts 15 and Pauline Halakhah," *RB* 102 (1995): 72–101, opts for a middle ground, claiming that the teaching is not explicit in the rabbinic writings before the second century, but the teaching is clear in some antecedent Jewish texts, such as Jubilees.

Donaldson believes that Paul went through a significant reassessment of his convictions but never entirely abandoned his Jewish roots. For the pre-conversion Paul,

> the broad framework of Paul's initial convictional world was provided by covenantal nomism. . . . Within the broad framework of covenantal nomism, Paul is to be located specifically within the more stringent and zealous forms of Pharisaism and, in particular, among those who felt that the one hope gentiles had of sharing in the salvation of the age to come was by becoming full proselytes to Judaism in this age.[9]

Earlier, in Jerusalem before the Damascus Road experience, Paul encountered Christians and began an ambitious program to persecute them. Donaldson states:

> His characterization of this persecuting activity as a manifestation of zeal indicates that it resulted not simply from some general and indeterminate antipathy, but more precisely because he perceived the Christian movement as posing a threat to the Torah. . . . The message that the Messiah had appeared in advance of the age to come, and that salvation was dependent on recognizing Jesus as this Messiah, implied an alternative way of determining the community of the "righteous," namely, by adherence to Christ, rather than to the Torah.[10]

For Donaldson, Paul's vitriolic reaction against the Christians revolved around the Christian diminution of the Torah: "To the extent to which the early Christian movement was prepared to include as members those who were lax about Torah observance, simply on the basis of the adherence to Christ, they were implying that Torah was not necessary. . . . Christ was functioning as a de facto replacement for the Torah as a membership requirement."[11]

I cannot fully concur with Donaldson on this point. At this juncture early in the history of Christianity, it seems unlikely that the Jerusalem Christians saw far enough ahead to recognize the break with the Torah. The Jerusalem Christians were messianic Jews who had not broken fellowship with non-Christ-believing Jews. If we follow the Acts of the Apostles, they still attended to the ritual practices in the temple and were Torah compliant.

---

9. Donaldson, *Paul and the Gentiles*, 295–96.
10. Donaldson, 296.
11. Donaldson, 297.

At this point, early in the Christian movement, the Jewish Christians had no intent to abandon the Torah and to swing the doors open widely to gentiles. Paul, in fact, later in life was the first to realize the ramifications of Christ's work as it related to the Torah, and he was one of the first to dive headlong into a ministry among the gentiles. His ministry to the gentiles eventually brought him into conflict with other Jews and Jewish Christians. Even following Paul's so-called third mission, upon his return to Jerusalem, James warned Paul: "You see, brother, how many thousands there are among the *Jews of those who have believed*, and they are all zealous for the Law" (Acts 21:20; also Acts 15:1–2).

Rather, I see Paul's persecution of the Christians as stemming from the negative Pharisaic reaction to Jesus's teachings against the Pharisees and their actions. Jesus denigrated the Pharisaic interpretation of the Torah while still supporting the Torah itself. Jesus clearly stated that he would not abolish the Torah but had come to fulfill it (Matt 5:17). He crit icized the righteous, arrogant pride and the hypocrisy of the Pharisees (Matt 6:1–18). Paul, himself a Pharisee, was probably in Jerusalem during Jesus's ministry in Galilee. Word of the popular country preacher in Galilee reached the ears of the esteemed Pharisees in Jerusalem, and their opposition to Jesus in the final days certainly contributed to the crucifixion. In the Gospels, the Pharisees' strong, vehement opposition to Jesus was a reaction to the challenge that Jesus presented to Pharisaic authority. The controversy stories in the Gospels reek of the pride and jealousy of a sect that was challenged and put on the spot. Jesus's teachings undermined the authority that the sect had long enjoyed among the common people. At the time of Paul's persecution of the Christians, there was no mission to the gentiles and no evident Christian opposition to the Torah. Paul opposed the Christians for the same reason the other Pharisees opposed Jesus: power and prestige.

After the Damascus Road experience, when Paul realized that Jesus was both Messiah and Savior,

> Paul did not so much abandon his native convictional world as reconstruct it around a new center. . . . He was forced to let go of Torah in that role. But quite a few of his native convictions—God, the election of Israel, Israel's role as a light to the Gentiles, the consummation of God's reign in the age to come, and others—were not directly implicated.[12]

12. Donaldson, 297.

FIGURE 69. Fresco of Paul and his books. Cave of Paul and Thela, Ephesus. See gallery for color version.

Nevertheless, "In his conversion, Paul came to a different understanding of the means of righteousness: Christ, not Torah, served as the entrance requirement and boundary marker of the community."[13]

In the first century, Paul was theologically advanced compared to his fellow Jews and Christians. At an early date, the convert Paul was able to navigate the theological ramifications of what Jesus had done on the cross. While other early Christians were still coming to grips with the supernatural reality of the resurrection, Paul was a chapter ahead. For Paul, the appearance of the Savior on the Damascus Road was confirmation that the Lord had risen. Now Paul set about figuring out how that truth transformed his former Jewish beliefs. While operating within a broader Jewish frame of mind, he realized that the Torah had performed its purpose. As a tutor (παιδαγωγός), the Torah's purpose was to convey the servants of God to the fount of the faith—Jesus (Gal 3:24–25). Once that task was finished, the Torah had completed its purpose and thus was no longer binding.

Later, as Paul began to share this new faith with Jews and gentiles in Cyprus, Anatolia, Macedonia, and Greece, he began to receive opposition. This opposition arose not only among unbelieving Jews but also among Jewish believers in Christ. Hundreds of years of embedded theology could not be erased easily, and cherished Jewish beliefs lingered in the early Christian communities. Even though the sacrifice of Christ did away with the sacrifice of bulls, goats, and sheep, the early Christians continued to congregate in the temple (Acts 2–3). Why? Did the early Christians believe that sacrifices were still necessary? Evidently, some did.

This point was addressed in the tenth chapter of Hebrews: "It is impossible for the blood of bulls and goats to take away sins" (v. 4). The emphasis on the singular sacrifice of Christ highlights the fact that some Jewish Christians still thought that temple observance and sacrifice were efficacious.

> By this will we have been sanctified through the offering of the body of Jesus Christ *once* for all. (v. 10)
>
> But he, having offered *one* sacrifice for sins for all time, sat down at the right hand of God. (v. 12)
>
> For by *one* offering he has perfected for all time those who are sanctified. (v. 14)

Although Hebrews was not written by Paul, the letter nonetheless accentuates that some Jewish Christians were still clinging to their past Jewish

13. Donaldson, 298.

traditions and beliefs. Paul needed to dispel thoughts of the now antiquated sacrificial system and the perceived need for the Torah.

When Paul and Barnabas returned to Antioch from their mission in Cyprus and Galatia, they encountered Jewish Christians who opposed Paul and Barnabas, insisting that gentile believers must be circumcised and ordered to observe the Torah (Acts 15:1–2). Similarly, at the end of Paul's final mission when he returned to Jerusalem, James met with Paul, saying: "See, brother, how many thousands there are among the Jews of those who have believed, and they are all zealous for the Law; and they have been told about you, that you are teaching all the Jews who are among the Gentiles to forsake Moses, telling them not to circumcise their children nor to walk according to the customs" (21:20–21). The apostle Peter and Barnabas also struggled with the issue, so much so that Paul publicly rebuked Peter in Antioch (Gal 2:11). Peter withdrew from table fellowship with gentile believers, since they did not observe the dietary restrictions of the Torah. Barnabas and other Jewish Christians were enticed to do the same "fearing the party of the circumcision" (2:11–13). The issue of integrating the gentile believers into the church became a prickly issue as long as the Torah stood in the way.

FIGURE 70. Glass dish of column with Christogram flanked by Peter and Paul. 4th c. AD. Metropolitan Museum of Art, New York. See gallery for color version.

Judaism already had a process for gentiles to become Jews. A proselyte was born as a gentile but converted to Judaism. Proselytes are frequently mentioned in Matthew's Gospel and the Acts. It is thought that a person who wished to become a Jew would undergo a trial period during which the candidate would be Torah compliant, followed by adult circumcision and immersion in a Jewish ritual bath (mikvah). It seems that these opponents of Paul expected gentile believers to go through the customary procedure of proselytism before they could be saved and embraced into the Christian covenant community. The concept of a Torah-free and circumcision-free acceptance of the gentiles was out of the question for them. For Paul, however, his apocalypse (Gal 1:12) made this clear, and his ministry experiences in Cilicia and Galatia confirmed that this was true.

Writing to the Galatians, Paul countered the false teachings of people known as the Judaizers. These quasi-Christians were probably the same as, or associated with, the people whom Paul opposed in Antioch (Acts 15:1–2). They may have retraced Paul's journey into Galatia to correct his teaching among the churches. These were Jewish Christians who did not fully understand the gospel and did not realize that the Torah had completed its purpose. They followed Jesus's teachings and believed that he was the Messiah. Many of them probably believed Jesus's work on the cross brought about redemption for sin. However, coming from a rich Jewish heritage that celebrated the law of Moses as a cornerstone of the faith, and from a Jewish culture that believed circumcision was the rite of passage into the covenant community, these people clung to ancient Jewish traditions. For Paul, however, their teachings were anathema. These Judaizers were teaching a "different gospel" (1:6) and had "bewitched" the Galatians (3:1).

In Galatians, immediately after his standardized introduction, Paul launched into an attack on the teachings of the Judaizers: "I am amazed that you are so quickly deserting Him who called you by the grace of Christ, for a different gospel; which is really not another, only there are some who are disturbing you and want to distort the gospel of Christ" (1:6–7). He proceeded to declare that anyone preaching a different gospel should be accursed. Later, in chapter 3, he detailed the purpose of the law and the abrogation of the Torah. Continuing in chapters 5 and 6, he declared that circumcision no longer had any purpose (5:6; 6:15) and went so far as to impugn circumcision as mutilation (5:12).

From the beginning of the letter, Paul insisted that his gospel was not appropriated from the teachings of others. Instead, his understanding of the gospel was independent of the apostles, prophets, rabbis, and others. His gospel was received as a direct revelation (apocalypse) from the Lord himself. Although Paul was known as a Pharisee, he taught a gospel that was antithetical to Pharisaic teaching. Paul, well connected to the apostles in his later years, shared a gospel that no one else was proclaiming. He asserted that he was an apostle "not sent through the agency of man, but through Jesus Christ and God the Father" (1:1).

He asked, "Am I seeking the favor of men or God?" (1:10). The rhetorical question needed no response. Paul was not looking for the approval of others, regardless of how esteemed they might be. He was doing God's bidding. He continued with a second rhetorical question: "Am I striving to please men?" The two statements are not a tautology. Two different verbs are used in these phrases: (πείθω and ἀρέσκω). Martyn correctly observes that the two rhetorical questions are antithetical. Martyn adds:

> Paul draws a contrast between two parts of his own life. . . . He implies that in that life he was, as Epictetus would have said, the slave of those he was trying to please (*Diss.* 4.1). Now with the termination of that period, he has oriented himself solely to Christ, being in fact Christ's slave and therefore liberated from the impulse to please other human beings.[14]

The verb in the second question, ἀρέσκειν, translated "to please," coupled with ἀνθρώποις (men), refers to a servile relationship. Foerster states that the compound word ἀνθρωπάρεσκος described one who "born of fear and quite natural in slaves, is striving to please those who are in superior authority."[15] Bietenhard expresses it more strongly, saying that ἀνθρωπάρεσκος is used only in reference to the service of slaves.[16]

Addressing household slaves, Paul used this compound word with parallel expressions in his letters to the Ephesians and Colossians.

> Slaves be obedient to those who are your masters according to the flesh, with fear and trembling in the sincerity of your heart as to Christ; not by way of eye-service, as men-pleasers [ἀνθρωπάρεσκοι], but as slaves of Christ. (Eph 6:5–6)

> Slaves, in all things obey those who are your masters on earth, not just as eye-service, as those who merely please men [ἀνθρωπάρεσκοι], but with sincerity of heart, fearing the Lord. (Col 3:22)

Paul, freed from bondage to his former human master, had now voluntarily become the slave of Christ. Through baptism, Paul became united with Christ, and "having been freed from sin and enslaved to God," he now served a new master (Rom 6:22).

The issue of striving to please, placate, or appease men may have been the Judaizers' attack on Paul *ad hominem*.[17] By undermining Paul's servile status, they questioned not only his teaching but also his apostleship. By

---

14. Martyn, *Galatians*, 139–40.
15. W. Foerster, *TDNT* 1:456.
16. H. Bietenhard, *NIDNTT*, 2:817.
17. "They had misrepresented certain acts of his past life . . . perhaps with an indirect reference to the marks of persecution which he bore on his body (τὰ στίγμα τοῦ Ἰησοῦ, vi. 17)." J. B. Lightfoot, *The Epistle of St. Paul to the Galatians* (Zondervan, 1957), 79.

offering a Torah-free gospel to the gentiles, Paul was acting as he formerly had, appeasing his Roman master. However, Paul finished verse 10 with a contrary-to-fact conditional sentence: "If I was still continuing to appease men [in a servile manner], I would not be a slave of Christ." The contrast between the protasis and the apodosis is stark. The word "still" is revealing. If Paul was still serving his human master, he could not be a slave of Christ. The addition of the word "still" in the protasis concedes that the former condition was true, but as a contrary-to-fact condition, it was no longer true. The apodosis declares that the current status of the apostle is only true because his former status was no longer valid.

Paul's identification as a "slave of Christ" is elsewhere found in his introductory remarks at the beginning of his letters to the Romans (1:1), Philippians (1:1), and Titus (1:1). In Galatians 1:10, however, the description is different. Paul was not using a standardized title to introduce himself but rather was describing his current status in contrast to his past bondage to a human master. However much scholars may claim that Paul is repeating expressions that were used of Moses (2 Kgs 18:12; 21:8) and David (2 Kgs 19:34; 20:6) as servants of God,[18] Galatians 1:10 is different. This does not stand as an honorific title or as an expression of his official status but rather as a description of the transition that Paul experienced. Paul was a slave serving a human master. He was manumitted, and now he voluntarily served a new master.

Paul's Apocalypse

Following up on his claim that he was appointed as an apostle not by the authority of any man (Gal 1:1), Paul took up the issue again in 1:11–12. He insisted that his gospel was not according to man (v. 11). He asserted that he did not receive it or was taught it from others, but rather, he received it as a revelation from Jesus Christ (v. 12). The term "revelation" (ἀποκάλυψις) is the same term used at the beginning of Revelation. The term connects Paul's experience with the apocalyptic literature common during the intertestamental period and the first century. The intertestamental apocalyptic writers commonly had otherworldly experiences in which they were taken up into the heavens where they saw and heard things from God. In Revelation, John wrote: "I looked, and behold, a door standing open in heaven,

18. Moo, *Galatians*, 84.

and the first voice which I had heard, like the sound of a trumpet speaking with me, said, 'Come up here, and I will show you what must take place after these things.' Immediately I was in the Spirit; and behold, a throne was standing in heaven, and One sitting on the throne" (Rev 4:1–2).

Paul reported a similar experience when he wrote to the Corinthians: "I know a man in Christ who fourteen years ago—whether in the body I do not know, or out of the body I do not know, God knows—such a man was caught up to the third heaven" (2 Cor 12:2). This was part of Paul's so-called boast to the Corinthians to assert his apostolic ministry. Second Corinthians was written around AD 55. If we subtract fourteen years from AD 55, this event took place in AD 41. Thus, this took place during the seven- to nine-year period when Paul was sent back to Tarsus and Cilicia (roughly AD 36–45) while he was still learning the faith.

This apocalyptic transport into the third heaven must be what Paul referred to in Galatians 1:12 when he described his reception of the gospel as an "apocalypse." His insistence on not receiving his teaching from people is emphatic and needlessly repetitious:

> Not sent from men nor indirectly from men, but through Jesus Christ and God the Father. (1:1)
>
> The gospel preached by me is not according to man. (1:11)
>
> I neither received it from man, nor was I taught it. (1:12)
>
> I did not immediately consult with flesh and blood. (1:16)
>
> I did not see any of the other apostles, except James. (1:19)
>
> I assure you before God that I am not lying. (1:20)

Paul's vehement denial of human involvement in his understanding of the gospel underscores his radical departure from his Pharisaic teaching and his forceful declaration of an apocalyptic gospel.

Paul's Apocalypse and the Gentiles

Josephus claimed the Pharisees believed that everything was decreed by fate (εἱμαρμένη). "The Pharisees who . . . hold the position of the leading sect, attribute everything to Fate and to God; they hold that to act rightly or otherwise rests, indeed for the most part with men, but that in each action

Fate cooperates."[19] "Though they postulate that everything is brought about by fate, still they do not deprive the human will of the pursuit of what is in man's power."[20] Josephus ought to have known their views on the topic since he had once joined the sect.

This belief was echoed elsewhere in first-century Judaism. The Essenes likewise believed that Torah compliance and fate determined an individual's destiny. This was harshly expressed in Jubilees 15.26:

> Anyone who is born whose own flesh is not circumcised on the eighth day is not from the sons of the covenant which the Lord made for Abraham since (he is) from the children of destruction. And there is therefore no sign upon him so that he might belong to the Lord because (he is destined) to be destroyed and annihilated from the earth and to be uprooted from the earth because he has broken the covenant of the Lord our God.

The Qumran community believed that people's destiny was set at birth according to their astrological signs.[21] The scroll 4Q186 Horoscope describes the fate of people based on their birth signs and appearance. The scroll declares that an individual's spirit consists of nine parts and one's fate is determined by how many parts of the spirit dwell in the House of Light or the House of Darkness. This understanding of the spirit could account for various degrees of holiness among people. Devout Jews would have eight parts of their spirit in the House of Light, while nominal Jews might have only five or six. Gentiles, however, were born with four or fewer parts in the House of Light and as many as eight in the House of Darkness. The destiny of all people was understood to have been determined at birth, based on their place in the zodiac. The Community Rule also reflects the sectarians' beliefs:

> The Levites shall curse all the men of the lot of Belial. They shall begin to speak and shall say: "Accursed are you for all your wicked, blameworthy deeds. May God hand you over to terror by the hand of all those carrying out acts of Vengeance. May he bring upon you destruction by the hand of all those who accomplish retributions. Accursed are you, without mercy, according to the darkness of your deeds, and sentence you to the gloom of everlasting fire. May

19. Josephus, *J.W.* 2.163.

20. Josephus, *Ant.* 18.13; also 13.171.

21. At least six synagogues from the Byzantine period in Galilee had zodiac circles on their floors.

God not be merciful when you entreat him. May he not forgive by purifying your iniquities. May he lift the countenance of his anger to avenge himself on you and may there be no peace for you by the mouth of those who intercede."
(1 QS 2.4–9)

The fundamental importance of the Torah was highlighted by *Liber antiquitatum biblicarum* (also known as Pseudo-Philo):

> I will give light to the world and illumine their dwelling places and establish my covenant with the sons of men and glorify my people above all nations. For them I will bring out the eternal statutes that are for those in the light, but for the ungodly a punishment. . . . I have given an everlasting Law into your hands and by this I will judge the whole world. For this will be a testimony. For even if men say, "We have not known you, and so we have not served you," therefore I will make a claim upon them because they have not learned my Law. (11.1–2)[22]

The understanding among most Jews was that since the gentiles did not have the Torah, it was impossible for them to be saved on judgment day. This was what Paul himself formerly believed. Writing to the Ephesians, he claimed, "You were at that time separate from Christ, excluded from the people of Israel, and strangers to the covenants of the promise, *having no hope* and without God in the world" (Eph 2:12).

However, the apocalypse reset Paul's understanding of the gentiles and their place in the coming kingdom.

> But now in Christ Jesus you who previously were far away have been brought near by the blood of Christ. For He Himself is our peace, who made both groups into one and broke down the barrier of the dividing wall, by *abolishing in His flesh the hostility, which is the Law* composed of commandments expressed in ordinances, so that in Himself He might make the two one new person, in this way establishing peace; and that He might reconcile them both in one body to God through the cross. (Eph 2:13–16)

The dawning of this revelation had sweeping consequences for Paul's theology and mission. It also created obstacles for other Jewish Christians who had not the benefit of Paul's apocalypse. The place of the Torah within Judaism at this time cannot be overstated. The Torah was the bedrock of Jewish faith and was considered the most sacred part of Scripture. The Sadducees, who did not believe in the inspiration of the historical and prophetic

22. J. Harrington, trans., "Pseudo-Philo," in *Old Testament Pseudepigrapha*, ed. James H. Charlesworth, vol. 2 (Doubleday, 1985), 318.

FIGURE 71. Lintel from church depicting the archangel Raphael and St. Paul. Byzantine period. Uşak Archaeological Museum. See gallery for color version.

books of the Hebrew Bible, held tightly to the Torah as the only Scripture. Thus, the Torah was the common bond that united all Jews.

For Jewish and Jewish Christian ears, it was shocking to hear Paul say that the Torah was abolished.[23] Moreover, for Paul to imagine that "the dividing wall," probably a reference to the wall dividing the Court of the Gentiles from the Court of Israel in the Jerusalem temple, was broken down, such words bordered on blasphemy. Reconciling the gentile people with Jewish people and creating one body was practically incomprehensible at that time. The notion that some people were fated to salvation (Jews) while others were fated to damnation (gentiles) was deeply embedded within first-century Judaism. Yet, this was the substance of Paul's revelation during the seven- to nine-year period in Tarsus and Cilicia.

23. Converted gentiles, known as proselytes, were required to obey the Torah and be circumcised. "That proselytism involves the acceptance of the Torah . . . is to say that it involves entrance into the Jewish community. . . . The emphasis in the literature on the proselytes' experience as one of separation or estrangement from their communities of origin is therefore not surprising." Donaldson, *Paul and the Gentiles*, 57–58. Similarly, Donaldson quotes Shaye Cohen: "As far as is known no (non-Christian) Jewish community in antiquity accepted male proselytes who were not circumcised" (59). Cf. Shaye J. D. Cohen, "Crossing the Boundary and Becoming a Jew," HTR 82 (1989), 27.

Paul expressed the freedom that Christ was offering to the gentiles in stark terms, which recalled the experiences that he himself felt as a slave.

Paul's Apocalypse and Zealotry

Paul's understanding of this apocalyptic gospel brought about a change, not only in his theology but also in his worldview and lifestyle. He reminded his audience of his former life persecuting the church "beyond measure" and his attempts to destroy the faith (1:13). He was advancing in Judaism beyond his peers and was "an extraordinary Zealot for my ancestral traditions" (1:14).[24] Proof of his zealotry was found in his persecution of what he thought to be a schismatic distortion of his ancestral traditions. The underlying premise of the Zealot movement was to safeguard the Torah and to maintain the purity of the Jewish faith.

We can trace three developmental stages of Paul's zealotry. During the first stage, Paul acquired an extremist, militant faith in God from his parents and kinfolk in Gischala of Galilee. This understanding of the Jewish faith was cultivated, in part, by the earlier militant Jewish faith that led to the Maccabean Revolt and the liberation of the Judean state during the Hasmonean period. Those hopes were dashed by the Roman occupation of Palestine in the last half of the first century BC. Devout Jews kindled hopes that another militant uprising would bring them freedom. These Zealots were committed to safeguarding the sanctity of the Torah and preserving the faith. They regarded the Romans and their collaborators as threats. The highest expression of one's faith, in the minds of these pious rebels, was to take up arms and shed blood in order to drive out the Romans and restore Jewish independence.

As Josephus records, many of these rebel villages were sacked by the Romans, and the residents were sold in the slave markets. Paul's family was among them. An unknown Roman citizen from Tarsus purchased the family, probably as a unit. The fortune of slaves was dependent on their master. Some were consigned to hard labor and brutal treatment. However, literate, educated slaves who possessed skills useful to their master generally enjoyed fair treatment. Some such slaves thrived in such conditions.

---

24. Most modern translations modify this expression: "being extremely zealous." However, Paul used the noun "Zealot," connecting his activity with the well-known Zealot movement active throughout the first century. He described his former life as an extremist. See Fairchild, "Paul's Pre-Christian Zealot Associations," 514–32.

Slaves taken in war would be predisposed to loathe Roman rule, and one can imagine that Paul's family felt the same. However, after serving their overlord for several years, Paul's family learned that the Romans, with few exceptions, were fair and just. Paul learned that he could practice his faith unimpeded and that the Roman penal code punished sinful behaviors. This is reflected in Paul's comments on Roman rule in the letter to the Romans (13:1–7). Additionally, dutiful service was rewarded with freedom and Roman citizenship. This realization brought about the second phase of Paul's zealotry. The Romans were no longer thought to be the threat he had once perceived.

At this stage, Paul's zeal to serve God was not dampened; rather, it increased as he was manumitted, moved to Jerusalem, and began training under the noted Pharisaic scholar Gamaliel. While in Jerusalem, however, Paul became aware of a new threat that was sweeping through Galilee and Judea—the Jesus movement. The majority of the population was illiterate, and the persuasive upstart Jesus challenged the rabbis' teachings. The followers of Jesus expanded, as it was widely believed that he was the Messiah. Jesus's denunciation of these rabbinic traditions, held in high esteem by the Pharisees and the people, was a direct challenge to Paul and his associates. Even though the author of the new faith was crucified, the Christian community exploded in the months and years afterward.

Here is where Paul found a new channel for his righteous zeal. Paul was instrumental in the death of Stephen, and now he threw himself into an attack on the followers of Jesus. As Acts notes, "Saul began ravaging the church, entering house after house; and dragging off men and women, he would put them in prison" (8:3). Looking back, Paul described this as evidence of his zealotry: "I used to persecute the church of God beyond measure and tried to destroy it . . . being an extraordinary Zealot for my ancestral traditions" (Gal 1:13); "as to zeal, a persecutor of the church" (Phil 3:6).

While engaged in the persecution of the church, Saul set out for Damascus, where many of the Christians had fled. On the road, Christ appeared to Saul alive, and this appearance brought about another radical transformation. He realized that the followers of Jesus were right. In short order, Saul's persecution of the Christians ended, and the soon-to-be apostle recognized that his Zealot bloodlust was once again misdirected. Christians were not the infidels that he once thought. Instead of desecrating the teachings of the Torah, Christians were now understood as bringing about the fulfillment of the Torah, revealing the true meaning of the Torah, and providing a proper understanding of the Jewish tradition.

FIGURE 72. Tarsus city street. 1st c. AD.

Paul's zealous service for God did not end there. In fact, Paul once again redirected his zealotry. This was the third stage of the apostle's zealotry. Previously, Saul expressed his zealotry as a guardian of his ancestral traditions, a defender of the sanctity of the Torah. In his service, Saul sought to advance Judaism through violence. Now, the apostle Paul realized with Christ that our battle is not against flesh and blood but rather against spiritual forces of evil in spiritual realms (Eph 6:12). Consequently, the battle is a battle within the soul. Winning this battle involves putting the deeds of the flesh to death. In harmony with this battle, Paul realized that physical suffering is an outward expression of the inner battle. Perhaps it was this zeal, coupled with a sense of remorse for his attacks on the faith, that drove Paul to persevere in his ministry regardless of the physical abuse that he received. Paul's penance was to follow Christ's example and take up his cross. "I have been crucified with Christ, and it is no longer I who live, but Christ lives in me" (Gal 2:20). The purpose of willingly bearing persecution was to cleanse, purge, and wash away the sinful self, resulting in freedom from slavery to sin. "Our old self was crucified with Him in order that our body of sin might be done away with, so that we would no longer be slaves to sin" (Rom 6:6). The zealotry which was formerly outwardly directed in hostility to others was now inwardly directed to eradicate sin and to free the soul.

FIGURE 73. Tarsus ancient city excavations.

Does Understanding Paul as a Former Slave Augment Our Understanding of the Gospel?

What difference does it make that Paul was once a slave? How, if at all, does this bear on his message? First, as we have discussed while examining the individual passages, this understanding helps us see that Paul's words were not detached comments on slavery as an outsider; rather, they were a passionate understanding of life from the inside, a recognition that slavery was an all-consuming incarceration that haunted him for the rest of his life.

The Torah and Slavery

This frame of mind reminded Paul that diverse forms of slavery surround us in devious ways that encumber us in life. Several of Paul's references have a double meaning, one abstract and the other personal. For instance, in the complex discussion of Galatians 4, Paul united himself with the Galatian Christians in their pre-Christian lives (as little children), describing that period as slavery. In the latter part of the chapter, Paul described his Torah-bound Jewish opponents as slaves, the descendants of Hagar. "This Hagar is Mount Sinai in Arabia and corresponds to the present Jerusalem, for she is in slavery with her children" (v. 25). On the other hand, Paul described the uncircumcised gentile Galatians as descendants of the free woman (by implication, Sarah). "Brethren, we are not children of a bondwoman, but of the free woman" (v. 31). With the pronoun "we," Paul, a Jew, continued to identify himself with the freed gentile Galatians. He experienced that freedom twice: once from a human master and then again freedom from the constraints of the Torah. Paul's words are telling: "As at that time he who was born according to the flesh [Ishmael] persecuted him who was born according to the Spirit [Isaac], so it is now also" (v. 29). What was the past and present mentioned here? According to Genesis, Ishmael never persecuted Isaac. Rather, Paul here described his own persecution of the church while enslaved under the Torah. Paul was speaking autobiographically. The words "so it is now" referred to the current trouble with the Judaizers who tried to impose Torah compliance on the Galatians. For Paul, the Torah had become an onerous slave master from whom one should seek release.

Paul did not write simply to cast aspersions on his fellow Jews. Indeed, as the apostle wrote, "I have great sorrow and unceasing grief in my heart. For I could wish that I myself were accursed, separated from Christ for the sake of my brethren, my kinsmen according to the flesh" (Rom 9:2–3). Again, "my heart's desire and my prayer to God for them is for their salvation" (Rom 10:1). Paul's continual practice of preaching *first* in the synagogues of cities and towns was a practice that he repeated until his dying day. Indeed, his passion for fellow Jews was evident in every way; he even suffered beatings at the hands of synagogue officials when, as a Roman citizen, he should not have been so treated. Yet, Paul's experience with the risen Christ taught him that the Torah had become an impediment to a personal faith with God.

I have argued earlier that Paul's frequent and unusual use of first-person pronouns—I, we, us, our—in sections of his letters to the Galatians and Romans should not be understood as a simple literary device. Instead, Paul was including his personal experiences in these passages. He employed slave terminology to describe the conversion he experienced to become free of the Torah, as he pleaded with others to make the same transition, and as he autobiographically connected his early life to the discussion.

Sin and Slavery

Paul made use of slave terminology to describe freedom from the Torah. But more commonly, he applied the same language to refer to sin and enslavement to Satan. Here, the apostle did not describe attachment to sin as a habit or even an addiction. Instead, he described it as something much more sinister: slavery. An addiction may be resolved through practice, counseling, and accountability. However, slavery was another matter beyond one's control. Paul described it as war.

Again employing first-person verbs and pronouns in Romans 6–7, Paul mingled war and military terminology with slavery and freedom expressions to aptly describe what was common in the first-century Roman world and what Paul himself personally experienced—the conquest of territories and the enslavement of populations. For centuries, scholars have debated Paul's bitter struggle with sin as described in Romans 7:14–24. Was Paul describing his former life in Judaism? Was he describing his current inability to practice righteousness? Or was he describing life in Christ without the abiding and empowering presence of the Holy Spirit? In my mind, none of these is sufficient to account for Paul's language. Twice, Paul stated, "I am doing what I do not want. I am no longer the one doing it, but sin dwelling in me" (7:16–17, 20). Paul was describing his life as a slave. This interpretation is reinforced in 7:23: "I see a different law in the members of my body, waging war against the law of my mind and making me a prisoner of the law of sin which is in my members." Paul recounted the trauma of his family's past. The "law" here is not a reference to the Torah but rather the entrenched practice of Roman enslavement. Here again, we see a dual reference. Paul described a struggle with sin, but in these verses, he also described an impossible victory over sin. He could not be describing his pre-Christian life, which he claimed was blameless (Phil 3:6). He could not be describing the victorious Christian life. Instead, he merged his futile early life as a slave with the seemingly impossible struggle over sin. The only way out was through the supernatural intervention of God's Spirit: "The law of the Spirit of life in Christ Jesus has set you free from the law of sin and of death" (8:2).

Slavery to the Elemental Principles of the World

Once again, we encounter one of the difficult expressions in Paul's writings. Within the span of seven verses (Gal 4:3, 9), Paul wrote "elemental things" (στοιχεῖα) twice. At first, he wrote, "As little children we were made slaves under the elemental principles [στοιχεῖα] of this world." Later, he expressed it as "the weak and worthless elemental principles, to which you desire to be enslaved all over again." As we noted in an earlier chapter, both of these examples describe the detested enslavement to these elemental

FIGURE 74. Votive relief of a family offering a sacrifice to Asclepius. A young slave crouches with a lamb at the altar. From the Asclepeion of Piraeus, 4th c. BC. Athens National Archaeological Museum.

principles. Paul used the inclusive "we" in verse 3, claiming that both he and the Galatians were previously made slaves to these elemental principles. Later, in verse 5, Paul described these elemental principles as "weak and worthless." In the context of this passage, the expression referred to the encumbrance of the Torah that the Judaizers were trying to foist on the gentile Galatians, who probably had little acquaintance with the Jewish law. Paul, having jettisoned the Torah previously, recognized that the Torah was weak and worthless. In verse 3, however, the expression is much broader. The Galatians would not have been encumbered by the Torah in their earlier years, although Paul was. Yet, both Paul and the Galatians would have been burdened by Roman laws that supported slavery and oppression. I have argued that "elemental principles" (στοιχεῖα) was a broad expression of institutional laws and customs that enslaved the people—both Jews and gentiles. Paul carried the burden of slavery in Tarsus in addition to the burden of being Torah compliant in Jewish circles. These were the elemental principles that subjugated Paul. The Galatians' servitude to the divine Caesar forced them to submit to weak and worthless pagan practices. For them, these were the elemental principles that enslaved them. World affairs are beyond our control, yet we are subject to the authorities that rule over us. Paul was calling the Galatians to recognize a higher authority who could free them from the practices that impeded their ability to serve a higher master.

Paul was writing to gentiles, describing how both Jews and gentiles were caught up in secular and religious systems, systems that enslave them in detrimental ways. How could he encapsulate these enslaving principles with an appropriate word that includes the Jewish Torah and a Roman system of laws and practices that support slavery? These systems were backed by a worldview that never even questioned the legitimacy of slavery. The word στοιχεῖα (elementary principles) was the term Paul chose.

The Institution of Slavery

Why did Paul not explicitly condemn slavery in all its forms? Here, it is important to understand the first-century Roman world. The institution of slavery was deeply embedded in the economy and customs of the ancient world. From the beginning of time, people enslaved other people. Few who were free raised objections to the practice. Simply put, a deeply entrenched institution strongly supported by the rich and powerful could not be eliminated in short order. Even the traumatic slave revolts that periodically plagued the Romans could not stop the unrelenting forces that drove people into servitude.

Christianity was a beginning. Paul set in motion a critique of slavery that snowballed into a movement, ultimately leading to the condemnation that still echoes throughout the civilized world today. Paul's letters to churches filled with slaves and former slaves began a subtle critique of slavery as utterly sinful. His tactfully worded letters were tempered by an understanding of the repercussions that a more brazen attack on slavery would bring on the new Christian faith, which was already under attack throughout the empire. As time progressed and the Christian faith took deeper root in the Mediterranean world, the emerging abolitionist movement gained momentum.

But with massive slave populations throughout the Mediterranean world in the first century, Paul did not want to cause an uprising that would result in the loss of life and the subsequent suppression of Christianity. The Romans were sensitive to perceived subversive movements that might bring about revolts. Paul knew that Roman law and governance were good as long as they administered justice in a manner that corresponded with God's standards of righteousness. His words in Romans 13:1–7 indicate that Christianity could coexist within the secular parameters of Roman rule. Obviously, Paul knew that the Roman system had flaws, but he recognized that it was better than what could be.

Paul encouraged slaves to gain their freedom if possible (1 Cor 7:21). He ordered the Corinthians, "Do not become slaves of men" (7:23). But to avoid causing disturbances, he thrice said, "Let each man remain in that condition in which he was called" (7:17, 20, 24). For those entrapped in slavery, Paul stated that Christian slaves were the Lord's freedmen and that those Christians who were free were Christ's slaves (7:22). No one was free to freelance; as Christians, we are bound to a master of justice and righteousness.

Slavery and Humility

The humble state of the slave corresponds to the humble life that Christ has called us to. Christians are not to strive for the control of others. The request of John and James on the road to Jerusalem was promptly dismissed (Mark 10:35–45). The brothers approached Jesus, asking to be installed in positions of power at the coming of the kingdom. Jesus's reply indicated that this might be the way of the world, but it was contrary to God's kingdom: "It is not so among you, whoever wishes to become great among you shall be your slave, and whoever wishes to be first among you shall be slave of all" (vv. 43–44). This was illustrated by Jesus himself at the Last Supper. Taking a towel and basin of water, Jesus took the role of a slave and washed the feet of his disciples, saying, "I gave you an example that you also should do as I did to you. Truly, I say to you, a slave is not greater than his master" (John 13:15–16).

Although Paul was not taught by Jesus, he undoubtedly knew many of Jesus's teachings. One of Jesus's most commonly repeated teachings was the need for servants of God to function as servants of one another. Christians were not to aspire to positions of power to control the actions of others. Instead, they were to lead from the bottom of society's social hierarchy. Blessed are the poor in spirit, for theirs is the kingdom of God. Disciples of Christ can serve their Lord while free or enslaved.

Following Jesus's lead, Paul explained, "For though I am free from all men, I have made myself a slave to all, so that I may win more" (1 Cor 9:19). The all-embracing objective of a disciple is to share the life-giving hope of freedom from sin and the richer freedom of salvation in Christ's kingdom. As a former slave, the title that Paul adopted was "Slave of Christ," a moniker that epitomized his life and teachings.

| 10 |

Paul's Vocabulary: The Use of Linguistic Statistics for the Study of Paul

THE CONCLUSIONS OF THIS VOLUME rest primarily on knowledge gleaned from ancient historical sources, an understanding of the social conditions 2,000 years ago, statements from Jerome and Josephus, clues dropped in the Acts of the Apostles, and statements from Paul himself. However, another underlying premise of this book is that a person's vocabulary and word frequency can be used to determine a person's background. After several conversations with another person, one should have a sense of the person's level of education, political leanings, religious inclinations, and perhaps even occupation. The more we listen, the more we learn. These details can be discerned even if they are not directly addressed.

We are fortunate that Paul wrote a great deal of the New Testament. According to the traditional view, Paul wrote thirteen letters and 32,408 of the 138,020 words in the Greek New Testament. That is 23.48 percent of the New Testament, second only to Luke's 37,932 words (27.48 percent). By studying these writings, scholars are able to describe Paul's Jewish background and training as well as his level of involvement in the Greco-Roman world.

Only recently has the dust settled on the old debate regarding Paul's primary worldview. Paul identified himself as an educated and esteemed Jew. Thus, many have found the source of Paul's thought embedded in Judaism.[1] However, his language and thoughts indicate a significant

---

1. W. D. Davies, *Paul and Rabbinic Judaism: Some Rabbinic Elements in Pauline Theology* (Fortress, 1980); Segal, *Paul the Convert*; and Chilton, *Rabbi Paul.*

understanding of the Greco-Roman world, mystery religions, and philosophy. Since Paul spent his early years in Tarsus, an intellectual and philosophical center, some have viewed Paul chiefly as a Hellenist.[2] Today, most scholars recognize that the apostle drew his water from two troughs, Jewish and Hellenistic.[3] The issue is largely dependent on the apostle's vocabulary and worldview.

Based on words and expressions, the German philologist Richard Reitzenstein attempted to anchor Paul's thought world in Gnosticism and the mystery religions. Although few scholars today agree with all of Reitzenstein's conclusions, his approach to studying Paul underscored the importance of vocabulary and philology to find the underpinnings of the apostle's thought.

> As rarely as this is stressed, I see precisely herein the justification of the philological labor in the area of the *history* of religions; it is necessary, for what is involved in these linguistic investigations is much more than language and words alone. Our religious feeling is wordless, but its conceptual elaboration and arrangement in our thought is done in words. . . . Only with the instruments of his language could even a Paul render comprehensible his tremendous religious experience and make it the foundation of his belief; the pre-condition is provided by the conceptual world of his time.[4]

> The sphere of philological labor does not extend to the ultimate origin; it can approach the very innermost personality and the experience of the individual man only by intimation and inference.[5]

---

2. Wilfred L. Knox, *St. Paul and the Church of the Gentiles* (Cambridge University Press, 1939); Alfred Wikenhauser, *Pauline Mysticism: Christ in the Mystical Teaching of St. Paul* (Herder and Herder, 1960); Rudolf Bultmann, *Theology of the New Testament*, 2 vols. (Scribner's Sons, 1951–55); Hyam Maccoby, *Paul and Hellenism* (Trinity Press International, 1991); Richard Reitzenstein, *Hellenistic Mystery-Religions : Their Basic Ideas and Significance*, trans. John E. Steely (Pickwick, 1978); and Abraham J. Malherbe, *Paul and the Popular Philosophers* (Fortress, 1989).

3. Despite his title, Troels Engberg-Pedersen states: "The book aims to situate Paul's thought firmly within the ancient ethical tradition as this was inaugurated by Plato's Socrates, developed by Aristotle and given classic shape in Stoicism. . . . The position is that there is a reading here which helps to solve a number of issues and that should be seen as complementing other recent interpretations of Paul—not least those stressing his Jewish profile—rather than as a substitute for them." *Paul and the Stoics* (Westminster John Knox, 2000), ix. So also Witherington, *Paul Quest*.

4. Reitzenstein, *Hellenistic Mystery-Religions*, 537–38 (emphasis original).

5. Reitzenstein, 539.

Our language is a fingerprint of our identity, a verbal DNA of the mysteries of our past.

Statistical data reinforces the conclusions of this book. Paul's vocabulary and conceptual world are disproportionately tilted toward words and their cognates related to slavery, freedom, and adoption. This alone does not prove that Paul was a slave. At a minimum, it tells us that Paul was in all respects familiar with slavery. This would suggest that Paul was either involved in the slave trade in some capacity or the victim of such trade.

The Data

Scholars who study Paul's writings generally fall into one of three camps. The traditional position, which many believe, is that the apostle wrote all thirteen letters attributed to him in the New Testament. Others do not believe that Paul wrote the Pastoral Epistles (1–2 Tim; Titus), considering them pseudepigraphal writings written by Paul's followers and falsely attributed to him. These scholars believe there are only ten authentic Pauline letters. Still others, for various reasons, are also skeptical of Ephesians, Colossians, and 2 Thessalonians, believing that Paul wrote a total of only seven letters in the New Testament.

The Greek New Testament text contains 138,020 words. If Paul wrote thirteen letters (32,408 words) in accordance with the traditional view, then he wrote 23.48 percent of the New Testament. If he wrote ten letters (28,920 words), not including 1–2 Timothy and Titus, then he wrote 20.95 percent of the New Testament. If Paul wrote only seven letters (24,093 words), then he wrote 17.46 percent of the New Testament.

Percentage of Pauline Letters in the NT[7]

Paul as author	Total word count in NT	Percentage of NT text
13 (traditional view)	32,408 words	23.48%
10 (minus 3)	28,920 words	20.95%
7 (minus 6)	24,093 words	17.46%

I have further broken down the total number of words in Paul's letters into three broad concepts: "slavery," "freedom," and "adoption" (cognates

7. Nestle Aland 27 Greek New Testament.

and associated words are lumped together in these three categories) as follows:

Slavery
ἀνθρωπάρεσκος (man-pleaser)
δουλαγωγέω (to make a slave, to treat as a slave)
δουλεία (slavery, bondage)
δουλεύω (to be a slave, to be subject)
δοῦλος (adj., slave)
δοῦλος (noun, slave, servant)
δουλόω (to enslave) / καταδουλόω (to enslave)
οἰκονομία (stewardship, management) / οἰκονόμος (steward, manager, administrator)

Freedom
ἀπελεύθερος (emancipated slave, freedman)
ἀπολύτρωσις (ransom, deliverance)
ἐλευθερία (freedom, liberty)
ἐλεύθερος (freedom)
ἐλευθερόω (to set free)
ἐξαγοράζω (buy back, redeem)
ῥύομαι (rescue, redeem, set free)

Adoption
υἱοθεσία (adoption)

The statistics below demonstrate that Paul used these terms of "slavery," "freedom," and "adoption" more than twice as often as writers of the other NT books. This strongly suggests that these concepts were distinctive characteristics of Paul's thought world. For example, according to the traditional view, Paul wrote 23.48% of the NT. Yet, he accounts for 49.25% of the slavery, freedom, and adoption terms found in the NT. For those scholars who do not believe that Paul authored 1 and 2 Timothy and Titus, Paul wrote 20.95% of the NT. For those holding this view, Paul accounts for 44.74% of the slavery, freedom and adoption terms. Likewise, for those scholars who subscribe to the belief that Paul wrote only seven letters, he wrote 17.46% of the NT, yet he is responsible for 34.96% of the usage of these terms in the NT. In other words, regardless of one's view of Pauline authorship, the statistics demonstrate that Paul disproportionately used slave, freedom, and adoption terminology more than twice as often as the authors of the rest of the NT.

Number of Times Terms Used in Paul's Letters Versus All of NT			
Term	In Paul's Letters	In NT	Paul's % of NT
"Slavery"	13 letters: 75x	NT: 188x	39.89%
	10 letters: 68x	NT: 188x	36.17%
	7 letters: 51x	NT: 188x	27.13%
"Freedom"	13 letters: 51x	NT: 73x	69.86%
	10 letters: 48x	NT: 73x	65.75%
	7 letters: 38x	NT: 73x	52.05%
"Adoption"	13 letters: 5x	NT: 5x	100%
	10 letters: 5x	NT: 5x	100%
	7 letters: 4x	NT: 5x	80%
Total Times	**13 letters: 131x**	**NT: 266x**	**49.25%**
	10 letters: 119x	**NT: 266x**	**44.74%**
	7 letters: 93x	**NT: 266x**	**34.96%**

Below is a comprehensive glossary of Greek terms related to slavery, freedom, adoption, and redemption used in Paul's letters and in other places in the New Testament. Following are descriptions of these terms and their location in Paul's letters and the New Testament.

Greek term	Brief translation	# in Paul	# in NT
ἀνθρωπάρεσκος	man-pleaser	2	2
ἀπελεύθερος	emancipated slave, freedman	1	1
ἀπολύτρωσις	ransom, deliverance	7	10
δουλαγωγέω	to make a slave, to treat as a slave	1	1
δουλεία	slavery, bondage	4	5
δουλεύω	to be a slave, to be subject	17	25
δοῦλος (δοῦλα)	slave (adj.)	2	2

Greek term	Brief translation	# in Paul	# in NT
δοῦλος	slave, servant	30	124
δουλόω	to enslave	6	8
ἐλευθερία	freedom, liberty	7	11
ἐλεύθερος	free	16	23
ἐλευθερόω	to set free	5	7
ἐξαγοράζω	buy back, redeem	4	4
καταδουλόω	to enslave	2	2
οἰκονομία	stewardship, management	6	9
οἰκονόμος	steward, manager, administrator	5	10
ῥύομαι	rescue, redeem, set free	11	15
υἱοθεσία	adoption	5	5

ἀνθρωπάρεσκος (man-pleaser): The term ἀνθρωπάρεσκος is used only in reference to slavery, representing the actions of a slave designed to please their master.[8] The compound word is split into two words in Galatians 1:10—ἀνθρώποις ἀρέσκειν—with the same meaning: "If I were still *trying to please men*, I would not be a slave of Christ."

Paul: Eph 6:6; Col 3:22

NT: None

ἀπελεύθερος (emancipated slave, freedman): The word occurs only once in the New Testament. As a compound word, ἀπελεύθερος (emancipated slave, freedman) combines the preposition ἀπό (from, away from) with ἐλεύθερος (freedom).[9] The term was a technical term for former slaves who had been manumitted.[10]

Paul: 1 Cor 7:22

NT: None

ἀπολύτρωσις (ransom, deliverance): "It means 'setting free for a ransom,' and is used of prisoners of war, slaves, and criminals condemned to

8. H. Bietenhard, *NIDNTT*, 2:817; Werner Foerster, "ἀρέσκω," *TDNT* 1:456.

9. J. Blunck, *NIDNTT*, 1:717–18; Heinrich Schlier, "ἐλεύθερος, ἐλευθερόω, ἐλευθερία, ἀπελεύθερος," *TDNT* 2:487–502.

10. Fee, *First Epistle to the Corinthians*, 353.

death. . . . In the NT ἀπολύτρωσις is always definitive [of] redemption or manumission."[11]

Paul: Rom 3:24; 8:23; 1 Cor 1:30; Eph 1:7, 14; 4:30; Col 1:14

NT: Luke 21:28; Heb 9:15; 11:35

δουλαγωγέω (to make a slave, to treat as a slave): "'To lead into slavery,' 'to cause to live the life of a slave.' This is a rare word."[12]

Paul: 1 Cor 9:27

NT: None

δουλεία (slavery, bondage): "Δουλεία implies obedience to the will of another. In this case, whether voluntarily or compulsorily, ἐλευθερία [freedom] is lost and the state of dependence reached which constitutes the situation of the δοῦλος [slave]."[13]

Paul: Rom 8:15, 21; Gal 4:24; 5:1

NT: Heb 2:15

δουλεύω (to be a slave, to serve, to be subject): In contrast to δουλόω, which is the act of enslaving, δουλεύω generally functions to express the service of a slave. "It is precisely the concept of *douleuo*, in contrast to that of *diakoneo* (serve), that emphasizes the obligatory character of the service for God and to one's neighbour that is the duty of the community of those who have been set free by Jesus Christ."[14]

Paul: Rom 6:6; 7:6, 25; 9:12; 12:11; 14:18; 16:18; Gal 4:8, 9, 25; 5:13; Eph 6:7; Phil 2:22; Col 3:24; 1 Thess 1:9; 1 Tim 6:2; Titus 3:3

NT: Matt 6:24 (2x); Luke 15:29; 16:13 (2x); John 8:33; Acts 7:7; 20:19

δοῦλος (adj.; slave): Technically, δοῦλος is an adjective, but in the two times it is used in the New Testament, the adjective functions substantively like the noun.

Paul: Rom 6:19 (2x)

NT: None

---

11. F. Büchsel, "λύτρωσις, ἀπολύτρωσις, κτλ," *TDNT* 4:352, 351–56. Cf. J. Schneider and C. Brown, *NIDNTT*, 3:189–200.

12. Karl H. Rengstorf, "δοῦλος, δουλεία, δουλόω, κτλ," *TDNT* 2:279–80.

13. Rengstorf, *TDNT* 2:274. Cf. Rudolf Tuente, "Slave–δοῦλος," *NIDNTT*, 3:592–98.

14. Tuente, *NIDNTT*, 3:592–98; Rengstorf, *TDNT* 2:261–79.

δοῦλος (noun; slave, servant): Not surprisingly, this is by far the most common term in the New Testament related to slavery.[15] Most of these occur in the Gospels (72/124, or 58.06 percent). Of these, most are in the Gospels of Matthew and Luke (56/124, or 45.16 percent) and the Q material. If the gospel source Q came from Galilean Christians,[16] like Paul, they would have been traumatized by the Roman conquest of Galilee and the enslavement of friends and neighbors. This may account for why they disproportionately recalled and incorporated slave teachings into Q and the Jesus accounts. Mark's Gospel only has five references to this term. Even though the Gospels skew the percentages, the number of uses of δοῦλος in Paul's writings still exceeds the percentage of Paul's writings in the New Testament (30/124 = 24.19% vs. 23.48%).

> **Paul:** Rom 1:1; 6:16 (2x), 17, 20; 1 Cor 7:21, 22 (2x), 23; 12:13; 2 Cor 4:5; Gal 1:10; 3:28; 4:1, 7; Eph 6:5–6, 8; Phil 1:1; 2:7; Col 3:11, 22; 4:1, 12; 1 Tim 6:1; 2 Tim 2:24; Titus 1:1; 2:9; Phlm 16 (2x)

> **NT:** Matt 8:9; 10:24, 25; 13:27–28; 18:23, 26, 28, 32; 20:27; 21:34, 35, 36; 22:3, 4, 6, 8, 10; 24:45, 46, 48, 50; 25:14, 19, 21, 23, 26, 30; 26:51; Mark 10:44; 12:2, 4; 13:34; 14:47; Luke 2:29; 7:2, 3, 8, 10; 12:37, 43, 45, 46, 47; 14:17, 21, 22, 23; 15:22; 17:7, 9, 10; 19:13, 15, 17, 22; 20:10, 11; 22:50; John 4:51; 8:34, 35; 13:16; 15:15, 20; 18:10, 18, 26; Acts 2:18; 4:29; 16:17; Jas 1:1; 1 Pet 2:16; 2 Pet 1:1; 2:19; Jude 1; Rev 1:1 (2x); 2:20; 6:15; 7:3; 10:7; 11:18; 13:16; 15:3; 19:2, 5, 18; 22:3, 6

δουλόω (to enslave): Δουλόω refers to the act of enslaving another person or object.[17] In Paul's writings, the term is always used figuratively. The word is used in Romans to refer to the voluntary act of enslaving oneself to "righteousness" and "God." In 1 Corinthians, Paul claimed that the believer is not enslaved to their unbelieving spouse (7:15). Later, in 1 Cor 9:19, he asserted that he made himself a slave to all people in order to win others to

---

15. Tuente, *NIDNTT*, 3:592–98. "*Doulos* and its cognates appear very frequently in the Pauline writings in comparison to the rest of the NT," 595. Rengstorf, *TDNT* 2:261–79.

16. "It is, therefore, tempting to assume that the redaction of Q took place somewhere in Galilee and that the document as a whole reflects the experience of a Galilean community of followers of Jesus." Helmut Koester, *Ancient Christian Gospels: Their History and Development* (Trinity Press International, 1990), 164. See also John Dominic Crossan, *The Historical Jesus: The Life of a Mediterranean Jewish Peasant* (HarperSanFrancisco, 1992), 429; Dale C. Allison Jr., *The Jesus Tradition in Q* (Trinity Press International, 1997), 53; and William E. Arnal, *Jesus and the Village Scribes: Galilean Conflicts and the Setting of Q* (Fortress, 2001).

17. Rengstorf, *TDNT* 2:279.

Christ. In Galatians, Paul used the word to describe his childhood: "While we were children, we had been enslaved under the basic principles of the world" (4:3).

Paul: Rom 6:18, 22; 1 Cor 7:15; 9:19; Gal 4:3; Titus 2:3

NT: Acts 7:6; 2 Pet 2:19

ἐλευθερία (freedom, liberty): The noun ἐλευθερία is never used with regard to political freedom but rather was used in reference to freedom in contrast to slavery or freedom from the Torah. In these contexts, the Torah was usually depicted as a slave master.[18]

Paul: Rom 8:21; 1 Cor 10:29; 2 Cor 3:17; Gal 2:4; 5:1, 13 (2x)

NT: Jas 1:25; 2:12; 1 Pet 2:16; 2 Pet 2:19

ἐλεύθερος (free): As an adjective, ἐλεύθερος carries similar meanings as the noun and was most commonly used as a substantival adjective: "free man" or "free woman."[19]

Paul: Rom 6:20; 7:3; 1 Cor 7:21, 22, 39; 9:1, 19; 12:13; Gal 3:28; 4:22, 23, 26, 30, 31; Eph 6:8; Col 3:11

NT: Matt 17:26; John 8:33, 36; 1 Pet 2:16; Rev 6:15; 13:16; 19:18

ἐλευθερόω (to set free): Another cognate of ἐλευθερία, the verb ἐλευθερόω describes the action of setting free. "The vb. *eleuthero* is used in the NT exclusively for the act which occurs or has occurred through Jesus: 'The truth will make you free' (Jn. 8:32), 'having been set free from sin' (Rom. 6:18, cf. 22)."[20]

Paul: Rom 6:18, 22; 8:2, 21; Gal 5:1

NT: John 8:32, 36

ἐξαγοράζω (buy back, redeem): A compound word combining the preposition ἐκ with ἀγοράζω, ἐξαγοράζω carries the meaning of making a purchase from the agora, in particular, the purchase of a slave from a slave market. The word has similar connotations to the practice of sacral

---

18. Blunck, *NIDNTT*, 1:715–21; Schlier, "ἐλεύθερος, ἐλευθερόω, ἐλευθερία, ἀπελεύθερος," *TDNT* 2:487–502.

19. Blunck, *NIDNTT*, 1:715–21; Schlier, *TDNT* 2:487–502.

20. Blunck, *NIDNTT*, 1:717; Schlier, *TDNT* 2:487–502.

manumissions practiced at the Delphic Oracle; however, it is the crucifixion of Christ (Gal 3:13) and not a monetary payment to Apollo that brings about freedom.[21]

Paul: Gal 3:13; 4:5; Eph 5:16; Col 4:5

NT: None

Καταδουλόω (to make a slave, to enslave): "Καταδουλόω is to some extent a stronger form of δουλόω. The basic meaning is 'to make a slave,' 'to enslave.'"[22]

Paul: 2 Cor 11:20; Gal 2:4

NT: None

οἰκονομία (stewardship, management): The word οἰκονομία refers to the responsibility of managing the home and business of a wealthy person.[23] Wealthy people during the first century hired individuals (οἰκονόμος, "steward") to manage their affairs and businesses. In practically every instance, the stewards were slaves. Paul repeatedly referred to his stewardship of the gospel. "I have a stewardship entrusted to me" (1 Cor 9:17; cf. Eph. 1:10; 3:2, 9; Col. 1:25).

Paul: 1 Cor 9:17; Eph 1:10; 3:2, 9; Col 1:25; 1 Tim 1:4

NT: Luke 16:2, 3, 4

οἰκονόμος (steward, manager, administrator): In the first century, the steward or household manager was generally a slave. "The term *oikonomos* was used to designate those slaves who worked as stewards of households or businesses; they were sometimes plantation managers or financial bursars. . . . A careful study of the term, however, shows that for the early Roman imperial period it usually indicated a slave or freed manager. . . . Landvogt claims, however, that by the early Roman period the situation had completely changed and that the *oikonomoi* were without exception taken from the slave populations."[24]

---

21. David H. Field, "Buy, Sell, Market–ἀγοράζω," *NIDNTT*, 1:267–68; Büchsel, "ἀγοράζω, ἐξαγοράζω," *TDNT* 1:124–28.

22. Rengstorf, *TDNT* 2:279.

23. Jürgen Goetzmann, "House–οἰκονομία," *NIDNTT*, 2:253–56; Otto Michel, "οἰκονομία," *TDNT* 5:151–53.

24. Martin, *Slavery as Salvation*, 15–16. Peter Vandvogt, *Epigraphische Untersuchung über den Oikonomos*, 8, 13; J. Goetzmann, *NIDNTT*, 2:253–56; O. Michel, *TDNT* 5:149–51.

Paul: Rom 16:23; 1 Cor 4:1–2; Gal 4:2; Titus 1:7

NT: Luke 12:42; 16:1, 3, 8; 1 Pet 4:10

ῥύομαι (to rescue, save, redeem, set free, deliver): In the New Testament, "in content it always means 'to save,' men are always the object, and God is always the author of salvation."[25] Two words for the act of salvation ("to save") are common to the New Testament. The more common word σώζω is used 114 times in the New Testament, but ῥύομαι only occurs fifteen times. In the Septuagint, the word ῥύομαι is used 141 times.[26] In several passages, ῥύομαι is used to describe rescue from bondage. "I will *free* you from slavery. I will also redeem you" (Exod 6:6 LXX). "Has any one of the gods of the nations *freed* his land from the hand of the king of Assyria?" (2 Kgs 18:33, also Isa 36:19). "Go out from Babylon, flee from Chaldea, declare this with a shout of joy, proclaim it, send it forth to the end of the earth; say, 'The Lord has *freed* his slave Jacob!'" (Isa 48:20 LXX). "Was it not you who dried up the sea, the waters of the great deep; who made the depths of the sea a way for the *redeemed* to cross over?" (Isa 51:10 LXX). The term often has connotations of rescuing or freeing from slavery.

Paul: Rom 7:24; 11:26; 15:31; 2 Cor 1:10 (2x); Col 1:13; 1 Thess 1:10; 2 Thess 3:2; 2 Tim 3:11; 4:17–18

NT: Matt 6:13; 27:43; Luke 1:74; 11:4; 2 Pet 2:7, 9

υἱοθεσία (adoption): The word υἱοθεσία is rare and never occurs in the Septuagint.[27] The fact that Paul used the word five times suggests that he was well aware of the concept and procedure of adoption.

Paul: Rom 8:15, 23; 9:4; Gal 4:5; Eph 1:5

NT: None

Conclusion

It cannot be denied that each person has a unique vocabulary and writing style. By exploring *how* authors communicate and what words they choose, it is possible to discover more than what is written. Over the past century scholars have pored over the New Testament writings to discover the

25. Wilhelm Kasch, ῥύομαι, *TDNT* 6:1002.

26. Schneider and Brown, *NIDNTT*, 3:200–204; W. Kasch, *TDNT* 6:998–1003.

27. Bauer, *NIDNTT*, 1:287–89; Peter Wülfing von Martitz and Eduard Schweizer, "υἱοθεσία," *TDNT* 8:397–99.

unique vocabulary of their authors. With documents much smaller than the Pauline corpus, researchers are confident that they have a sense of each of the gospel writers' vocabulary, syntax, and chief theological convictions.

One of the chief reasons why most scholars discount Paul's authorship of the letter to the Hebrews is its vocabulary and syntax, which differ significantly from the genuine letters of Paul. Additionally, many of the concepts communicated in Hebrews differ from those found in Paul's letters. Some scholars also see differences in the vocabulary of the Pastoral Epistles in relation to Paul's other letters as a reason to dismiss them as authentic. Likewise, a chief reason many scholars believe that the Apocalypse was written by a different person named John is that its vocabulary and syntax differ from what we read in John's Gospel and letters. On a much smaller scale, some scholars question the authenticity of 2 Peter, based in part on verbal differences. Scholars may question authorship based on the vocabulary of a text, or if one maintains the authenticity of a document, one must account for the peculiarities of its vocabulary. Nevertheless, however one deals with the issues of authorship, it is necessary to account for the vocabulary of the authors.

The argument regarding the statistics of vocabulary can be turned in either direction. Those defending Pauline authorship of the Pastorals, the authorship of Revelation by John, and even Pauline authorship of Hebrews can dismiss the value of examining the vocabulary of these writings. However, ignoring the data seems careless and impetuous. There is some legitimacy in studying statistics. One must account for the data in some way.

However, the argument for using word statistics can be overplayed. If the sample size is not large enough, the data leads us nowhere. There must be a sizable amount of literature addressing a somewhat similar topic to conduct any meaningful analysis. The arguments can sometimes be convoluted. In some cases, authenticity has been discounted because of too many similarities. Some have argued that the vocabulary in the letters to the Ephesians and the Colossians is so similar that one or the other must be a pseudepigraphal document written by someone mimicking Paul's style. This belief has gained a great deal of traction, even if it is understood that Paul wrote both letters from prison, at the same time, to churches in the same geographic region, dealing with similar problems and carried by the same person. Statistical analysis can be valuable, but it must be contextualized and used in conjunction with other supporting data. As Mark Twain famously said, "There are three kinds of lies: lies, damn lies and statistics." The statistics presented here are one leg of the argument.

We began this volume describing the value of circumstantial evidence and secondhand testimony. Most jury trials today depend entirely on such evidence. Crimes are generally not conducted in the presence of eyewitnesses. Investigators gather individual articles of evidence to exonerate or convict suspects. Although each piece of evidence may not directly prove a crime, when they are pieced together by skilled prosecuting attorneys, they create a compelling case for a conviction. Isolated apart from the broader narrative, the separate elements could be attributed to coincidence or random chance. But together, the collection of evidence may provide sufficient proof of the accusation.

In the case of the Paul, we are not dealing with a crime or a matter that would denigrate his character. So, the analogy of a criminal investigation is not a perfect parallel. Yet, the due diligence required in prosecuting a criminal case is necessary to investigate this issue. This is a matter of discovering an existential facet of the apostle tightly woven into his words, thoughts, and actions. Looking back to the distant past, it is a matter where much of the evidence has been lost. There is, however, evidence that remains. Some of it is circumstantial evidence and some of it is secondhand testimony. Fortunately, in our case, we do not have to meet the stringent standards of proof required by our legal system.

Our system of criminal justice depends on a high standard of proof for a conviction, and the term "beyond reasonable doubt" is the bar that must be crossed. Beyond reasonable doubt is the highest standard of proof in any court of law. The US Constitution does not define "beyond reasonable doubt," and the term is understood variously from person to person. Only one contrary person out of the twelve on a typical jury may cause a hung jury. Many criminal cases are unresolved because they fall short of this burden of proof.

Civil trials are different from criminal trials. In civil trials, the standard of "beyond reasonable doubt" is not necessary. Instead, civil cases hinge on "the preponderance of evidence." In these trials, the standard for the burden of proof must exceed 50 percent, which is much lower than in criminal cases. If the bulk of the evidence sustains the lawsuit or civil action, then the case may be proven and won. As with criminal cases, civil cases require the same diligence in the use of circumstantial evidence and secondhand testimony, but the bar for the burden of proof is reduced to the level of what is most probable.

In Paul's case, Jerome's testimony is important. He received information from earlier sources, and it is impossible to determine how far back the tradition can be traced. It is probable that Jerome received the tradition from Origen, the preeminent postapostolic scholar of his time. But where did Origen get the information? He had access to early Christian libraries at both Alexandria and Caesarea, but the trail dries up with Origen. Equally important is the circumstantial evidence from Acts 6–8. It is here that Paul first appears in Luke's narrative. The connection of Paul with the Synagogue of the Freedmen in Jerusalem (6:9), his involvement in the stoning of Stephen, and his subsequent persecution of Christians places him among the zealous diaspora Jews who returned to Jerusalem. The connection with the synagogue (implied with the reference to members from Cilicia) suggests that Paul was a freedman.

Some of the strongest testimony from Paul comes from his statements in Galatians 1:10 where he asserted that he was *no longer* a "man-pleaser" (a term used for slaves) but was rather a "slave of Christ." I have argued that in this letter (perhaps his earliest), the apostle revealed more of his past than in any other of his other known correspondence. Here, he frequently included first-person terms in the context of slavery and concluded the letter with a reference to the "brand-marks of Jesus" on his body. This was a physical mark, either a brand or tattoo, commonly applied by masters to their slaves to identify them as such.

It is not necessary to prove that all of Paul's references to slavery or freedom are specific recollections of the apostle's past experiences in slavery. Several of them are just that, especially in his letter to the Galatians and probably also in the letter to the Romans. His unnecessary inclusion of the first-person pronouns "I" or "we" justify the belief that Paul was making a personal connection to his early life. In other instances, however, Paul may not have been dealing directly with his past. Nonetheless, for one who had been conditioned or traumatized by slavery, it would have been impossible to escape from that frame of mind. This was the apostle's language, the pool of thought from which Paul drew concepts and meaning. The statistics from the last chapter that illustrated how slave terminology permeated Paul's vocabulary are compelling and must be explained by assuming that he had significant involvement in slavery as a slave, slave master, or slavetrader.

The conclusions of the earlier chapters lead us to the determination that Paul was indeed a slave, not metaphorically, but actually a slave during his early life. This conclusion is drawn from literary and historical sources, both Christian and non-Christian. It is drawn from Paul's own cautiously veiled statements sprinkled throughout his letters. It can also be drawn from the Acts of the Apostles, Paul's Roman name, his Roman citizenship, and his association with the Synagogue of the Freedmen. Independently, this data could be dismissed as hearsay or circumstantial evidence. Collectively, however, the information provides solid ground for the conclusion.

FIGURE 75. Funerary stele of Phylonoe. The woman's slave holds Phylonoe's baby who yearns for her deceased mother. Found at Psychiko. 4th c. BC. Athens National Archaeological Museum.

Bibliography

Abel, Ernest L. "The Myth of Jewish Slavery in Ptolemaic Egypt." *REJ* 127 (1968): 253–58.

Allison, Dale C., Jr. *The Jesus Tradition in Q*. Trinity Press International, 1997.

Appian. *Roman History, Volume III*. Edited and translated by Brian McGing. Loeb Classical Library 4. Harvard University Press, 2019.

Apuleius. *The Golden Ass, or Metamorphoses*. Translated by E. J. Kenney. Penguin, 1998.

Arnal, William E. *Jesus and the Village Scribes: Galilean Conflicts and the Setting of Q*. Fortress, 2001.

Atkinson, Kathleen M. T. "The Purpose of the Manumission Laws of Augustus." *Irish Jurist*, n.s. 1 (1966): 356–74.

Barrett, Charles Kingsley. *The Acts of the Apostles*. Vol. 1. ICC. T&T Clark, 1994.

———. *The First Epistle to the Corinthians*. HNTC. Harper & Row, 1968.

———. *Freedom and Obligation: A Study of the Epistle to the Galatians*. Westminster John Knox, 1985.

Barrier, Jeremy W. "Paul and His Master: Defining and Applying a Postcolonial Definition to Galatians 6:17." *CSSRB* 35 (2006): 34–38.

Barth, Markus, and Helmut Blanke. *The Letter to Philemon: A New Translation with Notes and Commentary*. ECC. Eerdmans, 2000.

Bell, Albert A., Jr. *Exploring the New Testament World: An Illustrated Guide to the World of Jesus and the First Christians*. Thomas Nelson, 1998.

Bennett, H. "The Exposure of Infants in Ancient Rome." *CJ* 18 (1923): 341–51.

Betz, Hans Dieter. *Der Apostel Paulus und die sokratische Tradition: Eine exegetische Untersuchung zu seiner "Apologie" 2 Korinther 10–13*. BHTh 45. Mohr, 1972

———. *Galatians: A Commentary on Paul's Letter to the Churches in Galatia*. Hermeneia. Fortress, 1979.

Bock, Darrell L. *Acts*. BECNT. Baker Academic, 2007.

Bockmuehl, Markus. "The Noachide Commandments and New Testament Ethics with Special Reference to Acts 15 and Pauline Halakhah." *RB* 102 (1995): 72–101.

Bömer, Franz. *Untersuchungen über die Religion der Sklaven in Griechenland und Rom*. 4 vols. F. Steiner, 1958–63.

Borgen, Peder. "Some Hebrew and Pagan Features in Philo's and Paul's Interpretation of Hagar and Ishmael." In *The New Testament and Hellenistic Judaism*. Edited by Peder Borgen and Søren Giverson. Aarhus University Press, 1995.

Bradley, Keith R. *Slavery and Society at Rome*. Cambridge University Press, 1994.

———. *Slaves and Masters in the Roman Empire: A Study in Social Control*. Oxford University Press, 1987.

Breytenbach, Cilliers, and Christiane Zimmermann. *Early Christianity in Lycaonia and Adjacent Areas: From Paul to Amphilochius of Iconium*. Early Christianity in Asia Minor 101. Brill, 2017.

Brown, Colin, ed. *New International Dictionary of New Testament Theology*. 4 vols. Zondervan, 1975–85.

Bruce, F. F. *The Epistle to the Galatians*. NIGTC. Eerdmans, 1982.

Brunt, P. A. *Italian Manpower 225 B.C.–A.D. 14*. Clarendon, 1987.

Buckland, William Warwick. *The Roman Law of Slavery: The Conditions of the Slave in Private Law from Augustus to Justinian*. Cambridge University Press, 1908.

Bultmann, Rudolf. *The Second Letter to the Corinthians*. Augsburg Fortress, 1985.

———. *Theology of the New Testament*. 2 vols. Scribner's Sons, 1951–55.

Burton, Ernest DeWitt. *Critical and Exegetical Commentary on the Epistle to the Galatians*. ICC. T&T Clark, 1921.

Byron, John. *Slavery Metaphors in Early Judaism and Pauline Christianity: A Traditio-Historical and Exegetical Examination*. WUNT 2.162. Mohr Siebeck, 2003.

Cadbury, Henry J. *The Book of Acts in History*. Black, 1955.

Cadwallader, Alan H. *Fragments of Colossae: Sifting Through the Traces*. ATF Press, 2015.

Callahan, Allen Dwight. "Paul's Epistle to Philemon: Toward an Alternative *Argumentum*." *HTR* 86 (1993): 357–76.

Charlesworth, James H., ed. *The Old Testament Pseudepigrapha*. 2 vols. Doubleday, 1983.

Chilton, Bruce. *Rabbi Paul: An Intellectual Biography*. Doubleday, 2004.

Ciampa, Roy E., and Brian S. Rosner. *The First Letter to the Corinthians*. PNTC. Eerdmans, 2010.

Cicero, M. Tullius. *De officiis*. Translated by Walter Miller. Cambridge. Loeb Classical Library 30. Harvard University Press,1913.

Cicero. *De oratore*. Translated by E. W. Sutton and H. Rackham. Loeb Classical Library 348. Harvard University Press, 1942.

Cicero, M. Tullius. *Pro Lege Manilia. Pro Caecina. Pro Cluentio. Pro Rabirio Perduellionis Reo*. Translated by H. Grose Hodge. Loeb Classical Library 198. Harvard University Press, 1927.

Cohen, Shaye J. D. "Crossing the Boundary and Becoming a Jew." *HTR* 82 (1989): 11–33.

Conzelmann, Hans. *Acts of the Apostles*. Hermeneia. Fortress, 1987.

Cranfield, C. E. B. *A Critical and Exegetical Commentary on the Epistle to the Romans*. Vol. 1. ICC. T&T Clark, 1975.

Crossan, John Dominic. *The Historical Jesus: The Life of a Mediterranean Jewish Peasant*. HarperSanFrancisco, 1992.

D'Andria, Francesco. *Hierapolis of Phrygia (Pamukkale): An Archaeological Guide*. Ege Yayınları, 2003.

Davies, W. D. *Paul and Rabbinic Judaism: Some Rabbinic Elements in Pauline Theology.* Fortress, 1980.

Deissmann, Adolf. *Light from the Ancient East: The New Testament Illustrated by Recently Discovered Texts of the Graeco-Roman World.* Translated by Lionel R. M. Strachan. Harper & Brothers, 1922.

Derrett, J. Duncan M. "'Bechuqey Hagoyim': Damascus Document IX, 1 Again." *RevQ* 11 (1983): 409–15.

deSilva, David A. *Honor, Patronage, Kinship and Purity.* IVP Academic, 2000.

de Souza, Philip. *Piracy in the Graeco-Roman World.* Cambridge University Press, 1999.

Dinkler, Erich. "Jesu Wort vom Kreuztragen." In *Neutestamentliche Studien für R. Bultmann: Zu seinem siebzigsten Geburtstag am 20. August 1954.* Edited by Walther Eltester. BZNW 21. Töpelmann, 1954.

Dio Chrysostom. *Discourses.* Translated by J. W. Cohoon and H. Lamar Crosby. Loeb Classical Library 358. Harvard University Press, 1940.

Dionysius of Halicarnassus. *Roman Antiquities.* Vol. 4, *Books 6.49–7.* Translated by Earnest Cary. LCL 364. Harvard University Press, 1943.

Dodd, Brian J. "Christ's Slave, People Pleasers and Galatians 1:10." *NTS* 42 (1996): 90–104.

Donaldson, Terence L. *Paul and the Gentiles: Remapping the Apostle's Convictional World.* Fortress, 1997.

Dunn, James D. G. *The Epistles to the Colossians and Philemon.* Eerdmans, 1996.

———. *Romans 1–8.* WBC 38A. Word, 1988.

Engberg-Pedersen, Troels. *Paul and the Stoics.* Westminster John Knox, 2000.

Epictetus. *Discourses, Books 1–2.* Translated by W. A. Oldfather. LCL 131. Harvard University Press, 1925.

———. *Discourses, Books 3–4.* Translated by W. A. Oldfather. LCL 218. Harvard University Press, 1925.

———. *Enchiridion.* Translated by W. A. Oldfather. Loeb Classical Library 218. Harvard University Press, 1928.

Euripides. *Fragments: Aegeus-Meleager*. Edited and translated by Christopher Collard and Martin Cropp. Loeb Classical Library 504. Harvard University Press, 2008.

Fairchild, Mark R. "Paul's Pre-Christian Zealot Associations: A Re-examination of Gal 1:14 and Acts 22:3." *NTS* 45 (1999): 514–32.

———. *The Underwater Basilica of Nicaea: Archaeology in the Birthplace of Christian Theology*. IVP Academic, 2024.

Fairchild, Mark R., and Jordan K. Monson. "Paul Unchained: What If the Apostle Grew Up a Slave? Would It Change the Way We Read Him?" *Christianity Today* 68.4 (2024): 34–47.

Fee, Gordon D. *The First Epistle to the Corinthians*. Rev. ed. NICNT. Eerdmans, 2014.

Finkelstein, Louis. "Some Examples of the Maccabean Halaka." *JBL* 49 (1930): 20–42.

Finley, Moses I. *Ancient Slavery and Modern Ideology*. Chatto & Windus, 1980.

Fitzmyer, Joseph A. *The Acts of the Apostles*. AB 31. Doubleday, 1998.

———. *First Corinthians*. AB 32. Yale University Press, 2008.

———. *The Letter to Philemon*. AB 34C. Doubleday, 2000.

———. *Romans*. AB 33. Doubleday, 1993.

Frank, Tenney. *An Economic Survey of Ancient Rome*. Vol. 1, *Rome and Italy of the Republic*. Johns Hopkins University Press, 1933.

Freyne, Sean. *Galilee: From Alexander the Great to Hadrian 323 BCE to 135 CE*. T&T Clark, 1980.

Friesen, Steven J. "Injustice or God's Will? Early Christian Explanations of Poverty." In *Wealth and Poverty in Early Church and Society*. Edited by Susan R. Holman. Baker Academic, 2008.

Fung, Ronald Y. K. *The Epistle to the Galatians*. NICNT. Eerdmans, 1988.

Furnish, Victor Paul. *II Corinthians*. AB 32A. Doubleday, 1984.

Gardner, Jane F. "The Adoption of Roman Freedmen." *Phoenix* 43 (1989): 236–57.

Garland, David E. *1 Corinthians*. BECNT. Baker Academic, 2003.

Garnsey, Peter. *Ideas of Slavery from Aristotle to Augustine*. Cambridge University Press, 1996.

Garnsey, Peter, and Richard Saller. *The Roman Empire: Economy, Society and Culture*. University of California Press, 1987.

Gaventa, B. R. "Galatians 1 and 2: Autobiography as Paradigm." *NovT* 28 (1986): 309–26.

Gibson, Elsa. *The "Christians for Christians" Inscriptions of Phrygia: Greek Texts, Translations and Commentary*. HTS 32. Scholars Press, 1978.

Haacker, Klaus. *Paulus: Der Werdegang eines Apostels*. SBS 171. Katholisches Bibelwerk, 1997.

———. "Zum Werdegang des Apostels Paulus: Biographische Daten und ihre theologische Relevanz." *ANRW* 26.2:833–40. Part 2, *Principat*, 26.2. Edited by Wolfgang Haase. De Gruyter, 1999.

Haenchen, Ernst. *The Acts of the Apostles: A Commentary*. Westminster John Knox, 1971.

Harris, Edward M. "Did Solon Abolish Debt-Bondage?" *ClQ* 52 (2002): 415–30.

Harris, Murray J. *The Second Epistle to the Corinthians: A Commentary on the Greek Text*. NIGTC. Eerdmans, 2005.

Harris, W. V. "Child-Exposure in the Roman Empire." *JRS* 84 (1994): 1–22.

———. "Towards a Study of the Roman Slave Trade." In *The Seaborne Commerce of Ancient Rome: Studies in Archaeology*. Edited by J. H. D'Arms and E. C. Kopff. Memoirs of the American Academy in Rome 36. American Academy in Rome, 1980.

Hengel, Martin. *Between Jesus and Paul: Studies in the Earliest History of Christianity*. Translated by John Bowden. Fortress, 1983.

———. *The Pre-Christian Paul*. Translated by John Bowden. SCM, 1991.

Hester, James D. "The Rhetorical Structure of Galatians 1:11–2:14." *JBL* 103 (1984): 223–33.

Hippolytus. *The Refutation of All Heresies*. Ante-Nicene Fathers.

Hock, Ronald F. "Paul's Tentmaking and the Problem of His Social Class." *JBL* 97 (1978): 555–64.

Holladay, Carl R. *Acts: A Commentary*. NTL. Westminster John Knox, 2016.

Horsley, Richard A. "Ancient Jewish Banditry and the Revolt Against Rome, A.D. 66–70." *CBQ* 43 (1981): 409–32.

———. *Galilee: History, Politics, People*. Trinity Press International, 1995.

———. *Jesus and the Spiral of Violence: Popular Jewish Resistance in Roman Palestine*. Fortress, 1993.

———. "Popular Messianic Movements Around the Time of Jesus." *CBQ* 46 (1984): 471–95.

———. "The Sicarii: Ancient Jewish 'Terrorists.'" *JR* 59 (1979): 435–58.

Horsley, Richard A., and John S. Hanson. *Bandits, Prophets and Messiahs: Popular Movements in the Time of Jesus*. Winston, 1985.

Hunt, A. S., and C. C. Edgar, trans. *Select Papri*. Vol. 2, *Public Documents*. LCL 282. Harvard University Press, 1934.

Jeffers, James S. *The Greco-Roman World of the New Testament Era: Exploring the Background of Early Christianity*. IVP Academic, 1999.

Jerome. *Commentariorum in Epistolam ad Philemonem liber*. Patrologia Latina.

———. *De Viris Illustribus* (*On Illustrious Men*). Nicene and Post-Nicene Fathers: Series II/Volume III.

Johnson, Allen Chester, Paul Robinson Coleman-Norton, and Frank Card Bourne. *Ancient Roman Statutes: A Translation with Introduction, Commentary, Glossary, and Index*. University of Texas Press, 1961.

Jones, C. P. "*Stigma*: Tattooing and Branding in Graeco-Roman Antiquity." *JRS* 77 (1987): 139–55.

Josephus. *Jewish Antiquities, Volume I: Books 1-3*. Translated by H. St. J. Thackeray. Loeb Classical Library 242. Harvard University Press, 1930.

———. *Jewish Antiquities, Volume V: Books 12-13*. Translated by Ralph Marcus. Loeb Classical Library 365. Harvard University Press, 1943.

———. *The Jewish War, Volume I: Books 1-2*. Translated by H. St. J. Thackeray. Loeb Classical Library 203. Harvard University Press, 1927.

———. *The Jewish War, Volume II: Books 3-4*. Translated by H. St. J. Thackeray. Loeb Classical Library 487. Harvard University Press, 1927.

———. *The Jewish War, Volume III: Books 5-7*. Translated by H. St. J. Thackeray. Loeb Classical Library 210. Harvard University Press, 1928.

Juvenal. *The Satires*. Translated by Niall Rudd. Oxford World's Classics. Oxford University Press, 1991.

Käsemann, Ernst. *Commentary on Romans*. Translated and edited by Geoffrey W. Bromiley. Eerdmans, 1980.

Kittel, Gerhard, and Gerhard Friedrich, eds. *Theological Dictionary of the New Testament*. Translated by Geoffrey W. Bromiley. 10 vols. Eerdmans, 1964–76.

Kleijwegt, Marc. "Debt Bondage and Chattel Slavery in Early Rome." In *Debt and Slavery in the Mediterranean and Atlantic Worlds*. Edited by Gwyn Campbell and Alessandro Stanziani. Routledge, 2013.

Knox, Wilfred L. *St. Paul and the Church of the Gentiles*. Cambridge University Press, 1939.

Koester, Helmut. *Ancient Christian Gospels: Their History and Development*. Trinity Press International, 1990.

———. *Introduction to the New Testament*. Vol. 2. Fortress, 1982.

Kudryavtseva, T. V. "Reconsidering the *imperium infinitum* of Marcus Antonius Creticus." *Vestnik of Saint Petersburg University* 64 (2019): 937–50.

Kyle, Donald G. *Spectacles of Death in Ancient Rome*. Routledge, 1998.

Laroche, Roland A. "Valerius Antias and His Numerical Totals: A Reappraisal." *Historia* 26.3 (1997): 358–68.

Légasse, Simon. "Paul's Pre-Christian Career According to Acts." In *Palestinian Setting*. Edited by Richard Bauckham. Vol. 4 of *The Book of Acts in Its First Century Setting*. Eerdmans, 1995.

Lenski, Noel. "Slavery in the Roman Empire." In *The Palgrave Handbook of Global Slavery Throughout History*. Edited by Damian A. Pargas and Juliane Schiel. Palgrave Macmillan, 2023.

Liddell, Henry George, Robert Scott, and Henry Stuart Jones. *A Greek-English Lexicon.* 9th ed. with revised supplement. Clarendon, 1996.

Lightfoot, J. B. *The Epistle of St. Paul to the Galatians.* Zondervan, 1957.

———. *Saint Paul's Epistles to the Colossians and to Philemon.* Zondervan, 1959.

Lindsay, Hugh. *Adoption in the Roman World.* Cambridge University Press, 2009.

Livy. *Ab Urbe Condita.* Oxford Classical Texts. Edited and translated by S. Conway and C. F. Walters. Clarendon Press, 1920.

Lohse, Eduard. *Colossians and Philemon.* Hermeneia. Fortress, 1971.

Lüdemann, Gerd. *The Acts of the Apostles: What Really Happened in the Earliest Days of the Church.* Prometheus, 2005.

Lüdemann, Gerd. *Early Christianity According to the Traditions in Acts: A Commentary.* Fortress, 1987.

Lührmann, Dieter. *Galatians: A Continental Commentary.* Fortress, 1992.

Lyall, Francis. "Roman Law in the Writings of Paul: Adoption." *JBL* 88 (1969): 458–66.

———. *Slaves, Citizens, Sons: Legal Metaphors in the Epistles.* Academie, 1984.

Lyons, George. *Pauline Autobiography: Toward a New Understanding.* Society of Biblical Literature, 1985.

Maccoby, Hyam. *Paul and Hellenism.* Trinity Press International, 1991.

MacMullen, Ramsay. "Late Roman Slavery." *Historia* 36 (1987): 359–82.

Madden, John. "Slavery in the Roman Empire: Numbers and Origins." *Classics Ireland* 3 (1996): 109–28.

Malherbe, Abraham J. *Paul and the Popular Philosophers.* Fortress, 1989.

Malina, Bruce J., and Jerome H. Neyrey, "Honor and Shame in Luke-Acts: Pivotal Values of the Mediterranean World." In *The Social World of Luke-Acts: Models for Interpretation*. Edited by Jerome H. Neyrey. Hendrickson, 1991.

Marshall, Peter. *Enmity in Corinth: Social Conventions in Paul's Relations with the Corinthians.* WUNT 2.23. Mohr Siebeck, 1987.

Martial. *Epigrams. Vol. 1, Spectacles, Books 1–5*. Edited and translated by D. R. Shackleton Bailey. Loeb Classical Library 94. Harvard University Press, 1993.

Martin, Dale B. "Slavery and the Ancient Jewish Family." In *The Jewish Family in Antiquity*, ed. Shaye J. D. Cohen. BJS. Scholars Press, 2020.

———. *Slavery as Salvation: The Metaphor of Slavery in Pauline Christianity.* Yale University Press, 1990.

Martyn, J. Louis. *Galatians*. AB 33A. Doubleday, 1997.

———. *Theological Issues in the Letters of Paul.* Abingdon, 1997.

McKeown, Niall. "Greek and Roman Slavery." In *The Routledge History of Slavery*. Edited by Gad Heuman and Trevor Burnard. Routledge, 2011.

Meeks, Wayne A. *The First Urban Christians: The Social World of the Apostle Paul.* Yale University Press, 1983.

Mitchell, Stephen. "The Cult of Theos Hypsistos Between Pagans, Jews, and Christians." In *Pagan Monotheism in Late Antiquity*. Edited by Polymnia Athanassadi and Michael Frede. Oxford University Press, 1999.

———. "Further Thoughts on the Cult of Theos Hypsistos." In *One God: Pagan Monotheism in the Roman Empire*. Edited by Stephen Mitchell and Peter Van Nuffelen. Cambridge University Press, 2010.

Moo, Douglas J. *The Epistle to the Romans*. NICNT. Eerdmans, 1996.

———. *Galatians*. BECNT. Baker Academic, 2013.

———. *The Letters to the Colossians and to Philemon*. PNTC. Eerdmans, 2008.

Murphy-O'Connor, Jerome. *1 Corinthians*. NTM 10. Liturgical Press, 1979.

———. *Paul: A Critical Life*. Oxford University Press, 1996.

Novak, David. *The Image of the Non-Jew in Judaism: An Historical and Constructive Study of the Noahide Laws.* Edwin Mellen, 1983.

———. "The Origin of the Noahide Laws." In *Perspectives on Jews and Judaism: Essays in Honor of Wolfe Kelman*. Edited by Arthur A. Chiel. Rabbinical Assembly, 1978.

O'Neill, J. C. *The Recovery of Paul's Letter to the Galatians.* SPCK, 1972.

Ormerod, H. A. "The Campaigns of Servilius Isauricus Against the Pirates." *JRS* 12 (1922): 35–56.

Patrologia Latina. Edited by J.-P. Migne. 217 vols. Paris, 1844–64.

Peterson, David G. *The Acts of the Apostles*. PNTC. Eerdmans, 2009.

Petronius. *The Satyricon*. Translated by P. G. Walsh. Oxford World's Classics. Oxford University Press, 1997.

Pew Research Center's Forum on Religion & Public Life. "The World's Muslims: Religion, Politics and Society." Pew Research Center, 2013.

Philo. *Every Good Man Is Free. Quod omnis probus liber sit.* Translated by F. H. Colson. Loeb Classical Library 363. Harvard University Press, 1941.

———. *On the Cherubim* (*De cherubim*). Translated by F. H. Colson and G. H. Whitaker. Loeb Classical Library 227. Harvard University Press, 1929.

Pleket, H. W. "Religious History as the History of Mentality: The 'Believer' as Servant of the Deity in the Greek World." In *Faith, Hope and Worship: Aspects of Religious Mentality in the Ancient World*. Edited by H. S. Versnel. Brill, 1981.

Rabinowitz, Jacob J. "Manumission of Slaves in Roman Law and Oriental Law." *JNES* 19 (1960): 42–45.

Radin, Max. "The Exposure of Infants in Roman Law and Practice." *CJ* 20 (1925): 337–43.

Rapske, Brian. *Paul in Roman Custody*. Vol. 3 of *The Book of Acts in Its First Century Setting*. Eerdmans, 1994.

Reitzenstein, Richard. *Hellenistic Mystery-Religions: Their Basic Ideas and Significance*. Translated by John E. Steely. Pickwick, 1978.

Reumann, John. *Philippians: A New Translation with Introduction and Commentary*. AB 33B. Yale University Press, 2008.

Richardson, Peter. *Herod: King of the Jews and Friend of the Romans*. University of South Carolina Press, 1996.

Riesner, Rainer. *Paul's Early Period: Chronology, Mission Strategy, Theology*. Translated by Doug Stott. Eerdmans, 1998.

Riesner, Rainer. "Synagogues in Jerusalem." In *Palestinian Setting*. Edited by Richard Bauckman. Vol. 4 of *The Book of Acts in Its First Century Setting*. Eerdmans, 1995.

Roetzel, Calvin. *Paul: The Man and the Myth*. Fortress, 1999.

Roloff, Jürgen. *Die Apostelgeschichte*. NTD 5. Vandenhoeck & Ruprecht, 1988.

Sanders, E. P. *Judaism: Practice and Belief*. Trinity Press International, 1992.

———. *Paul and Palestinian Judaism: A Comparison of Patterns of Religion*. Fortress, 1977.

Sandmel, Samuel. *Judaism and Christian Beginnings*. Oxford University Press, 1978.

Scheidel, Walter. "Human Mobility in Roman Italy, II: The Slave Population." *JRS* 95 (2005): 64–79.

———. "The Roman Slave Supply." In *The Cambridge World History of Slavery*. Vol. 1, *The Ancient Mediterranean World*. Edited by Keith Bradley and Paul Cartledge. Cambridge University Press, 2011.

Scheidel, Walter, and Steven J. Friesen. "The Size of the Economy and the Distribution of Income in the Roman Empire." *JRS* 99 (2009): 61–91.

Schnabel, Eckhard J. *Acts*. ZECNT. Zondervan, 2012.

———. *Paul the Missionary: Realities, Strategies and Methods*. IVP Academic, 2008.

Schowalter, Daniel N., and Steven J. Friesen, eds. *Urban Religion in Roman Corinth*. HTS 53. Harvard University Press, 2005.

Schreiner, Thomas R. *Romans*. BECNT. Baker Academic, 1998.

Schweizer, Eduard. "Slaves of the Elements and Worshipers of Angels: Gal 4:3, 9 and Col 2:8, 18, 20." *JBL* 107 (1988): 455–68.

Scott, James M. *Adoption as Sons of God: An Exegetical Investigation into the Background of Huiothesia in the Pauline Corpus*. WUNT 2.48. Mohr Siebeck, 1992.

Segal, Alan F. *Paul the Convert: The Apostolate and Apostasy of Saul the Pharisee*. Yale University Press, 1990.

Soards, Marion L. *The Speeches in Acts: Their Content, Context, and Concerns*. Westminster John Knox, 1994.

Sommers, Tamler. *Why Honor Matters*. Basic Books, 2018.

Stegemann, Wolfgang. "War der Apostel Paulus ein römischer Bürger?" *ZNW* 78 (1987): 200–229.

Strabo. *Geography*, Volume I: Books 1-2. Translated by Horace Leonard Jones. Loeb Classical Library 49. Harvard University Press, 1917.

Telford, Lynda. *Sulla: A Dictator Reconsidered*. Pen & Sword Military, 2014.

Theissen, Gerd. *The Social Setting of Pauline Christianity: Essays on Corinth*. Translated by John H. Schütz. Fortress, 1982.

Thielman, Frank. *Romans*. ZECNT. Zondervan, 2018.

Thiselton, Anthony C. *The First Epistle to the Corinthians: A Commentary on the Greek Text*. NIGTC. Eerdmans, 2000.

Thompson, F. H. *The Archaeology of Greek and Roman Slavery*. Bloomsbury, 2003.

Thrall, Margaret E. *A Critical and Exegetical Commentary on the Second Epistle to the Corinthians*. Vol. 1. ICC. T&T Clark, 1994.

Treggiari, Susan. "*Contubernales* in *CIL* 6." *Phoenix* 35 (1981): 42–69.

Urbach, E. E. "The Laws Regarding Slavery as a Source for the Social History of the Period of the Second Temple, the Mishnah and Talmud." In *Papers of the Institute of Jewish Studies, London*. Edited by J. G. Weiss. Magnes, 1964.

van Unnik, W. C. *Tarsus or Jerusalem: The City of Paul's Youth*. Translated by George Ogg. Epworth, 1962.

Vincent, Marvin R. *A Critical and Exegetical Commentary on the Epistles to the Philippians and to Philemon*. ICC. T&T Clark, 1972.

Vlassopoulos, Kostas. "Slavery in Ancient Greece." In *The Palgrave Handbook of Global Slavery Throughout History*. Edited by Damian A. Pargas and Juliane Schiel. Palgrave Macmillan, 2023.

Wallace, Daniel B. *Greek Grammar Beyond the Basics: An Exegetical Syntax of the New Testament*. Zondervan, 1996.

Westermann, William L. *The Slave Systems of Greek and Roman Antiquity*. American Philosophical Society, 1955.

Wickham, Jason Paul. "The Enslavement of War Captives by the Romans to 146 BC." PhD diss., University of Liverpool, 2014.

Wikenhauser, Alfred. *Pauline Mysticism: Christ in the Mystical Teaching of St. Paul.* Herder and Herder, 1960.

Williams, Sam K. "*Promise* in Galatians: A Reading of Paul's Reading of Scripture." *JBL* 107 (1988): 709–20.

Witherington, Ben, III. *The Acts of the Apostles: A Socio-Rhetorical Commentary.* Eerdmans, 1998.

———. *Grace in Galatia: A Commentary on Paul's Letter to the Galatians.* Eerdmans, 1998.

———. *The Paul Quest: The Renewed Search for the Jew of Tarsus.* IVP Academic, 1998.

Ziolkowski, Adam. "The Plundering of Epirus in 167 B.C.: Economic Considerations." *Papers of the British School at Rome* 54 (1986): 69–80.

Index

Color Gallery

FIGURE 22. Funerary relief. "Farewell, Kallikrite."

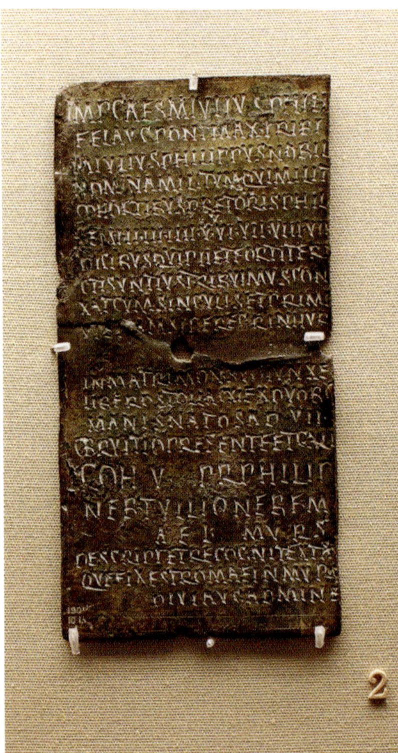

Clockwise, from top left: FIGURE 16. Terracotta lamp with slaves carrying a barrel. FIGURE 25. Venetio gladiator contest with *noxii*. FIGURE 19. Funerary stele of Ameinokleia leaning on her slave. FIGURE 32. Bronze diploma granting citizenship to a retired soldier.

FIGURE 33. Bronze diploma granting citizenship to Decurion Reburrus.

FIGURE 34. Bronze diploma granting citizenship to Dasmenus Azalus.

FIGURE 70. Glass dish of column with Christogram flanked by Peter and Paul.

FIGURE 14. Relief of a slave trader and three bound slaves.

FIGURE 62. Funerary relief of a family of freedmen.

FIGURE 17. Small bronze statue of emaciated slave Eudamidas.

FIGURE 10. Funerary relief of Paramonos and Serapas.

FIGURE 45. Synagogue at Gischala (modern Jish), home village of Paul's parents in Galilee.

FIGURE 3. Sumerian box with shell and lapis lazuli.

FIGURE 71. Lintel from church depicting the archangel Raphael and St. Paul.

FIGURE 69. Fresco of Paul in the Paul and Thecla cave, Ephesus.